Gerri Kimber, Janet Wilson (eds.)

Re-forming World Literature

Katherine Mansfield and the Modernist Short Story

STUDIES IN WORLD LITERATURE

Editors:	Advisory Board:
Prof Janet Wilson, University of Northampton, UK	Dr Gerd Bayer, University of Erlangen, Germany
Dr Chris Ringrose, Monash University, Australia	Dr Fiona Tolan, Liverpool John Moores University, UK

The book series STUDIES IN WORLD LITERATURE is devoted to the analysis of global literature, and the multiple, sometimes contradictory, tendencies it accommodates. Its field of enquiry is the 'new' world literature, a category currently emerging through multiple changes from the old Romantic concept of *Weltliteratur*, attuned to the challenges posed by postcolonialism and multiculturalism, the increasing globalisation of literature (but also its reverse trend, regionalisation), and the diversification of the market place. STUDIES IN WORLD LITERATURE encourages research which celebrates and critically assesses a phenomenon that can be understood, as Pheng Cheah points out, as the 'literature of the world—imaginings and stories [...] that track and account for contemporary globalization as well as older historical narratives of worldhood'.

World literature can be brought into dialogue with postcolonial writing through scrutiny of how it is written, read, circulated, and received transnationally within the contemporary circuit of global cultural capital. The series also responds to the need to examine the inherent contradictions in the concept of a world literature and dependence on a hegemonic (often English-centred) literary and critical discourse.

The series seeks to address these tensions, and consequently welcomes:
1) volumes which debate such matters theoretically (including definitions of what counts as 'world literature' and the place of postcolonial literary production within this larger category);
2) comparative studies of texts and genres from different countries and cultures under common headings or concepts such as memory, ethics, and human rights.

Volumes on national literatures, when these are set in a world/comparative or generic context, will also be considered, and the series will include discussions of other complementary aspects of discourse, narratology, and media. While writing by 'canonical' authors will be covered, the series will additionally propose wider cultural and intellectual genealogies for 'minor' or occluded writers. A key aim of this series is to redeploy the familiar rhetoric of postcolonial theory and discourse in relation to concepts relevant to world literature by introducing arguments that will be integrated with the evidence of individual literary practice. This emphasis on contesting definitions of 'diasporic' or 'postcolonial' writing, 'transnational' or 'transcultural' literatures and 'world' literature as used by writers, critics and thinkers may lead to a reconsideration of the boundaries that divide and intersections that link these related fields.

Recent volumes:

2 Vincent van Bever Donker
Recognition and Ethics in World Literature
Religion, Violence, and the Human
ISBN 978-3-8382-0847-3

3 Bruce King
From New National to World Literature
Essays and Reviews
ISBN 978-3-8382-0856-5

4 Gareth Griffiths, Philip Mead (eds.)
The Social Work of Narrative
Human Rights and the Cultural Imaginary
ISBN 978-3-8382-0858-9

5 Johanna Emeney
The Rise of Autobiographical Medical Poetry and the Medical Humanities
ISBN 978-3-8382-0938-8

Gerri Kimber, Janet Wilson (eds.)

RE-FORMING WORLD LITERATURE

Katherine Mansfield and the Modernist Short Story

ibidem-Verlag
Stuttgart

Bibliografische Information der Deutschen Nationalbibliothek
Die Deutsche Nationalbibliothek verzeichnet diese Publikation in der
Deutschen Nationalbibliografie; detaillierte bibliografische Daten sind im
Internet über http://dnb.d-nb.de abrufbar.

Bibliographic information published by the Deutsche Nationalbibliothek
Die Deutsche Nationalbibliothek lists this publication in the Deutsche Nationalbibliografie;
detailed bibliographic data are available in the Internet at http://dnb.d-nb.de.

Cover picture:
Nova totius terrarum orbis tabula Amstelodami, ex officina G. a Schagen (1682). Source: Wikimedia Commons. Public Domain.

∞

Gedruckt auf alterungsbeständigem, säurefreien Papier
Printed on acid-free paper

ISBN-13: 978-3-8382-1113-8

© *ibidem*-Verlag
Stuttgart 2018

Alle Rechte vorbehalten

Das Werk einschließlich aller seiner Teile ist urheberrechtlich geschützt. Jede Verwertung
außerhalb der engen Grenzen des Urheberrechtsgesetzes ist ohne Zustimmung des Verlages
unzulässig und strafbar. Dies gilt insbesondere für Vervielfältigungen,
Übersetzungen, Mikroverfilmungen und elektronische Speicherformen sowie die
Einspeicherung und Verarbeitung in elektronischen Systemen.

All rights reserved. No part of this publication may be reproduced, stored in or introduced into a retrieval
system, or transmitted, in any form, or by any means (electronic, mechanical, photocopying, recording or
otherwise) without the prior written permission of the publisher. Any person who does any unauthorized act
in relation to this publication may be liable to criminal prosecution and civil claims for damages.

Printed in the EU

CONTENTS

Acknowledgements 7

Abbreviations 9

Introduction 11

Global Modernisms

Enda Duffy
Mansfield, Soma, and the Burning Dress of Modernism 29

Ruchi Mundeja
Of Parvenus and Pantheons: Mansfield's Short Fiction as
a "Reading Back" 51

Maurizia Boscagli
The Art of Work: Katherine Mansfield's Servant and Perception ... 71

UK and US Modernisms

Ailsa Cox
Slippery British: Katherine Mansfield's Legacy in the UK 93

Janet Wilson
"Kew Gardens" and "Miss Brill": Virginia Woolf and
Katherine Mansfield as Short Story Writers 113

Sydney Janet Kaplan
Katherine Mansfield's American Legacy:
The Case of Margery Latimer 139

Poetry, Suffering and the Self

Claire Davison
On First Looking into Mansfield's Heine: Dislocative Lyric
and the Sound of Music 161

Todd Martin
Constructing Jealousy, Exacting Revenge: Allusions to Robert
Browning's "My Last Duchess" in Katherine Mansfield's "Poison"..185

Erica Baldt
Katherine Mansfield: Homeostasis, Equanimity, and Fiction..........209

Fairy Stories and War

Gerri Kimber
Katherine Mansfield, Fairy Tales and Fir Trees: "the story is
past too: past! past!—that's the way with all stories".................231

Elsa Högberg
Consuming Identifications: Food Politics in Mansfield's
"A Suburban Fairy Tale"..251

Aimee Gasston
Treasure and Rot: Preservation and Bequest in
Mansfield's Short Fiction 271

Janka Kascakova
Death by Ink: The Symbolism of Ink in Katherine Mansfield's
"The Fly"..287

Notes on Contributors...**305**

Index...**309**

Acknowledgements

The editors would like to thank the following individuals and institutions: Valerie Lange at *ibidem*, for her advice and guidance during the preparation of the manuscript; Chris Ringrose, for helping to prepare the final texts for publication; the Alexander Turnbull Library, Wellington, New Zealand and especially Linda McGregor and Fiona Oliver; Ralph Kimber, for preparing the index; Peter Brooker and Rishona Zimring for their endorsements.

Abbreviations

Unless otherwise indicated, all references to Katherine Mansfield's works are to the following editions and abbreviated thus:

CP
Gerri Kimber and Claire Davison, eds. 2016. *The Collected Poems of Katherine Mansfield.* Edinburgh: Edinburgh University Press.

CW1 and CW2
Gerri Kimber and Vincent O'Sullivan, eds. 2012. *The Edinburgh Edition of the Collected Works of Katherine Mansfield.* Vols 1 and 2—*The Collected Fiction.* Edinburgh: Edinburgh University Press.

CW3
Gerri Kimber and Angela Smith, eds. 2014. *The Edinburgh Edition of the Collected Works of Katherine Mansfield.* Vol. 3—*The Poetry and Critical Writings.* Edinburgh: Edinburgh University Press.

CW4
Gerri Kimber and Claire Davison, eds. 2016. *The Edinburgh Edition of the Collected Works of Katherine Mansfield.* Vol. 4—*The Diaries of Katherine Mansfield, including Miscellaneous Works.* Edinburgh: Edinburgh University Press.

Letters 1–5
Vincent O'Sullivan and Margaret Scott, eds. 1984–2008. *The Collected Letters of Katherine Mansfield.* 5 vols. Oxford: Clarendon Press.

Notebooks 1–2
Margaret Scott, ed. 2002. *The Katherine Mansfield Notebooks.* 2 vols. Minneapolis, MN: University of Minnesota Press.

Introduction

Gerri Kimber and Janet Wilson

This collection of essays by modernist critics and scholars of Katherine Mansfield from across the world aims to engage with and challenge the widely held view that the short story is an under-researched and overlooked genre in the current understanding of world literature. By this we mean the critical evaluation of literature undertaken by critics (Damrosch 2003; Casanova 2004; Moretti 2000; Cheah 2016), through revisionary approaches to Goethe's original *Weltliteratur*. This new departure is prompted by the challenges posed by the dynamic circulation of texts in the global marketplace, the diversification of media (print, electronic, downloadable, open access), production processes, and cultural forces such as postcolonialism and multiculturalism.[1] In reexamining the short story genre in order to challenge the perception of its relative obscurity when compared to the novel in current evaluations of world literature, this collection focuses on the stories of the New Zealand writer Katherine Mansfield, who is often viewed as a "minor" modernist. Being considered minor by virtue of genre, output or impact, does not of course preclude entry into postcolonial and world literature studies, although the lack of critical attention to writing in such genres is a limitation of these fields that is often overlooked, as the editors of a special issue of the *Journal of Postcolonial Writing* point out (Munos and Ledent 2018, 1). The contributors to this volume collectively argue from a range of critical perspectives that the continuing impact of Mansfield's work and reputation is such that, despite her publishing exclusively in a minor genre, her stories can be read in terms of the

---

[1] As evidence of how this field has taken root see, for example, the *Journal of World Literature,* founded in 2016. Its Editors-in Chief are David Damrosch, Theo D'haen, Jale Pala, and Zhang Longxi.

new configurations of the global marketplace that have led to the revival and rethinking of the category "world literature."

It is perhaps not surprising that the novel continues to be privileged in research and theorizing in this recent shift to a new framework of analysis. Disciplines which proclaim a challenge to familiar binary concepts like postcolonial studies (metropolitan centre/colonial periphery) or diaspora studies (homeland/hostland, relocation/dislocation, departure/return), can be seen as yielding ground to the more universalist category of a world literature, but without undermining the genre's dominance. In terms of a public preference, the novel's primacy has been unassailable since the 19th century, despite competition from other genres like biography and autobiography. Indeed, the *English Catalogue of Books* shows that as a popular form it was enthroned in the hierarchies of genre while the short story, with its shorter length and more limited scope, was relegated to a minor place (Battershill 2018, 63). In the new millennium some overlap between the different critical frameworks of analysis means that continuities of such preference are also likely, as the same texts are often approached through more than one theoretical lens. Critics and theorists of world literature seem to ignore questions of genre when considering this recently revised category as one that principally emanates from the rapid mobilization of culture under globalization: David Damrosch (2003), for example, claims that a text enters into world literature by "circulating out into a broader world beyond its linguistic and cultural point of origin" (6). Likewise Pheng Cheah (2016) claims that we can understand a text's worldliness by treating it as "an object of circulation in a global market of print commodities or as the product of a global system of production" (24).

The short story's diminished status as the poor cousin to the novel (the genre against which literary developments and fashions are usually measured), and frequently at odds with its centring, normative impetus that reflects and refracts social order, is often iterated in discussions of national or regional story types. Philip Holden (2010), for example, argues that the way the short story interrupts and interrogates the national narrative deserves greater attention

(442, cited by Munos and Ledent 2018, x), while Ernest Emenyonu (2013) complains that the African short story, like much short fiction around the world, is still an under-researched genre (1). Yet world literature criticism can, and does, accommodate so-called lesser writers associated with minority genres, whose work may be occluded due to the relative obscurity of their national traditions or to limited publication opportunities. The global perspective that ignores the hierarchization of genre, instead attends to the stories and narratives of worldhood that account for the past as well as the contemporary moment, and stresses the spread of a writer's work though translation, adaptation, and various modes of dissemination.

Mansfield's oeuvre is by any standards an exception to the usual conditions under which the short story genre is viewed as "minor", for its publishing history and reception demonstrate all the salient features of a world literature: in her lifetime, and particularly after her early death in 1923, she had a growing following world-wide, in England, in Europe, especially in France where she lived for periods,[2] New Zealand and Australia, Russia,[3] and the Far East.[4] Her work has never been out of print and soon after her death was translated into other languages. Throughout the 20th century her reputation as a great writer who "raised up higher" the story as a genre was such that even a detractor like Frank O'Connor (1963) put her alongside the literary greats of modernism like Proust (140). Her crowning place among the elite of short story writers appears in various indicators of preference; for example, in *Fifty Great Stories* selected by William Crane as the "world's finest fiction" (first published in 1948, and often reprinted as a mass market paperback), her story "The Garden Party" opens the volume. But she remains controversial when nationality is weighted in such selections. As Ailsa Cox points out in her essay, she

---

[2] On Mansfield's reception in France, see Kimber (2008).
[3] On the translation of her works into Russian, first in 1922, followed by two collections in 1923, see Woods (2001, 248–49).
[4] The first translation of Mansfield's writing into Chinese, by Xu Zhimo, was published shortly after her death in May 1923, in *The Short Story Magazine* (Gong 2001, 12).

was excluded from *The Penguin Book of the British Short Story* (Hensher 2015), because she was seen as a writer "conferring merit on [her] place of birth [i.e. New Zealand] rather than [her] residence [i.e. England]" (xiii; cited by Cox, 93). And the fact remains that her small oeuvre of approximately 216 stories and story fragments (Kimber 2015, 2), means that she often seems insignificant, and when not regarded as "minor" is seen as marginal, as, for example, writing in a "feminine" tradition. As Bonnie Kime Scott (1996) notes, "she was marginalised in particular ways during her lifetime and in rather different ways after her death" (299; cited by Kimber 2015, 3).

Mansfield's entitlement to a place in the pantheon of world literature was something that she instinctively, even unconsciously sought through her capacity for cultural and linguistic exchange and a chameleon-like quality, partly due to her capacity to assume different guises and personae. Her work is able to occupy more than one cultural space, to move between places, attracting diverse readerships in multiple contexts of reception. As a modernist who distanced herself from any explicit associations with nationality and national definitions, she cultivated a certain ambiguity by omitting signposts that might associate her work with a particular country, place, or historical moment.[5] Such placelessness and lack of a specific chronology are crucial to the cosmopolitan modernist identity for which she was known in the 1920s and 30s. There is also her passion for languages, including her facility in speaking European languages which made her more multi-lingual than most of her peers (Davison 2015, 1). Her curiosity about the "expressivity" of language, the ways that words and phrases shift and cross cultural borders, can be found refracted in numerous ways in her texts. Mansfield as translator and translations of Mansfield's work are the subject of the essays in the recently published volume *Mansfield and Translation* (Davison, Kimber and Martin 2015).

---

[5] For example, a comparison of "The Aloe" with its revised version as "Prelude" shows that she removed all markers of nationality (e.g. Australia and New Zealand); she rarely if ever references New Zealand (with the exception of "A Truthful Adventure"); and often omits place names by which a city or country can be identified.

Among her many literary initiatives was her work as an avid translator of texts from French, Russian and Polish—the latter two with her collaborators, S.S. Koteliansky, a professional translator and friend, and her lover, Floryan Sobieniowski—and this substantial body of work was until recently largely unexplored and unpublished;[6] as Claire Davison points out, such a discovery sheds new light on Mansfield the writer (*CW*3, 149; 2015, 3). This openness to the malleable, plastic properties of language is a quality in her work that makes it receptive to translation, in the way that Stephan Helgesson (2014) describes as "a circulational phenomenon that moves across languages and literary fields" (484). In fact the literary innovations and transpositions that her stories have inspired among her successors and followers can be associated with translation in its widest sense, as her work is interpreted and lives on in the compositions of others; this includes its adaptation into alternative media, such as drama, cinema, music and the visual arts. Such transformations and transmedial adaptations of her writing, a rich component of her literary legacy, are evidence of how Mansfield's influence has expanded by means of different types of translation or imitation, so making it worthy of its place among the diverse literary, generic and media repertoires of world literature.

In pointing to the global production and dissemination of short stories, and in particular the growing reception of Mansfield's work worldwide, drawing on new scholarship that has emerged in the last decade following the founding of the Katherine Mansfield Society in 2008 (www.katherinemansfieldsociety.org), this volume of essays reveals how literary modernism can be read in a myriad of ways in terms of the contemporary category of new world literature. Indeed, the resurgence of interest in Mansfield has taken the form of a reexamination of the political, historical and cultural framings of modernism, with the recognition that these can be reinterpreted in broader terms of categories and definitions that were not used even a decade ago, as the essays by Ruchi Mundeja and Todd Martin make clear.

*****

---

[6] Collated by Gerri Kimber and published together for the first time in *CW*3.

Re-forming World Literature: Katherine Mansfield and The Modernist Short Story, then, offers new and innovative ways of reading Mansfield's work that show her position in the multiply-constructed field of world literature, and that seem a logical development in the current critical revival of interest in this modernist author. The collection has been divided into four sections: "Global Modernisms", "UK and US Modernisms", "Poetry, Suffering and the Self", and "Fairy Tales and War", reflecting the breadth of topics addressed by the contributors' chapters.

In "Global Modernisms", three chapters offer new and dynamic reasons for affirming Mansfield's position as a modernist who encompasses a global reach. Enda Duffy's truly groundbreaking chapter, "Mansfield, Soma, and the Burning Dress of Modernism", reads Mansfield as the inventor of "a new law of attraction, and communion" namely, "tenderness" (31). Comparing Mansfield's work to that of Virginia Woolf and James Joyce, Duffy points out that "the modernist prose of each of these writers became experimental in the first instance to record with an unprecedented accuracy the physical sensations, the spasms, the reactions of bodies to stimuli, of the characters it displayed" (33). The somatic response to such sensations experienced by the characters of all three authors, and Mansfield in particular, such as fluctuations in body temperature, rates of heartbeat and breathing, the ways we sense excitement and stress, all are captured in the best modernist writing as a symptomology of fluctuating life as it is lived, so that intense human energy—soma—rather than deep human feeling, becomes the goal. For Duffy, the short-story form itself, developed it has been said as material to be read during a standard train commuting time, is the literary form engaged in a race against time and for attention, and is thus the perfect soma text, a measuring machine of the pulsation of human energy, where Mansfield's nervy, tempo-shifting writing can be read as a new literary form, in which modernism's dream of high energy can be understood. Ruchi Mundeja in her chapter establishes a dialogue between the divergent critical discourses of postcolonial and world literature studies by addressing

Mansfield's colonial origins, arguing that "parvenus and arrivistes" (55) from the periphery resist the mainstream and so may "tilt [...] 'the literary balance of power'" of world literature (Mundeja 53, citing Casanova 2004, 43). Mansfield's "ex-centric" positioning enables her to contest assumptions of metropolitan modernism and its lingua franca. Pointing to her preference for the short story with its potential to subvert dominant social or cultural values, Mundeja argues that Mansfield offers a "reading back" (rather than a writing back) to the metropolitan centre, in an "excoriating of European epistemologies, seen as precursors to the more enabling writerly instantiations of postcolonial agency" (53). Her example of how modernism is critiqued by the outsider's "postcolonial" perspective is Mansfield's narcissistic anti-hero, Raoul Duquette, the literary poseur of "Je ne parle pas français", whose "parodic performance" in his enactment of modernism "becomes a conduit to its blindspots" (59). Maurizia Boscagli turns to another socially marginal type, the servant, claiming that Mansfield shows a greater interest in the working class than many of her contemporaries. In noting the influence of Flaubert's realism, especially in "Flaubertian elements" that she adapts (74) to her satire on the bourgeoisie, and identifying by contrast, in Woolf's modernist text *To the Lighthouse*, the limited interiority of the caretaker figure Mrs McNab, Boscagli argues that Mansfield introduces sentimentality into modernist writing, and transforms it into a way of accessing "a new form of perception" (85). She examines "Ma Parker" for the way the story's "affective excess" (88) lingers so that the reader experiences a "close distance" (86) from its emotions, rather than catharsis. Mansfield's stylistic juxtapositions—of high modernism, realism and sentimentality—undermine the commonly assumed link between women and mass culture in which sentimentality is associated with the low brow and vulgar. Her focus on the female servant, Boscagli concludes, shows Mansfield reworking sentimentality nd melodrama to "unmake the opposition of high and low that defines so much of male modernism" (88).

The section on "UK and US Modernisms" focuses on the legacy of Mansfield and her influence in the work of other writers, both in the UK and in the USA. Ailsa Cox's essay specifically addresses Mansfield's legacy in the UK, with a consideration as to whether she is in fact a "British" author, as some critics have positioned her. With a comparative reading of stories by contemporary British female authors, A. S. Byatt, Candia McWilliam, Janice Galloway, Ali Smith and Tessa Hadley, Cox traces the themes and techniques in their work that link them to Mansfield, affirming that "there is so much that all these writers take from Mansfield; it is difficult to imagine the British short story without her" (110). Janet Wilson compares Katherine Mansfield and Virginia Woolf as modernist short story writers by examining their "public garden" stories, "Kew Gardens" and "Miss Brill", reading the latter's dark vision as a deliberate contrast to the former's vibrant impressionistic celebration of nature. She identifies the epistolary exchanges, reviews and other communications in the early friendship between Mansfield and Woolf to elaborate Antony Alpers's claim that Mansfield may have inspired the theme for "Kew Gardens". Intertextual allusions to Woolf's acclaimed story in Mansfield's story "A Dill Pickle", and another possible link in "The Escape", the chapter claims, suggest an ongoing conversation between the writers over issues of sexuality, betrayal and marriage. Both contributed in different ways to the flourishing of the modernist short story in the early 20th century: Woolf's story, more radically experimental, has been much admired and often reprinted, while Mansfield's is one of her most memorably affective. Sydney Janet Kaplan focuses on Mansfield's legacy in the work of American author Margery Latimer, who had been influenced by John Middleton Murry's construction of the legendary figure of Mansfield through the posthumous editing of his wife's notebooks and letters. Murry's introductions to those collections emphasized several aspects of Mansfield's life and work that would have resonated with Latimer: her youthful revolt against provincialism, her desire to escape to London, and the interconnection between her passionate devotion to the art of writing and her personal suffering. The extent to which Latimer's writing resembles (and contrasts with) Mansfield's is demonstrated through a comparison between Latimer's story, "The Family", and Mansfield's "Prelude". The chapter argues that where Latimer's interpretation of family relations differs from Mansfield's, it is propelled by her underlying critique of American ideology. Kaplan concludes that "Latimer's recognition of an emotional and aesthetic affinity with Mansfield is most fully revealed in the similarity of their personal spiritual quests" (152), and especially their relationship with A. R. Orage.

Three authors address other aspects of Mansfield's work through the framework of a world literature, including the European literary and Eastern philosophical heritages which Mansfield accessed through various pathways and at different stages of her life, in the section on "Poetry, Suffering and the Self". Claire Davison's pioneering chapter on the influence of the 19th-century German poet Heinrich Heine on Mansfield confirms the importance she accorded her own poetry-writing, especially in her early years as a writer. Her copy of Heine's *Buch der Lieder* (*Book of Songs*) was a constant companion throughout her life, and Davison's chapter explores some of the poems in the collection, tracing their influence on the literary apprenticeship of Mansfield, not only in her own poetry and early tone-poems, but in decidedly Heine-esque themes and styles that would evolve into figures of enchantment in her later, modernist stories: "the essential tension and strangeness of the lyric [...] in turn lends itself splendidly to the dynamics of nascent modernism" (180–1). Todd Martin takes another 19th-century poetic heavyweight—Robert Browning—focusing specifically on what he sees as allusions to Browning's celebrated poem "My Last Duchess" in Mansfield's short story "Poison", exploring how she uses such allusions to enhance the theme of jealousy inherent in her story. Martin's approach to Mansfield's appropriation of a well-known European literary form, the dramatic monologue, written by a master of the genre, stresses how "a particular text fits within and reacts to a global literary tradition" (186). Via close textual analysis, and drawing on David Damrosch's view that works of art refract rather than reflect their cultures (2009, 2), Martin offers an illuminating comparison between the final printed story and the original typescript, highlighting the connection between her story and Browning's poem: in so doing, Mansfield makes an artistic choice which "capitalizes on the connections in order to establish a dialogue between the two texts, one that not only adds meaning to her own story, but which also places her within the framework of world literature" (206). Erica Baldt's chapter, "Katherine Mansfield: Homeostasis, Equanimity, and Fiction", explores the ways in which Mansfield uses the short story form as a vehicle by which to interrogate concepts of mysticism as they were commonly understood and promulgated in London at the time she was writing, especially towards the end of her life. Specifically, she focuses on how "Mansfield's ability to achieve what she always sought—what the *Bhagavad Gita* calls 'serenity at last'—was severely limited by pain and illness" (211). Through an analysis of several stories, Baldt demonstrates how "even as the suffering itself seems to put her further from a place of physical balance, it allows her the 'privilege' of seeing in a new way, of writing in a new way" (226).

In the final section, "Fairy Stories and War", four chapters examine Mansfield's stories from multiple perspectives: the fairy tale, both as a genre and a symbol; the notion of "treasure" as literary inheritance; and the symbolism of ink in a story about the horrors of war. As familiar literary tropes and categories, they all resonate beyond any particular cultural or national source, confirming that many of Mansfield's sources and inspirations are rooted in a pan-European mythology, symbolism and literary practice—all indicative of her universalising appeal. The origins of the fairy tale in oral folk literature, and its importance to the short story genre are implied by world literature critic Pheng Cheah who says "stories do not originate from the teller. They come into being in response to the world and to the coming of the other. [...] stories can only be told if there is a listener" (2016, 298). Gerri Kimber's chapter discusses the impact of fairy stories, and other children's literature within a global context, on Mansfield's oeuvre, with a particular focus on the fairy tales of Hans Christian Andersen and the Victorian children's book *Christmas-Tree Land* by Mrs Molesworth. Brought up in far away New Zealand, Mansfield was deeply affected by—and related to—these very European tales, and Kimber demonstrates the resonances of their impact on Mansfield's adult writing life; as Kimber reveals, "the marvellous itself, as Mansfield knew instinctively, is inherent in modernity, since modernity consists of an interplay between enchantment and disenchantment" (250). In "Consuming Identifications: Food Politics in Mansfield's 'A Suburban Fairy Tale'", Elsa Högberg argues that Mansfield's work illuminates the crucial role of the modernist short story as a socio-political force. In her reinvention of the short story form, Mansfield explores animism and telepathy as aesthetic devices that cause an uncanny blurring of the subject-object boundary. With a particular focus on the politics of hunger and food in her 1919 story "A Suburban Fairy Tale"—Mansfield's outraged response to the postwar famine in Germany, and the British indifference to this crisis—Högberg explores her aesthetic creation of animist and telepathic relations as an effective way of addressing social and political injustice. Aimee Gasston's essay considers the notion of legacy in Mansfield's work, where decay and mortality are carefully counterbalanced by art's capacity to preserve. She argues for the modernist short story innovated by Mansfield as primarily concerned with preservation and bequest, seeking to pass on "treasure" as literary inheritance; an activity in opposition to the fleetingness inherent to the short form. She also considers whether the materiality of Mansfield's work is itself bound up with notions of endowment, considering those rights and obligations passed on to both writers and readers through the stories she left behind. Taking the story "At the Bay" as one example of many, this chapter looks at the ways in which "rot" (a word which beats throughout Mansfield's stories) is juxtaposed with "treasure", setting up a conceptual dichotomy that parallels the author's defiant work to attain posterity in the face of permanent change, brevity, disintegration and decay. For Gasston, Mansfield's legacy is "both profound and manifold—a refulgent literature containing a myriad of carefully chosen objects, to each of which a 'discreet, tenacious meaning' attaches" (282). In the final chapter, Janka Kascakova analyses the symbolism of ink in Mansfield's celebrated short story "The Fly". Kascakova explores the possible symbolical meanings of ink in the story, arguing that its appearance and use are highly significant and closely connected to the circumstances surrounding the beginning and progress of the Great War. Mansfield's story is, among other things, "an expression of her belief that beyond the bullets, grenades, shrapnel, gas, tanks and disease, her brother and thousands of other young men and women were, in fact, killed by ink" (301). The fly's death thereby reflects on many aspects of human activity whose writing (that is "using ink") contributed to the demise of such an unprecedented number of young men: the politics, the bureaucracy, the war propaganda but also education, literature and science.

*****

Pheng Cheah has recently explored a "radical rethinking of world literature as literature that is an active power in the making of worlds, that is, both a site of processes of worlding and an agent that participates and intervenes in these processes" (2016, 2). This reformulation offers just one more perspective that might be tested further in relation to the continuous circulation and growing impact of Mansfield's short story oeuvre as testimony to how worlding happens while actively contributing to this process. The chapters in this collection show that Mansfield's is a multivalent voice, and she the supreme example of a writer positioned between different borders and boundaries—between modernism and postcolonialism; between the short story and other genres (like the novella or poetry, or non-fiction such as letters, diaries, reviews and translations); between Europe and New Zealand. This gives her work a ubiquitousness that Vincent O'Sullivan (1994) attributes to "rejection of the centre, rejection of the borders as well, the sense of discomposure everywhere, the play of feeling present and absent at the same time in almost any place" (13). In terms of the recent attempts to reconcile postcolonialism and world literature (Cheah, 2016; Ashcroft 2013; Helgesson, 2014) her stories might be seen, according to Bill Ashcroft, as belonging to a system of world literature which she entered through the network of imperial and economic power and whose "dominant discourse of imperial control" she helped to transform—even as, Ruchi Mundeja points out, by destabilizing the "literary Greenwich meridian" (67, citing Casanova 2004, 4). But Mansfield transcends such categorisations as well, because of her linguistic agility, multiple masks and guises, and ability to read the foreign; while the placelessness which makes her resist pigeonholing into any single cultural category means her stories move between multiple places and locations, open to being interpreted by different readerships according to different cultural codes and specificities. The chapters here locate up-to-date scholarship on modernism and Mansfield, synthesizing them with the different paradigms of world literature to show that despite being often identified as a minor figure within the literary canon, Mansfield, with her increasingly worldwide reputation as a short story writer par excellence, can not only be recuperated for inclusion in a global literary framework but can offer ways of reading beyond it.

Bibliography

Ashcroft, Bill. 2013. "Beyond the Nation: Australian Literature as World Literature." In *Scenes of Reading: Is Australian Literature a World Literature?*, edited by Rob. Dixon and Bridget Rooney, 34–46. Melbourne: Australian Scholarly Publishing.

Battershill, Claire. 2018. *Modernist Lives: Biography and Autobiography at Leonard and Virginia Woolf's Hogarth Press*. London: Continuum.

Casanova, Pascale. 2004. *The World Republic of Letters*. Translated by M.B. DeBevoise. Cambridge, MA: Harvard University Press.

Cheah, Pheng. 2016. *What is a World? On Postcolonial Literature as World Literature*. Durham, NC and London: Duke University Press.

Damrosch, David. 2003. *What is World Literature?* Princeton, NJ: Princeton University Press.

Davison, Claire, Gerri Kimber, and Todd Martin, eds. 2015. *Katherine Mansfield and Translation*. Katherine Mansfield Studies, 7. Edinburgh: Edinburgh University Press.

Davison, Claire. 2015. "Introduction." *Katherine Mansfield and Translation*, edited by Claire Davison, Gerri Kimber and Todd Martin, 1–11. Katherine Mansfield Studies, 7. Edinburgh: Edinburgh University Press.

Emenyonu, Ernest. 2013. "Editorial: 'Once Upon a Time Begins a Story…'." *African Literature Today* 31: 1–7.

Gong, Shifen. 2001. "Introduction." *A Fine Pen: The Chinese View of Katherine Mansfield*, edited and translated by Shifen Gong, 11–38. Dunedin: Otago University Press.

Helgesson, Stephan, 2014. "Postcolonialism and World Literature: Rethinking the Boundaries." *Interventions* 16 (4): 483–500.

Hensher, Philip. 2015. "General Introduction." In *The Penguin Book of the British Short Story*. Vol. 2, edited by Philip Hensher, xiii–xxxviii. London: Penguin

Holden, Philip. 2010. "Reading for Genre: The Short Story and (Post)colonial Governmentality." *Interventions: International Journal of Postcolonial Studies* 12 (3): 442–58.

Kimber, Gerri. 2008. *Katherine Mansfield: The View from France*. Oxford and New York: Peter Lang.

---. 2015. *Katherine Mansfield and the Art of the Short Story*. London: Palgrave MacMillan.

Moretti, Franco. 2000. "Conjectures on World Literature." *New Left Review* 1 (January–February). https://newleftreview.org/II/1/franco-moretti-conjectures-on-world-literature.

Munos, Delphine, and Bénédicte Ledent. 2018. "'Minor' genres in postcolonial literatures: New webs of meaning." In "'Minor' genres in postcolonial literatures," edited by Bénédicte Ledent and Delphine Munos. Special issue of *Journal of Postcolonial Writing* 56 (1): 1–5.

O'Connor, Frank. 1963. *The Lonely Voice: A Study of the Short Story*. London; Macmillan.

O'Sullivan, Vincent. 1994. "Finding the Pattern: Solving the Problem: Katherine Mansfield, the New Zealand European." In *Katherine Mansfield: In from the Margin*, edited by Roger Robinson, 9–24. New Orleans: Louisana State University Press.

Scott, Bonnie Kime, ed. 1990. *The Gender of Modernism: A Critical Anthology.* Bloomington, IN: Indiana University Press.

Woods, Joanna. 2001. *Katerina: The Russian World of Katherine Mansfield.* Harmondsworth: Penguin.

Global Modernisms

Mansfield, Soma, and the Burning Dress of Modernism

Enda Duffy

> [T]his woman who, living intensely in all the beauty she found around her, fought so bravely against her illness. She seemed to cut through any falseness or furry edges sharply, yet always with an underlying tenderness. (Ida Baker [1985, 157] on Katherine Mansfield)[1]

> Energy is eternal delight. (William Blake)

This is a paper about tenderness. It might seem difficult, on first touch, to think of Katherine Mansfield as the modern poet of tenderness, yet I am struck by how the word "tenderness" turns out to be secreted at the heart of so many of her stories. "Oh, why did she feel so tender towards the whole world tonight?" thinks Bertha during her dinner-party in "Bliss" (Mansfield 2010, 68). Then here is Linda on Stanley in "Prelude": "And how tender he always was at times like these, how submissive, how thoughtful" (62). Or Raoul to Mouse in "Je ne parle pas français": "'But I'm sure you do,' I answered, so tender, so reassuring, I might have been a dentist about to withdraw her first little milk tooth" (98). In each of these cases, there is a tentativeness around naming the tenderness, a sense of the possible distance between the attachment being expressed and the expression of it.

Tenderness has been around for a long time in English literature, perhaps nowhere more famously than in Keats's "Ode to a Nightingale": "Already with thee! tender is the night", which was recalled by

---

[1] Interestingly, Baker speaks of Mansfield in terms of a medical metaphor: "Katherine was no nurse or doctor, rather a surgeon, cutting through the outer surface, under which most of us hide, to find and expose the truth of each personality. From this she derived an insight that could lead her to compassionate understanding" (204). I am grateful to Prof. Janka Kascakova, Catholic University, Ružomberok, Slovakia, for drawing my attention to Baker's work.

F. Scott Fitzgerald in 1934 for the title of his last novel. In *Hamlet*, Ophelia refers to the *tendresse* in tenderness but also opens the way to the word's contractual implications, when she tells her father of Hamlet that "He hath, my lord, of late made many tenders / Of his affection to me" (Shakespeare, *Hamlet*, 1. 3.98–99, 298). Polonius seizes on these meanings of "tender" as contract: he chides her for "having taken these tenders for true play", he orders her to "Tender yourself more dearly", or otherwise, he notes, "You'll tender me a fool" (1.3.108). "Tender", crossing over from Middle French, was already in use in Chaucer (2008), where it commonly means "youthful": it occurs as such in the sixth line of the Prologue to *The Canterbury Tales*, where April is praised as the month of "the tender croppes, and the yonge sonne" (32). "Tender" as "young", then, "tender" as "soft" or "sympathetic", "tender" as "contract" and as "legal tender": this word, index first in Middle French of a version of intense feeling, was hardened out in English to include lifespans ("tender" as "young"), contractual arrangements ("tender me . . ."), and the effects of such contracts on the economic level ("legal tender").

All of these meanings are subsumed by Katherine Mansfield in her letters to John Middleton Murry, where "tenderness" is one of her most valued words:

> Last night, there was a moment before you got into bed. You stood, quite naked, bending forward a little—talking. It was only for an instant. I saw you—I loved you so—loved your body with such tenderness—Ah my dear—And I am not thinking now of "passion". No, of that other thing that makes me feel that every inch of you is precious to me. Your soft shoulders—your creamy warm skin, your ears, cold like shells are cold—your long legs and feet that I love to clasp with my feet—the feeling of your belly—and your thin young back.—Just below that bone that comes out at the back of your neck you have a little mole. It is partly because we are young that I feel this tenderness. (*Letters* 1, 86)

Tenderness, here, twice: the power of these lines, I propose, comes not just from their palpable intimacy, but because Mansfield is doing something amazing: she is inching, in her language of intimacy, away from more conventional 19th-century languages of love and towards one built around physical sensation and affect. It is not, as she says, "passion", by which she means sexual desire, the force that fascinated many (mostly male) modernists, from Freud to D.H. Lawrence to Joyce. Neither is it quite "love", whether we think of that feeling within the classical categorizations as *eros* or *agape*, as an invention of the "amour courteous" tradition, or in terms of the bourgeois version of love at the service of the family romance plot. That bourgeois, 19th-century romantic version of love is what Joyce ([1922] 1986) satirizes in *Ulysses*, with the interpolation "Love loves to love love [...] Constable 14A loves Mary Kelly", after Bloom, arguing with the drinkers in Barney Kiernan's public house, has unconvincingly defined love as "I mean the opposite of hatred" and is derided by one of his interlocutors as "A nice pattern of a Romeo and Juliet" (273).

No, Mansfield's tenderness, this essay claims, is a new, modernist version of human connection. It is a filiation nurtured from an intense physicality. We have many words in modernism for the opposite to "tenderness": ennui, alienation, modernist angst. Modernist art teems with glamorizations of this opposite phenomenon and of its dark allure, from Edvard Munch's "The Scream" to T.S. Eliot's "The Love Song of J. Alfred Prufrock" to Thomas Mann's *Death in Venice*. Katherine Mansfield, in stories such as "Miss Brill" and "Je ne parle pas français", and in the trick ending of "Bliss", often appears to be working in that predictable modernist idiom, looking down upon lonely, loveless existences. (At least Mann's Aschenbach in *Death in Venice* finds his Tazio, and Prufrock dreams of mermaids; Mansfield's Miss Brill has only her boxed fur collar in her bedsit.) Nevertheless, I think the real pleasure of Mansfield's stories, and certainly of her letters, strangely, is the opposite. Amongst the modernist cavalcade of proofs of the impossibility of real human connections, she is the unlikely witness to—or possibly the inventor of—something quite opposite: a template, of a new law of attraction, and communion. She took a word, tenderness, bandied about in English literature for almost a millennium, and made it the name of a new life-register. Katherine Mansfield, then: the inventor of modern tenderness.

To clarify: this essay does not claim that Mansfield, as the "woman writer", is simply being more empathetic, kind or caring than the rest, that, as they rushed to delineate modernist angst, she championed an alternative empathy. (It claims, *au contraire*, that she was *more* completely and profoundly modernist than they.)[2] To begin to sketch the scope and significance of Mansfield's tenderness-text, let us juxtapose it with the achievement of Virginia Woolf and James Joyce. In a diary entry in 1941, Virginia Woolf (1984) wrote the following:

> Joyce is dead. I remember Miss. Waver, bringing *Ulysses* [...]. And the pages reeled with indecency. I put it in the drawer of the inlaid cabinet. One day Katherine Mansfield came and I had it out. She began to read, ridiculing: then suddenly said, "still there is something in this: a scene that should figure I suppose in the history of literature" [...]. I bought the blue paper book and read it here one summer I think, with spasms of wonder, of discovery. (352–53)[3]

The encounter described here between Joyce's *Ulysses*, Woolf, who would soon write the short story that would eventually become *Mrs. Dalloway*, and Mansfield, soon to write "Bliss", is surely a key node both of modernist anxiety-of-influence and of modernist cross-inspiration.[4] Note, however, not merely Woolf's acknowledgement of her jealousy, both of the innovative power of Joyce's writing and of Mansfield's ability to appreciate it, but her description of this jealousy

---

[2] For an excellent work on the relation between sentiment and modernity, see Illouz (2007), Ch. 1, "The Rise of *Homo Sentimentalis*" (1–39).

[3] For extensive and interesting discussions of Woolf-Joyce relations, see Canani and Sullam (2014).

[4] For the famous letter in which Mansfield speaks of envying Woolf ("How I envy Virginia"), see *Letters* 3, 127–28. T.S. Eliot might also be included in this circle of envy, respect and influence. Eliot wrote in praise of "Bliss", calling it "brief, poignant, and in the best sense, slight" (1934, 35–36).

as a spasm. Naming the experience a spasm, she recognized it primarily as a physical sensation, an experience that passed over her body. William James, older brother of the proto-modernist novelist Henry James and a towering figure in the history of modern psychology, had in 1884 written the key essay "What is an Emotion?" in which he professed to solve one of the oldest controversies in the study of feelings when he declared that emotions were first experienced upon the body and then, recognizing them, one knew one had had that emotion (1884, 188–205). That is, emotions were not first mental recognitions, of which one then noted symptoms upon one's body. Woolf's spasm of jealousy exactly followed this logic: the physical sensation precedes the acknowledgement of the feeling. More, I want to suggest that it was that same logic at work in Joyce's prose that Katherine Mansfield noticed when she declared that "still there is something in this: a scene that should figure I suppose in the history of literature". Here, if you will, is a moment of cultural transmission: Mansfield, on reading Joyce, brings out even more in the texture of her own writing the very embodied "tenderness" she was already predisposed to celebrate; Woolf, in describing her own discovery of what Joyce was attempting as a "spasm" she herself experienced, was still putting into practice, years later in her diary, the commitment to recording a particular kind of embodied and tender experience that she had first seen Mansfield acknowledge as the greatness of Joyce's prose. In this sense the throwaway term "spasm" may be Woolf's acutely accurate way of putting her finger on exactly what Joyce, Mansfield and herself had each achieved in modernist prose.

Hence to this essay's thesis: the modernist prose of each of these writers became experimental in the first instance to record with an unprecedented accuracy the physical sensations, the spasms, the reactions of bodies to stimuli, of the characters it displayed. To show how this worked on the page, consider a single scene in *Ulysses*—let us imagine it was the one Mansfield read—the end of the "Lestrygonians" episode. Here Bloom, after his lunch of a gorgonzola cheese sandwich and a glass of wine, has just turned the corner into Kildare St., when he sees Blazes Boylan, the man who will soon be in bed with Molly, Bloom's wife. Bloom panics:

> Mr. Bloom came into Kildare St. First I must. Library.
> Straw hat in sunlight. Tan shoes. Turned-up trousers. It is. It is.
> His heart quopped softly. To the right. Museum. Goddesses. He swerved to the right.
> Is it? Almost certain. Won't look. Wine in my face. Why did I? Too heady. Yes it is. The walk. Not see. Get on.
> Making for the museum gate with long windy steps he lifted his eyes. Handsome building. Sir Thomas Deane designed. Not following me?
> Didn't see me perhaps. Light in his eyes.
> The flutter of his breath came forth in short sighs. Quick. Cold statues: quiet there. Safe in a minute.
> No. Didn't see me. After two. Just at the gate.
> My heart! ([1922] 1986, 150 [*U*8: 1167–1179])

Bloom could have stood his ground, confronted Boylan—and transformed the plot. But he doesn't. He scuttles away, and Joyce, writing like a zealous movie cameraman who wants to capture every tremble and fluctuation of a victim's body and face, gives us not deep thoughts on Bloom's cowardice, not a report on Bloom's feelings, certainly not a wistful hymn to Bloom's lost love (as Conrad, James or Hardy would each have done). Rather, he gives us a second-by-second account of the exact symptoms of body changes Bloom exhibits. We witness his reddening face, his shortening, panting breaths, his faster-beating heart, and the exact movements of his fluttering hands. The key line is "His heart quopped softly": the central physical experience that is being recorded here is Leopold Bloom's rising and wavering heartbeat. It is flanked by a quick note of Bloom's sudden blush ("Wine in my face"), his altered gait ("Swerved"), his shortened breath ("with long windy steps"), and his now pounding heart ("Moment more. My heart!"). All are unmistakable, transmitted in telegraphically-brief sentence-fragments.

If this is a primary pillar of Joyce's *Ulyssean* modus, Virginia Woolf in his wake accomplished a similar turn even more thoroughly, in her own style. In fact, when Clarissa Dalloway, at the denouement of *Mrs. Dalloway*, faces a crisis less immediate but even more resonant than that from which Bloom fled, Woolf launches nothing less than a mini-manifesto for this kind of writing. At her party, Clarissa hears of Septimus Smith's suicide:

> Always her body went through it first, when she was told, suddenly, of an accident: her dress flamed, her body burned. He had thrown himself from a window. Up had flashed the ground; through him, blundering, burning, went the rusty spikes. There he lay with a thud, thud, thud in his brain, and then a suffocation and blackness. For she saw it. But why had he done it? ([1925] 1990, 184)

"Always her body went through it first" is a summation of William James's account of emotion; then comes "her dress flamed, her body burned". Here is the flaming dress of modernism. Djuna Barnes (1937), in an even more accurate phrase in her novel *Nightwood*, terms it "the trepidation of the flesh" (41). Here, in *Mrs. Dalloway*, it delineates merely a rise in body temperature, a hot flush, an intense version of Bloom's "wine in my face". Yet this simplicity belies a Jamesian revolution in the representation of human well-being in the novel in English, in which the annotated somatics preceded any account of motivation as a means to get at feelings. The key is that Woolf transmits feeling, emotion, by delineating physical sensation. The logic of an older narrative form is reversed: now we as readers get the annotation of somatic reaction from which we can if we wish infer emotion, what we call feeling, and from which we assume we can discern motivation. The soma-text fronts, or substitutes for, the feeling-text.

Next, let us consider how this works in the stories of Katherine Mansfield. Our text-case will be the story that takes a somatic state for its title—"Bliss", written in 1917:

> What can you do if you are thirty, and turning the corner of your own street, you are overcome suddenly by a feeling of bliss—absolute bliss!—as though you'd suddenly swallowed a bright piece of the late afternoon sun and it burned in your bosom, sending out a little shower of sparks into every particle, into every finger and toe? (2010, 68)

This is the second paragraph of "Bliss". In this story Mansfield trumps Woolf's "burning dress" in advance with her evocation of the whole body as incendiary device. There is an avant-garde joke from 1915 by Francis Picaba, in which he entitles a drawing of an electrical spark plug, taken from a technical manual, "Portrait of a Young American Woman in a State of Nudity" (see Duffy 2009, 14–16). In "Bliss", Bertha Young's body functions literally as a kind of spark-plug, a point at which forces and currents of energy converge and are transformed and transmitted. First, as in Joyce, the text allows us to consider affects by reading soma-symptoms evident in, and generated in, Bertha's body, where they are first read by Bertha herself. To the extent that the story operates as a stream-of-consciousness narrative, it offers a continuous close reading by Bertha of the symptoms of her own body:

> But in her bosom there was that bright, glowing place—that shower of little sparks coming from it. It was almost unbearable, she hardly dared to breathe for fear of fanning it higher, and yet she breathed deeply, deeply. She hardly dared to look in the cold mirror—but she did look, and it gave her back a woman, radiant, with smiling, trembling lips. (2010, 68–69)

Here, as in Joyce, is the measure of one's breathing, as it is annotated in modernist prose. Bloom's "long windy steps" is matched by Bertha's barely daring to breathe. Here too, very much in the terms outlined by William James, is a person knowing her emotion, and trying to name it, after it has first appeared upon her body. This is how the story names, in Bertha, "bliss".

But what is bliss? It is happiness, but intensified. Here is a story about an intensity, a nexus of undefined feelings. It is this intensity that Bertha calls "tenderness", when she asks, "Oh, why did she feel so tender towards the whole world tonight? Everything was good—was right. All that happened seemed to fill again her brimming cup of bliss" (76). This tenderness, then, is not a heightened state of some known feeling (such as "love" or even "joy"), but rather a heightened state of intense physical being—an extra aliveness. This intense aliveness manifests itself in the story in an excess of energy. In *Ulysses* and *Mrs. Dalloway*, the somatic symptoms being recorded evidence themselves upon the bodies of flâneurs—which is to say, upon moving bodies. In "Bliss" this movement is upgraded to the point where it is registered as a continuous expenditure of energy from the body of each character, and in each case the somatic symptoms manifest themselves as modulations of the characters' energy. Energy, as tenderness's charge, is under scrutiny in "Bliss".

Mansfield's story, I propose, is primarily concerned with the project of annotating aliveness, which it denominates "bliss". It effects this by marking the signs of energy in Bertha's dynamic body in particular. Joyce's text, as we saw, annotates the symptoms of human response upon Bloom's body in movement; Woolf goes further, but, as a close reading of many passages in her work would show, her symptom-textuality is constrained by attention to matters of possible motivation as she lays out Clarissa's stream of consciousness. We might think of Woolf's modernist prose project as a writer's struggle on the one hand to get beyond the dictates of the psychologist William James, with his stress on the primacy of the physiological and symptomological evidence of bodily changes, and on the other, to evade the example of his brother Henry James, whose prose wove elaborate speculations regarding possible motivations around every action and movement. Mansfield, instead, nowhere more than in "Bliss", hones in mercilessly on the reading of the human organism's own physical energy.

She is not, therefore, concerned primarily with feelings, or with the way in which new knowledge, gained during the story, alters how Bertha feels. The story is not an account of a woman who must control or conceal her feelings or who must gather more information to have insight—the terms in which "Bliss" is conventionally read. In such accounts the story exists to show up Bertha as a naïve young wife without knowledge, in a tale that is centrally about how she discovers that her husband is having an affair. In this reading, "Bliss" is a vignette of a blighted life; the title is ironic, and more likely than not refers to the phrase "ignorance is bliss". To read it as such, as a bitterly ironic snapshot of a blindly happy young wife who gets her comeuppance and is forced to face reality by the last page, is to see Bertha just as Leopold Bloom has often been seen: as a pathetic cuckold. I submit that just as *Ulysses* does not in the end care about Molly's affair, even if it hangs upon it whatever vestiges of conventional family-romance plot the novel contains, "Bliss" is not centrally concerned with Harry's affair with Pearl. The narrative of the cuckold is simply the oldest plot in the comic repertoire (favoured by Boccaccio in *The Decameron*, for example); here, in the early 20th century, it is pressed into service as the frame on which is draped matter much more interesting to the denizens of modernity. This matter is energy. Hence, to a thesis on these texts: in these modernist works, the old concern with feelings—with the inviolability of love, for example, the slow curdle of jealousy, the admirable sense of rootedness generated by the ability to trust—gives way to a new concern. It is one we are only coming to terms with as readers a century later: the issue of human energy. Energy, an intense aliveness as an end in itself, is what is celebrated in "Bliss".

It might be pointed out that the short story is the ideal vehicle for this modernist turn to human energy. The short story may be thought of as a closed economy, like a state or a company. Within this economy, forces circulate. Readers have been trained, given the modern short story's origins in the detective story from Poe to Conan Doyle, to think of this primarily as an economy of information. In terms of its account of information-impact, "Bliss" concerns Bertha's ignorance, and her discovery of her husband's lies. We tend to read the short story's feeling-displays as reinforcing the text's informational "revelation". Reading for feelings, "Bliss" reveals the superficiality of feelings among these affected bourgeois-bohemians. This reading of the text as a magical revelation of the fakery of feelings on display is mitigated only by intimations of queer desire between Bertha and Pearl. I want to suggest here, instead, that "Bliss" involves us in an economy of circulating energies. Like the atom, whose structure was uncovered by another New Zealander, Ernest Rutherford, in 1919 (see Kelman 1969), the story contains, and pulses with, energies. Readers track the economy of energy, and are energized by the text.

Consider "Bliss" as an energy vortex. The "bright glowing space in Bertha's bosom" with "its little shower of sparks coming from it" is only the beginning. First, there is the rush of Bertha's every move: as the story opens "She wanted to run instead of walk" (2010, 68); soon, "running up the steps, rattling the letterbox [...] she seized her bag and ran upstairs to the nursery" (69). Before the party, "Picking up the cushions [...] she threw them back on the couches [...] suddenly hugging [one] to her, passionately, passionately" (72); as the party begins "she flung down on a couch and pressed her hands to her eyes". The whole grammar of the story echoes Bertha's breathless rush. Next, the other versions of human excitement here act as her foils: her baby, who "saw her mother and began to jump" (69), her husband Harry, who worries that he will be five minutes late: "He loved doing things at high pressure..." (74). The guests too are mostly impressions built around their energies. Eddie stresses unlikely words in every exclamation, to exaggerate the account of his life lived *in extremis*, all coded as a specific rhythm of male queerness; Pearl Fulton, in contrast, is the languorous one with the "cool, sleepy voice": "What was there in that cool arm that could fan—fan—start blazing—blazing—the fire of bliss that Bertha did not know what to do with?" (75).

Pearl's cool arm, touching Bertha's hand: the energy in this energy economy is not contained exclusively in the characters' bodies. Rather, it radiates out into the very matter of the house, the garden, the meal, making it all vibrate. There is in the story an economy of heat and cold, of light and dark and of moon and fire that is not merely symbolic. Light effects, from cinema, are everywhere: "For the dark table seemed to melt into the dusty light and the glass dish and the blue bowl to float in the air" (69). Soon we are told: "The fire had died down in the drawing room into a red flickering 'nest of baby phoenixes', said Face" (77), while the enigmatic pear tree at the end of the garden "seemed, like the flame of a candle, to stretch up, the point, to quiver in the bright air" (77). Then, there is the story's economy of heat and cold: Bertha feels how "the cold air fell on her arms"(68), while Pearl Fulton, described by Harry as "cold like all blond women" is the one with "that cold arm" (71). This symphony of dark and light, heat and cold, maps the energy vectors in the atmosphere that is the medium for the characters' energies and languor. The enclosed space of the short story can barely contain this energy, this electricity, that pulses through the characters' bodies and across the air they breathe. The short story's style, with its dashes, repeated words, and telegraphic directness, monitors, seismograph-like, the energy relayed.

So is "Bliss," then, a vitalist tale? Is it a work of Britain's best-known vitalist offshoot, Wyndham Lewis's Vorticism? John Middleton Murry's modernist life virtually began when he moved to Paris and read the works of Henri Bergson. Yet it would be very faint praise indeed to describe "Bliss" as merely an exercise in modish vitalism. Nevertheless, it is a short story about Bergson's "élan vital". Both Mansfield's "Bliss" and Bergson's "élan vital", however, beg to be contextualized. One such context is the medico-scientific project, underway from the mid-19th century, to retheorize, literally, what it meant to be alive—to isolate and understand the continuous processes that implied aliveness.

Recently, a new environmentalist neo-vitalism has emerged, asking us to consider if apparently inert matter in nature—such as a rock or debris in the gutter—might not in fact be alive; around 1860, the simpler but much more daunting project was to isolate what kept living things alive. Key in this history was Claude Bernard (1974), who defined life as a struggle between the "milieu intérieur", the processes that go on inside your body, and those of the "milieu extérieur", the physical and other forces outside it (84). Darwin (1872), particularly in his final book, *The Expression of Emotion in Man and Animals*, gave a history of the mutation of some of these life processes, as they could be apprehended through the locomotive, and expressive, movements of organism's bodies: he discussed not only large locomotive movements, such as how we walk, but much more subtle ones that relate to emotion: how we laugh, sneer, and frown. The subsequent medico-scientific project to refine these definitions of life may be said to have had two stages. Doctors first focused on human energy as it was visible in human locomotion and physical movement (Rabinbach 1992); conversely, they attended too to the issues of slowed locomotion, the evidence of fatigue and exhaustion. This work coincided with the era in which physical labour, in which human energy as gross locomotive power, was harnessed as energy to drive the economy, as in factory or manual work. It was characterized by obsessive studies of human locomotion in all its details, all made more possible by new technologies of observation, recording and measurement; the most famous examples may be the stop-action photography sequences of Eadweard Muybridge in the US and Étienne-Jules Marey in France. This line of medical and social research culminated in Taylorism, the pseudo-science of efficient movement, and in Henry Ford's assembly line. The horrors of the assembly line were however, being satirized, in the inter-war years for example, by Charlie Chaplin in the film *Modern Times* of 1936.

The second phase of the medico-scientific project to define life, which matters more to modernism and which coincides with the various modernist experiments, emerged as the doctors began to attend to ever subtler human movements—trembling lips, rates of breathing and heart-beat, blinking eyes, the human breath. Now, feelings could be considered readable through subtle physical movements. "Nerves" had been a commonplace for over a century: Mrs. Bennett complains of her nerves on the first pages of *Pride and Prejudice*. But in 1881 Dr. James Beard published *American Nervousness*, in which he blamed modernity for causing "neurasthenia" or "nervous exhaustion"—a lassitude resulting from over-stimulation of the nerves (Beard 1881). Subsequent researchers included William James, who as we have seen, read emotions as observable effects upon the body, and, in the new century, his student Walter Cannon (1915), whose *Bodily Changes in Pain, Hunger, Fear and Rage* explores what he called "the bodily changes which occur in conjunction with pain, hunger and the major emotions" (vi). In other words, the years between 1850 and 1929 witnessed the takeover by medical science (and male scientists) of a field—the emotions, the passions, the feelings—that had, at least since the 18th-century Romantics, been regarded as the concern of culture, and devalued as the concern of women.

As we read Katherine Mansfield's short stories, and keep these contexts in mind, we may ask whether modernist literature, as it catches up with these new initiatives in the "life-sciences", merely following the scientists' lead, or is it going further? The new attention to the minutiae of the body's symptoms in Joyce, Woolf, Mansfield and many others, from Gertrude Stein (who as a student worked in the laboratory of William James) to D.H. Lawrence (whose peculiar late-imperial British amalgam of pastoral, post-Decadence and Futurism, all of which was familiar to Mansfield, can be grasped in these terms), parallels the early 20th-century stance of the scientists. Modernist experimental literary culture was thoroughly attuned to representing symptoms of emotions as they were displayed upon the moving human body. Is what I've called Mansfield's tenderness more attuned than the work of Beard or Cannon, or for that matter, William James or Henri Bergson, to vital modern life? Is it more profound in its account of it than theirs, and if so, how?

To begin to answer this, consider how the modernist era is bracketed by two striking and vastly influential events in the understanding of life and in the history of medicine. The first is the isolation, in 1903, at the start of the long modernist moment, of adrenaline (see Hoffmann 2013). Adrenaline's discovery and patenting, by Jochiki Takamine, a Japanese businessman and scientist who arrived in the US for the New Orleans exhibition, is a story worthy of H.G. Wells's novel *Tono Bungay*. Synthetic adrenaline was soon being sold as an energy booster—athletes took it before sporting contests. The account of its action on the body—the famous narrative of "fight or flight"—is an old story of heroics retooled for modernity. But this story made adrenaline nothing less than the body's proof that energy surges were the indices of life. Mansfield's "Bliss", with all its talk of running upstairs, of hugging cushions, of "that bright glowing space" in "Bertha's bosom [...] with that little shower of sparks coming from it", is certainly a story about adrenaline and its effects. It is the tale of an adrenaline rush. We might even be tempted to read the line about the "little shower of sparks" as a satire on the whole interest in adrenaline-powered intensity that was still circulating in the decade the text was written. I disclaim such an ironic reading; on the contrary, "Bliss" is a tale about an adrenaline rush made all the more intense because the plot allows neither fight nor flight. "Bliss" anticipates the discovery which, in my schema, is the second event, which coincides with the end of the modernist moment. This was the discovery by the Hungarian-Canadian doctor Hans Selye in 1936 of a syndrome he named "stress" (see, for example, Selye [1956] 1978). The term "stress" came from metallurgy, where it denoted the breaking point of metals. And, as with Beard's *American Nervousness*, so too with Selye's stress: almost at once, "stress" became more or less a key term to describe human well-being, or a relative lack of it. It instantly became both a medical diagnosis, and a term for how we live. This mass adoption of the idea of stress was a global phenomenon: the word entered many languages unchanged. Stress, so ubiquitous in our own lives, and in our thinking since, was only named in the late 1930s. Stress is a late-modernist invention. It may be the 20th century's major contribution to thinking conceptually about how we live in the world. Remarkably, no-one, until now, has spoken of it in literature.

  This silence is even more strange when you consider that virtually every modernist text—and every story by Katherine Mansfield—is a story about stress. *Ulysses* charts the rise and fall of Leopold Bloom's stress over a day in Dublin; *Mrs. Dalloway*, likewise, charts that of Clarissa. "Bliss", while it is clearly a tale of an adrenaline rush, is also very evidently a story in which that rush, brought on by excitement, is intensified, and has its energy diverted and pent-up, by stress. Many stories by Mansfield—consider "The Daughters of the Late Colonel", for example—are unmitigated stress-texts. Literature, then, has paralleled medical science and its envisioning of the meanings and rhythms of life. As cultural critics we must ask: with what meaning does the literary text imbue the adrenaline rush, and the stress-text, that science does not?

Recently the critic Franco Moretti (2016) pointed out that the real reason the humanities are fading is that for years all the truly big ideas have been had by scientists, so that the brightest students are inevitably attracted to science. If this is true, then we might want to claim that modernism represents the last time when the cultural realm still generated big ideas. Conversely, note that the modernist moment was one when science not only had vast new ideas about the universe, from the structure of the atom to the possibility of the atomic bomb, but also theorized the terrain of feelings that had formerly been left to culture. Science recast the concept of energy in these years, from the second law of thermodynamics to Einstein's "e=mc2" (kinetic energy equals matter multiplied by a constant, the speed of light, to the square of two); at the same time, from Beard to Selye, it fully reconceptualized human wellbeing, and what Darwin called "the expression of emotions" as the subject's energetic reaction to external stimuli. It deferred feeling to energy. Given the prevalence since of these ideas about our own well-being (we ask ourselves if we feel "energized," if we are "stressed") it would appear that the scientists stole a march on culture, offering a narrative of how it feels to be alive in modernity that gained instant widespread, even global acceptance, so that it is now wholly taken for granted and appears mundane.

Responses in the realm of culture, I want to claim, developed in two ways. First, as pursued by the Italian Futurists, and, in literature in English, in their different ways by D.H. Lawrence, Wyndham Lewis, Ezra Pound and many others, culture cast itself as a proselytizing vehicle for human energy—against a past, an establishment, or a bogey such as "bourgeois respectability" that was cast as stodgy, static, or, as prime symptom of what the young Joyce described in his native Dublin as "paralysis". Such stodginess was presumed to be the enemy of an over-policed and pent-up energy whose eventual surfacing was imagined as natural and possibly inevitable. In the work of Lawrence, for example, from his quasi-decadent first novel, *The White Peacock* (begun 1906, published 1911) to his poems written in Bandol, *Pansies* (1930),[5] this emerges as the last gambit of pastoral; to the extent that Mansfield is "Laurentian" (and there is always a trace element of Lawrence in her work, as with the heavy symbolism of the pear tree in "Bliss") she too indulges in this version of literary vitalism. On the other hand, one dominant modernist strain appears in general to launch a drawn-out lament that the old ways of feeling, under the immense tide of modern speed and hurry, are disappearing: from T.S. Eliot's "The Love Song of J. Alfred Prufrock" which concerns the inability to love, all the way to the Marxist critic Fredric Jameson's (1991) theory about postmodernism as witnessing what he call the final "death of affect", modernists and their successors have mostly lamented that, as we slower humans cannot keep up with the modern world's excitements, we have lost our ability to feel altogether, and become blasé. (The "blasé attitude" was one of the symptoms adduced by Georg Simmel (1960) in 1903 as the byproduct of modern urban living, in his essay "The Metropolis and Mental Life".) Neither is it difficult to read almost every Mansfield short story within these latter parameters. Her stories often come across as Chekhovian laments for, or satires of, the callousness, or the wholescale inability to feel and intuit, of modern people. The more modern one is in a Mansfield story, the less one can feel: Miss Brill has some shade of feeling left, which merely exposes her as pathetic as she returns to her lonely room, while the cool threesome of "Je ne parle pas français" are utterly without feeling.

---

5   See D.H. Lawrence, *The White Peacock* (1911), and *Pansies* (1929). For an interesting account of the censorship efforts around the *Pansies* MS, see Pollnitz (2005).

And yet: I think that neither Futurist-filtered vitalism nor Chekhovian lament over feeling's demise is the true pleasure of Mansfield's texts. Which is not to say that these elements are not both there: in "Bliss", for example, both the semi-secret lesbian union of Bertha and Pearl Fulton before the pear tree happens, and so does the revelation that the shimmering glamour of these people's lives is built upon a lie: that Bertha's husband and Pearl are having an affair. Yet the real pleasure of the text, I submit, and the source of Mansfield's big modernist idea, is otherwise: it is that stress, generated in the information economy (in "Bliss", the revelation of the affair), can be overcome by energy, as manifested in the way in which Bertha reacts to the excitement of her milieu and herself generates it, in her body, in her surroundings, and especially in those around her. This, I'd suggest, is not the only the pleasure of "Bliss" but even, in their own ways and channeled through their own complex symphonies of styles, of both *Mrs. Dalloway* and *Ulysses* as well. Clarissa overcomes her illness to generate an energy as sparking as the bourgeois experience of London itself; Bloom overcomes the stress of knowing of his wife's affair through the energy of his empathy. And Bertha? Bertha in this story has brought her intense energy to the point where, "For the first time in her life Bertha Young desired her husband" (79). We might not be comfortable with this, for example, as feminist readers. Nevertheless, note that the text does *not* state here that "For the first time in her life, Bertha Young *realized that* she desired him"; that is, this is not what in Joyce criticism would be called an epiphany, an injection of knowledge into the knowledge economy. Further, in the terms Mansfield used to Murry in her letter to him quoted earlier, neither is Bertha's response "just passion". It is simply, but more significantly, that she "desired". This beginning of desire, which potentially can include everybody and is boundless, is what is significant. It is the accession to feeling first felt upon the body. Certainly, it is not the "death of affect": in fact, it is the awakening of affect. The title "Bliss", then, is not satirical but literal: high energy, channeled, circulated, ricocheting off others, makes for an intense explosion of a very modern and direct affect.

One more point. Scientific experiments are like late-modernist minimalist art: they try to shave away all contexts, and thus cannot answer the question: why? In the context of our questions here: why, in the late 19th and early 20th centuries, did energy begin to replace the old architecture of feeling, of love, loyalty, jealousy, shame and the whole taxonomy of bourgeois sentiment that had sustained the family romance plot of the modern novel in particular?[6] Mansfield, Joyce and Woolf, by lining their evocations of energy with intense detail, imply, if not its causes, at least its contexts. In brief, in their texts, the adrenaline rush, and also the stressful moments for each character, results from anxiety about their husbands and wives: the old structures of social organization, and the feelings that go with them, are creaking. Next, note that each text centers on a party: "Bliss" is (like Joyce's "The Dead") a party-story; *Mrs. Dalloway* builds up to the party organized by Clarissa in her grand London home, while *Ulysses* culminates in the rowdy expressionist free-for-all in the "Nighttown" episode "Circe", set in the parlour of a Dublin brothel (Joyce [1922] 1986, 350–497). All three, in other words, are ostensibly about the energy we expend in leisure, and yet in each, work, and workers—especially servants—hover as an issue, just as servants hover as characters. This was the era when, in the west, factory work was being replaced by service work, when human energy expenditure was being reorganized, and the definition of the new "white-collar" worker, as salesperson or as teacher, for example, was that you emoted as the way you expended energy. Beyond this development, the implications of new technology also hover. Just as, in Eliot's "The Waste Land", a woman in a London bedroom is saying "My nerves are bad tonight", while outside is "a taxi, throbbing waiting" (2000, 293). In the texts of Mansfield, Joyce and Woolf too the telephone, taxis, the new city tram systems, and the airplane in *Mrs. Dalloway*, pitch the characters' energies against the new

---

[6] There is a scattered but growing critical literature that works to think in these terms. One early and highly original contribution is Brennan (2000); its focus on exhaustion suggests a cautionary counterpoint to the argument advanced here. Recent work relating affect, culture and politics includes Massumi (2002).

technological energies of the machines of movement. The worlds of energized human leisure face off against the massive forces of technologically-harnessed and -driven energy, which appears infinitely greater than any human energy. "Just then the light snapped on" may be the sentence at the center of "Bliss": the presence of that new thing in the early 20th century, widespread electricity, in itself massively inflated the energy economy described in these texts.

In this new order of vastly increased energy, where human energy is being put to new purposes in white-collar work, where any human energy appears puny in contrast to machine energy, it is not surprising that science, whether physics or medicine, became energy-obsessed, that the philosophy of Henri Bergson, Hans Dreisch (1914) and William James turned to vitalism, and that modernist fictions began to show their readers how to generate and calibrate their own energies in this new energy-scape. Hence "tenderness". Mansfield, I'm claiming, in "Bliss" and in many other stories, measures the human energy of her characters. Hers is energy writing. She shows in Bertha how a wild energy, expended, can conquer the stress of the discovery of her husband's callousness. Her adrenaline rush, and her stress, conditions her intense tenderness, an intense receptivity to other's energies as a value in itself. "Bliss" is one of the original works on how human beings can thrive in the new global energy economy. It paints the pleasure, and the excitement, of the flaming dress of modernism: an intense somatic receptivity, a passionate tenderness, as a result of an energy seized out of the atmosphere, refracted on others, celebrated at a party, making connections that are charged. "Bliss", in "Bliss", is the joy of energy expended. Mansfield's "Bliss" is itself alive, and energized, with the excitement of her discovery of a new way to be.

Bibliography

Baker, Ida. 1985. *Katherine Mansfield: The Memories of LM*. London: Virago.

Barnes, Djuna. 1937. *Nightwood*. New York: New Directions.

Bernard, Claude. 1974. *Lectures on the Phenomena of Life Common to Animals and Plants.* Translated by Hebbel E. Hoff, Roger Guillemin and Lucienne Guillemin. Springfield, IL: Charles C. Thomas.

Brennan, Teresa. 2000. *Exhausting Modernity: Grounds for a New Economy.* New York: Routledge.

Canani, Marco, and Sara Sullam, eds. 2014. *Parallaxes: Virginia Woolf Meets James Joyce.* Newcastle upon Tyne: Cambridge Scholars Publishing.

Cannon, Walter Bradford. 1915. *Bodily Changes in Pain, Hunger, Fear and Rage: An Account of Recent Researches into the Function of Emotional Excitement.* New York: D. Appleton and Co.

Chaucer, Geoffrey. 2008. *General Prologue to the Canterbury Tales.* Oxford: Oxford University Press, Oxford Student Texts Series.

Darwin, Charles. 1872. *The Expression of Emotion in Man and Animals.* London: John Murray.

Dreisch, Hans. 1914. *The History and Theory of Vitalism.* London: Macmillan.

Duffy, Enda. 2009. *The Speed Handbook: Velocity, Pleasure, Modernism.* Durham, NC: Duke University Press.

Eliot, T.S. 1934. *After Strange Gods: A Primer of Modern Heresy.* London: Faber and Faber.

---. 1991. *Collected Poems, 1909-1962.* New York: Harcourt, Brace, Jovanovich.

Hankin, Cherry, ed. 1991. *Letters between Katherine Mansfield and John Middleton Murry.* New York: New Amsterdam books.

Hoffmann, Brian B. 2013. *Adrenaline.* Cambridge, MA: Harvard University Press.

Illouz, Eva. 2007. *Cold Intimacies: The Making of Emotional Capitalism.* London: Polity, 2007.

James, William. 1884. "What is an Emotion?" *Mind* 9 (34): 188-205.

Jameson, Fredric. 1991. *Postmodernism, or, The Cultural Logic of Late Capitalism.* Durham, NC: Duke University Press.

Joyce, James. [1922] 1986. *Ulysses.* The Gabler Edition. New York: Vintage Books, Random House.

Kelman, Peter, and A. Harris Stone, eds. 1969. *Ernest Rutherford, Architect of the Atom*. Illus. by Henry Gorski. New York: Prentice-Hall.

Lawrence, D.H. 1911. *The White Peacock*. London: Heinemann.

---. 1929. *Pansies*. London: Martin Secker.

Mansfield, Katherine. 2010. *The Best Short Stories of Katherine Mansfield*. Edited by Enda Duffy. New York: Dover Books.

Massumi, Brian. 2002. *Parables of the Virtual*. Durham, NC: Duke University Press.

Moretti, Franco. 2016. "The Digital in the Humanities: An Interview with Franco Moretti." Conducted by Melissa Dinsman, March 2. https://lareviewofbooks.org/article/the-digital-in-the-humanities-an-interview-with-franco-moretti.

Pollnitz, Christopher. 2005. "The Censorship and Transmission of D. H. Lawrence's *Pansies*: The Home Office and the 'Foul-Mouthed Fellow'." *Journal of Modern Literature* 28 (3): 44–71.

Rabinbach, Anson. 1992. *The Human Motor: Energy, Fatigue, and the Origins of Modernity*. Berkeley, CA: University of California Press.

Selye, Hans. [1956] 1978. *The Stress of Life*. New York: McGraw Hill.

Shakespeare, William. 2001. *Hamlet*. London: The Arden Shakespeare, Thompson Publishing.

Simmel, Georg. 1960. "The Metropolis and Mental Life." In *Images of Man: The Classical Tradition of Sociological Thinking*, edited by C. Wright Mills, 36–62. New York: George Braziller.

Woolf, Virginia. 1984. *The Diary of Virginia Woolf*, Vol. 5, *1936–41*. Edited by Anne Olivier Bell, assisted by Andrew McNellie. New York: Harcourt Brace.

---. [1925] 1990. *Mrs. Dalloway*. New York: Mariner Books.

Of Parvenus and Pantheons:
Mansfield's Short Fiction as a "Reading Back"

Ruchi Mundeja

> From that very first afternoon, my childhood was, to put it prettily, "kissed away". I became very languid, very caressing, and *greedy* beyond measure. And so quickened, so sharpened, I seemed to understand everybody and be able to do what I liked with everybody [...]. [T]here's always an African laundress and an outhouse, and I am very frank and *bon enfant* about plenty of sugar on the little fried cake.
>
> "Je ne parle pas français" (Mansfield 2007, 66, 68: emphasis mine)

In her journal, Mansfield once wrote vis-à-vis one of her stories, "I want to use all my force even when I am taking a fine line" (Murry 1984, 256). It is this finesse of walking the fine line, negotiated with an unflinching, bare-all honesty (the "force" that Mansfield refers to), that I see animating the portrait of Raoul Duquette in "Je ne parle pas français", a story that plays itself out so perilously close to the threshold—between the record of a charlatan and an ethnography of the metropolitan avant-garde. In that regard, it is the epigraph above from Mansfield's story that made me pause in my reading of Raoul Duquette as an embodiment of unscrupulous literary ambition and led me to explore how perhaps Mansfield is not simply exposing him but, more provocatively, by deploying him as a penetrative reader-consumer of his milieu, performing an interrogatory reading of modernist discourse itself. What proves arresting in the above quote, making it a conceptual frame for this chapter, is the mention of the appetitive in Raoul. Raoul's hunger for sugared cakes is a veiled flaunting of an early and intimate familiarity with the forbidden, thus whetting his appetite for forays into the buried. In the encounters with the African laundress as he describes them, the libidinal and the appetitive come together. In fact, his literary career seems to unfold against the backdrop of cafés and salons where Raoul's various appetites—carnal, gastronomic, voyeuristic, aspirational—as "quickened" (in his telling) by his encounters with the African woman, crave satiation. Arguments such as those by Simon Gikandi (2003) show that modernism's artistic overhaulings depended on both the fetishization and the evacuation of the African subject (457). Mansfield's story, in its tactical deployment of Raoul's encounter with the African woman as the catalytic centrepiece, seems to lead us to this understanding. Those early brushes he sees as bringing him into line with the avant-garde's experimental agendas—he shows himself compulsively drawn to rummage for artistic inspiration under "the laundry baskets" in a bid to "stagger the critics" (Mansfield 2007, 67). Urmila Seshagiri (2010) offers a brilliant reading of the connection between the newly racialized European metropolises and the "begetting" of Raoul's modernist "mastery" (132–35). In the way Raoul establishes the early initiation into an understanding of the subterranean, he lays a claim to "the audacities of avant-gardism" (Begam and Moses 2007, 1). But there is another dimension to this idea of diving under the surface—Mansfield's story performs its own surreptitious drama of burrowing under and rifling through modernism's aesthetic closet. Probing this metacritical component in Mansfield's short fiction, I look at "Je ne parle pas français" and "The Escape" as dialogically engaging with the modernist literary scene.

After longstanding discussions about de-tethering the idea of the postcolonial from a strictly chronological bias, writers like Mansfield are now being considered through that rubric. As the "temporal horizons of the field" are debated and in its "present contours" the postcolonial is less a historical marker than a record of excentric voices, then the experience of dislocation that began with the spread of empire, and which Mansfield also felt, makes it possible for that lens to be turned to her fiction (Wilson et al. 2010, 1–2). In fact, it is the purpose of this essay to recover that ex-centricity in Mansfield's case. Carrying forward that line of thinking it argues for her fiction to be seen as expository rather than constitutive—as a reading rather than a writing back. I term it a reading back because I see the implicit invitation to a readerly excoriation of eurocentric epistemologies that these texts offer, as defining their status as a precursor to the more enabling writerly instantiation of postcolonial agency. Fiction such as Mansfield's that renders tenuous the boundary between modernism and the postcolonial is marked by its readerly disobedience—Said's (1979) idea of insubordination to the "imperial lingua franca" (213) modified here as scepticism towards, if one may call it that, the modernist lingua franca. If postcolonial writing is seen as "a site of radical contestation and contestatory radicalism" (Moore-Gilbert, Stanton and Maley 2013, 3), then in her skirmishes with the dominant literary idioms of her time, and her ability to see how these perpetuated an othering, even while purportedly and proclaimedly contesting it, Mansfield, as an ambivalently positioned writer, is certainly one of the voices that inaugurate the zone of "contestation".

It is this aspect of Mansfield's work, its interlocutory component vis-à-vis modernist discourse, that interests me. Thus, the premise of this essay is that instead of tracing homologies between metropolitan modernists and voices like Mansfield's that had travelled in from the colonial peripheries, one can alternatively explore how the colonial "interlopers" add a qualifying chapter to the modernist narrative. That is, rather than seeing the work of new modernist studies as illustrating expansion through incorporation into a modernist paradigm that bestows upon writers like Mansfield and Rhys (from the "margins") a place in the canon, "centering" them in other words, we might well turn to consider how fiction such as theirs de-centers certain assumptions underpinning metropolitan modernism itself. As we move towards the conceptual paradigm of a "world literature", reversing the lens—that is, seeing how the periphery modulates the center—might be a more interesting variant as opposed to a belated redressing of canonical inequities or in Pascale Casanova's (2004) words, tilting the "literary balance of power" (43). Indeed, Casanova stresses that the literary republic, the world of letters, is riven by the violence of "struggle and competition over the very nature of literature itself" (12).

The "expatriateness" of Mansfield and its effect on her negotiations with the surrounding metropolitan milieu intriguingly gives her work an edginess, an almost abrasive resistance to modernist formations. In many of her letters and journal entries Mansfield speaks of how she felt like an intruder in the imperial metropole, an inferior version of the imperial subject. She reprises the moment that a number of émigrés from the colonial borderlands testified to—warily perceived as they were of infusing a strain of outsiderness (miscegenation/pollution: racial and/or cultural) into the space of the imperial capital.

This idea of being treated circumspectly intersects with the genre that Mansfield chose to write in: the short story. The short story, as Adrian Hunter (2003) points out, has had to shake itself free of being perceived as a "miniaturized novel" (73). That the genre battled against being considered something of a literary parvenu when Mansfield came to it is stated in the editors' Introduction to *The British Short Story*, in that the story functioned at the level of a "'filler'" in the Victorian period (Liggins et al. 2011, 26). This resonates with Mansfield's, the colonial outsider's, own contentious relationship with the literary establishment of her time. Pertinent to my argument here, Paul March-Russell (2009) traces a connection to the short story's "lack of status" which "has appealed to writers at odds with the dominant values of their society" (70). This essay is an attempt to see whether and how the experience of a certain kind of marginality played upon Mansfield's deployment of the genre itself, so that it became in her hands not just a way to find belongingness within the metropolitan writerly milieu but in fact a launchpad into tactical skirmishes with it. Similar to what I propose of Duquette, Mansfield, in her chosen métier of the short story, reads modernism back to its progenitors.

Ali Smith (2007) points out that Mansfield's stories about writers are among her wittiest (xxv). Can one then cast her as an inveterate satirist of her literary world? It is this excoriating vision that I believe she invests in her otherwise compromised protagonist, Raoul; that is, she counterbalances his unscrupulous pursuit of literary success with his tongue-in-cheek portrayal of the "supercilious intellectualism" (Martin 2017, 8) of literary parlours complete with "cubist sofas" (Mansfield 2007, 70). How then does one read Duquette's insatiable greed—for food, for sex and, most revealingly, for feeding off the secret lives of others—as illuminating the modernist moment? In its zest for newness, metropolitan modernism purged itself of orthodoxy by digging into other spaces, other cultural idioms, thus coming dangerously close to reprising the colonial lust that it otherwise distanced itself from. From Kurtz's gaping mouth in *Heart of Darkness* to Woolf's perceiving giant oyster eye (in her essay "Street Haunting"), modernism's creative amplitude rested on a sensory and cerebral ingestion. In the insatiable appetites of both Kurtz and Raoul, in the images of Kurtz's devouring maw and of the appetitive in Raoul, one finds a problematic contiguity between colonialist rapacity and modernist voracity. In his never-satisfied hunger for sugared cakes, Raoul is Mansfield's grimly magnified image of that subtext of modernism, where all is spectacle and copy to him. Through Raoul's literary *flânerie*—his frequenting of salons and soirées—Mansfield indicates the vast, insatiable, sampling fetish of modernism.

This chapter finds its genesis in my increasingly sceptical engagement with the recent revisionary turn in modernist studies (see Mao and Walkowitz 2008). As literary curricula become more diverse and multi-locational, writers from locations other than the Anglo-American are welcomed into the ever-expanding folds of modernist syllabi. In this context, the question I ask in this chapter is whether the new turn in modernist studies might also be read through a similar prism of ingestion: its expansionist gestures, its incorporatory largesse, appropriating even that which is non-synchronous.

The fevered zeal with which the "parvenus and arrivistes" are inducted into the mainstream involves perhaps a reverse danger. If exclusion implies a silence, then there can be an insidious silencing even in gestures of inclusion. Thus I am drawn more towards probing that which in Mansfield's work is irreducible to a common modernist idiom. Where most critical commentaries on Mansfield argue for her place in the modernist pantheon, it is worth adding the caveat, without making a virtue of marginality, that such gestures might undermine the voice and vision of such writers with a divided positionality, and gloss over their more critical strain. What Woolf saw as the cheap or the acid-laden in Mansfield, for example, might just as well be interpreted as the dis-identificatory, the recalcitrant. In examining "Je ne parle pas français" and "The Escape", the critical endeavour is not to establish continuity between her work and modernism, but from a more sceptical standpoint, to probe the areas of non-synchronicity.

It is important then to bring to the fore statements from Mansfield that underline her awareness of an ex-centric positioning: "you see I am not a highbrow. Sunday lunches and very intricate conversations on 'Sex' and that 'fatigue' which is so essential [...] I flee from" (*Letters* 4, 324). Mansfield's deliberate embrace of a louche, low world can be read as an insightful commentary on some of the blind spots of the "highbrow". If both her uncertainly defined position within the colonial-metropolitan structure as well as her chosen genre (short stories) made her something of a parvenu, Mansfield here seems to wield that position as a challenge to modernism's self-constructions (and pretensions). Since it is in the stigmatized position of the marginalized outsider that this chapter's interest lies, this lens can be extended to study the short story.

While the modernist novel has arguably garnered more critical attention, recent critical work on the modernist short story sees the writers' deployment of the form as of a piece with their claims to resuscitate a moribund literary scene. Since Mansfield and Woolf, that "public of two", were literarily divided vis-à-vis Mansfield's exclusive association with the short story form, it is worth considering their relationship to the genre. Recent criticism—see, for instance, Skrbic (2004) and Hoberman and Benzel (2004)—makes a strong case against according a "step-motherly" treatment to Woolf's short stories or of reading them only within the framing penumbra of her experiments with the novel. While Woolf's quest for newness undoubtedly drew her to the form, some of her remarks subtextually imply that she also saw it as a release from the "greater" labour of writing a novel.

Her remark to Ethel Smyth betrays her dependence on generic hierarchies: "These little pieces [...] were written by way of diversion; they were the *treats* I allowed myself [...]. I shall never forget the day I wrote The Mark on the Wall—all in a flash, as if flying, after being kept stone breaking for months" (*Letters* 4, 231; emphasis added). Such statements betray a lurking self-consciousness about being a novelist hard at work, dabbling on the side with other forms. Again, a statement from a letter where Woolf declares that "it is very amusing to try with these short things" can be juxtaposed against her designation of her creative labour while writing *The Years*, a "corpulent and most obstinate novel" (Woolf *Letters* II, 167; V, 439). In the terms used, the *agon* of one against the *jouissance* of the other, can one see an internalization of the generic hierarchies that she otherwise strove to dislodge?

Tellingly, the fraught relationship between Mansfield and Woolf often involved oblique remarks and insinuating asides from both over their distinct fictional terrains: for instance, when Mansfield writes with purposeful indirection of how "anyone who has not himself written the eighty thousand-odd words [that constitute a novel]" would not "realize the grim importance of the fact that a novel is not written in a day" (*CW*3, 625), she seems to be uncomfortably aware of the successful pursuit of the established novelistic genre by her more renowned contemporaries. However, as McDonnell (2010) succinctly argues, while Mansfield seemed to self-consciously function under the mammoth, looming, presence of the modernist novel, her stance was often one of defiance rather than simply diffidence at the "lowliness" of her chosen craft (123, 127). Woolf, for her part, tried to put Mansfield in her place after the latter's review of *Night and Day*, by implying that her reviews of novels showed her as being out of her depth with the novel form (see McDonnell 2010, 121–22).

Furthermore, critiquing Mansfield's "drawbacks", the following comment made by Woolf in 1931 comes close to the crux of the debate:

My theory is that while she possessed the most amazing senses of her generation so that she could actually reproduce this room for instance [...] she was as weak as water, as insipid, and a great deal more commonplace, when she had to use her mind. That is, she can't put any thoughts, or feelings, or subtleties into her characters. (Woolf *Letters* III, 59)

Mansfield, Woolf's contemporary, would have been sensitive to the implicit hierarchization underpinning these unfavourable reflections from Woolf on the element of "lack" in her work, especially given the acute consciousness that each writer had of the other's career trajectory.

Keeping these multiple frames of "outsiderness" in mind is Raoul Duquette, albeit in all his reprehensibility, Mansfield's only reference point if the story be read as a "cry against corruption" (*Letters* 2, 54)? As a master mimic and reader of his artistic milieu, he is invested with the combative readerliness that I wish to foreground in Mansfield's work. His entire persona is built on inventing for himself a complex backstory sufficiently layered to guarantee entry into the art circles of his time. And it is there that his self-conscious performativity, carried to extreme lengths, becomes a measure of Mansfield's reading of the self-instantiation of the modernists. His image of himself as the customs official rifling through hidden caches is a deliberate toying with the modernist penchant for plumbing hidden depths.

Whether it be the terra incognita of Woolf's tunnelling process, or Freud's projecting himself as a "conquistador" (quoted in McHale and Stevenson 2006, 12), all imply an epistemological excavation of the uncharted and buried. The zealous pursuit of the submerged by canonical modernists is at one level trivialized by Raoul's sleazy images. And yet one cannot shrug off the feeling that the writer is not just pointing to the crassness of his observations. Mansfield's own deft exploitation of the labels of lowbrow and upstart suggests that she attributes a subversive vision to her protagonist, who enacts modernism and whose gleefully parodic performance becomes a conduit to its blindspots. Modernism's consuming interest in heightened mental states is grotesquely reflected in Raoul's voyeuristic cannibalizing of the lives of others for literary advantage. In his declared commitment to mining the substratum, Raoul becomes modernism's anti-hero. Mansfield recounts Raoul's abasement sans frills; but as a failed impresario he does provide an insight into the vanities of the artistic milieu he so darkly and macabrely mirrors. To that extent, this story lends itself to being interpreted schismatically: even as the reader is drawn into assessing the morally compromised protagonist, Duquette's own evaluations of the surrounding ethos take on a critical resonance.

In his self-specularity, in the unabashedness with which he fits himself out as a modern, Raoul mimes modernism's self-fashioning. Peter Brooker (2007), commenting on Mansfield's journey from New Zealand to the "playgrounds of Europe", speaks of how "Becoming a bohemian [...] was like stepping through a wardrobe" (107–08). The languorous panache with which Raoul uses borrowed robes (most of his clothes he confesses are "unpaid for") to cultivate an exotic style deserves further consideration. As he takes the bow in his kimono, his traversing of territory startlingly similar to that covered by Mansfield herself becomes more explicit.[1] It is that vantage point, from being both self-dramatizing participant and wry recorder, that links writer and character. Raoul fashions himself as a writer of the "submerged world" (Mansfield 2007, 67).

Duquette's comments seem saturated with malice and an entirely self-gratificatory venom, and yet there is a sceptical glance at some defining modernist tenets, such as how the quotidian often becomes a conduit to the epiphanic. In one of his asides he says of stray

---

1   Beci Carver (2015) offers an interesting reading of what she sees as the naivety of Mansfield's affectations such as her Japanese phase. Labelling it an "unscholarly" attitude, Carver contrasts it to the more scholarly interest of those like Pound in other cultures (305). While Mansfield cannot be exonerated from the charge of exploitation in flirting with alien modes as a version of role-playing, the non-scholarliness also made for a certain distance from which she could satirize these incursions, including her own.

observations made during his peregrinations: "one never knows when a little tag like that may come in useful to round off a paragraph" (Mansfield 2007, 63). He speaks of his moment of *"geste"* coming upon him suddenly in his haunting of cafés, when among the clichéd scrawls and stock love phrases scrawled on the pink, soggy blotting paper, "like the tongue of a dead kitten" (63), he chances upon that stale little phrase, "je ne parle pas français". If one were to interpret this through a literary lens, Raoul seems to imply a moment when the dead feebleness of narrative, its unvirile flaccidity, imaged in the tired notes inscribed onto the limp blotting paper, pulsates into life as his eyes alight on that phrase. That note of female helplessness—the phrase is associated in the story with Mouse, who is figured in tropes of passivity and sentimentalism—restores his confidence in his creative mastery. It leads Raoul to a sense of his creative prowess, suggesting how modernism's move towards a more robust aesthetic was coded along gendered lines. Can this be read, given the gendering, as an allegorized reference to modernism's triumphal distancing of itself from the uninitiated mass? In strongly libidinal imagery, Mansfield points to modernism's many claims to invigorate the literary scene, to inseminate it with surcharged vitality; limpness and bagginess are to be replaced by fecundity—expressed inimitably by Pound as "driving any new idea into the great passive vulva of London" (quoted in Brooker et al, 2010, 161). Interestingly the height of that epiphanic instant, reconfirming Raoul's artistic self valorization, is described in almost post-orgasmic terms: "And up I puffed and puffed, blowing off finally with: 'After all I must be first-rate. No second rate mind could have experienced such an intensity of feeling'" (Mansfield 2007, 64).

Mansfield places under the lens the modernist impulse towards appropriation, both along the lines of gender and race. To come to the transformative encounter with the African laundress, Raoul talks with a self-conscious flourish of how the experience "sharpened" something in him, so that he was "in a state of more or less physical excitement" most of the time (Mansfield 2007, 66, 67). Seshagiri notes that Raoul's attribution of his authorial talents to those childhood clandestine sexual trysts with the African woman can be linked to

Mansfield's offering a "retrospective view of the varied racial formations that enabled avant-garde development" (2010, 125). Raoul scarcely nods in the direction of his family background, saying he sees no point in mentioning it, but does circle back continually to the heavily sexualized nature of his brush with the laundress. Mansfield arranges almost a set piece of racial stereotypes—the frizzy hair, the buxomness, the sexuality oozing from every pore—as Raoul speaks of how his childhood was "kissed away" under her caresses (Mansfield 2007, 66). Mansfield's complex depiction of Raoul makes his statements reek of distorted emphasis such that one wonders how much is self-invention and how much is approximate to the truth. For instance, when he recounts the episode, saying: "I was tiny for my age, and pale, with a lovely little half-open mouth—I feel sure of that", the words point to how the past is being cast in a certain light—one that would lend Raoul the requisite degree of the enigmatic in his brushes with the illicit (66).

Raoul is Mansfield's dark paean to modernist self-birthing—the contemporary cult of artistic self-cultivation lurks in such statements as:

> I have no family; I don't want any [...]. In fact there's only one memory that stands out at all. That is rather interesting because it seems to me now so very significant as regards myself from the literary point of view. (Mansfield 2007, 66)

From here on, having established a back story that adds a murky depth to his "character", he stakes his claim to the writerly via his insight into the subterranean instincts that undergird civilization: "I am going to write about things that have never been touched before. I am going to make a name for myself as a writer about the submerged world" (Mansfield 2007, 67). He declares himself "rich" (67), because he is in possession of truths that others are not privy to. Raoul's experience of the other, the African woman, will, he believes, make him a pioneer into untraversed regions, à la Kurtz. The encounter with the African laundress is seen as the enabling condition for his forays into uncharted terrain in a twisted reprisal of modernism's appropriative courting of the primitive as a conduit to visionary expansion. The episode in fact speaks of a strange conjunction between the colonial and modernist frames. Raoul's description of the laundress is starkly close to how the imperial imaginary was cut through by racial thought, and on a parallel axis, how modernism thrived on difference to infuse novelty into the artscape. Gikandi (2003) speaks of modernism's "representational revolution" as haunted by "the schemata—and stigmata—of difference" (457). This is to suggest the schism between the pathological and the fetishized, a split that shadowed modernism's interest in the racial other. These are insights that postcolonial critics like Simon Gikandi would later build on.

And finally the title of the story brings us back to the self-consciousness of modernist coteries about how the epistemological finesse to read the "foreign", the linguistic felicity required of a many-tongued modernism as John Marx (2005, 2) designates it, rested with a select few and that for the philistines and the uninitiated, the foreign remained illegible. Revealingly, as against Mouse's foundering attempts at translational/ transcultural crossings, Dick and Raoul can be seen to embody the cerebral mobility of modernism, with each making studies of the literary traditions of the other's culture.

One sees the same engagement with the power politics embedded in modernist aesthetics written into a story like "The Escape", though the paradigm most conspicuously at the centre of this narrative has to do with the marital. The opening of the story lands us in a veritable battle zone, with an acrid, corrosive tone dominating the marital relationship. At an explicit level, it is the woman who comes off the worse. We are auditors to her self-centredness, her high-pitched complaints, her querulous tone.

The story makes for perplexing reading since one wonders where this stands within the group of Mansfield's stories that portray women's entrapment within the marital structure. In a story such as "Marriage à la Mode", Isabel is undeniably the subject of ironic scrutiny, but we are at the same time cognisant of how Mansfield walks the "fine line" in counterbalancing that by delineating the boredom and stasis in the lives of women like Isabel. 'The Escape" seems anomalous, then, in that the hysteria in the woman's voice is extreme to the point of being grating. And yet that over-dramatization itself begs a closer look; if one takes the perceiving consciousness to be the husband's, then the story might be read differently. There are points where Mansfield alerts us to the fact that the man is carefully watching his wife, in all her flailing rage. As the carriage in which they are travelling lurches dangerously, this comes to the reader through his almost dispassionate gaze: "He saw her eyes blaze at him, and she positively hissed, 'I suppose you are enjoying this?'" (Mansfield 2007, 200). It is his almost sublime indifference to her reactions that comes across here. Other details as filtered through his observing consciousness stand out: her phobic reaction to the "other", which in the immediate context is the working class children who run alongside the carriage (she "others" them as "horrid little monkeys" [199]), is set against the man's more "empathetic" attitude. The woman's self-absorption, I argue, is suspiciously overdone; it is through the (self-consciously) more refined sensibility of the man that she reveals herself as the repository of crass embourgeoisement. By paying closer attention to its structure we can see how the story's value as commentary becomes manifest—for instance, at the points at which the man's voice enters the story. When the woman seems to be on the brink of breakdown his voice enters to pathologize her display of emotion. As W.H. New (1994) points out, to over-read the hysteria in the woman's voice is to disregard "the functions and effects of the story's form" (104).

The story opens with the wife's litany of complaints at her husband's ineptitude, but just as we begin to feel we know who to identify with here, who the victim is, Mansfield brings us up short against the husband's misogyny and suppressed hatred (and given his reference to Egyptian burial rituals, perhaps bordering on the murderous). These are his thoughts as he looks at his wife's bag:

> The little bag, with its shiny, silvery jaws open, lay on her lap.
> He could see her powder-puff, her rouge stick, a bundle of

letters, a phial of tiny black pills like seeds. [...] He thought: "In Egypt she would be buried with those things." (Mansfield 2007, 197–98)

His vision of the bag with its gaping, devouring maw is indicative of his perception of his wife as emasculating, and the subsequent focus on the items of make-up is perhaps meant to underline her feminine shallowness. The random disarray of collectibles in her bag that his gaze especially designates, sets her up as an indiscriminate, undiscerning consumer. Interestingly, even as he frames her in this way, his own eclectic knowledge of other cultures (here Egypt), locates him within what Claire Davison (2015) identifies as "the cross-cultural, transpositional energies of the modernist era" (2). The woman's consumerism is seen as commercially circumscribed, and the husband in contradistinction is the cosmopolitanized connoisseur of the other. That the gendering might be read as Mansfield looking aslant at the hierarchies in modernist discourse is borne out by how the woman comes to represent the philistine, parochial, uninitiated mass, and the husband the modernist artist seeking an "escape" from these bourgeois constrictions. Tellingly, in both stories under consideration, the man's travel lust is dwelt upon. This recalls Raoul consistently associating images of voyaging with Dick, and at the end of "The Escape", the woman hints at her husband's seeking "escape" through travel.

Mansfield depicts the marital relationship as strife-ridden, and in fact it casts the reader in a rather voyeuristic mould, as we are privy to the constant friction between the couple. The parasol that catalyzes the quarrel which leads to the husband's "epiphanic" moment, we find out, is a gift from her mother and thus of emotional significance. Is the "extraordinary smile" that she detects on his face only her paranoid imagination or is it his patriarchal response to the community of women (given the matrilineal origins of the parasol), who disrupt the male way of being? Ali Smith notes that Mansfield's style often "suggests [...] that the narrative voice is expressing only one opinion, that there's flexibility of interpretation here" (2007, xx). Turning the critical gaze in the story around from the woman to the man, it can be argued that there is an implied denigration of women's communitarian bonds here. The epiphanic moment, when he is in a darkly contemplative mood after his wife tells him she must "escape" from him for some time, can be read as the counterpart to Bertha's figuration of the pear tree in "Bliss". He feels a silence enveloping him as he becomes aware of an immense tree and yet a female voice rises from behind the tree—initially soft and dream-like but ultimately configured as engulfing—to shatter the subliminal solitude he is on the brink of experiencing. Masculine self-sufficiency is again interrupted by the reminder of female presence, returning him to his mundane existence. Significantly, the interrupted epiphany is described through the imagery of constriction: "Something stirred in his breast. Something dark, something unbearable and dreadful" (Mansfield 2007, 202). The gendering of the force that stifles the visionary moment is crucial to the current argument.

The female voice initially seems part of the great silence yet he sees it as curtailing his autonomy: "He knew it would come floating to him from the hidden leaves and his peace was shattered" (Mansfield 2007, 202). Here one senses that the epiphanic moment is possibly another way that Mansfield shapes a counter-response to modernist tropes. She re-writes it to wrench it from its sublime axis. Modernism's penchant to mine everyday moments for their sublime potential is deliberately disrupted. That is, whereas for most modernists the mundane is the pathway to the ineffable, for Mansfield, epiphanic moments end anti-climatically—the philosophical is evoked only to be muffled in the immediacy of daily existence. The transcendent aspirations of the modernist artist seek a grandiose articulation while the woman's voice skims over quotidian details, marital disappointments and communicative lapses.

Can the story in fact be read as an allegorized take on the relationship between modernism and mass culture? The man's immersion in that exalted, solipsistic moment as against the trivial everydayness of his wife, who has already been set up as a consumer of mass products, as suggested by the wide maw of her bag? This wide maw could well be an image of the cannibalizing power of mass culture with which modernism had such a vexed relationship. Mansfield gives signs that problematize our first impression of the husband as the hapless victim. In fact, a number of ways in which Mansfield defines the man—his wanderer's spirit, his separateness, his contempt for his partner's myopic concern with the mundane, his self-consciousness about his relative openness to the other, his moment of contact with the ineffable—bring him close to the self-valorizing model of the modernist artist. And there are enough statements from the high modernists of how artistic pursuit depended on an "escape" from the provincialism of "the mealy mouths of Belgravia" (Woolf 2008, 138). The tale, in this reading, then expands into a comment on the classist politics of modernist coteries and their vision of art.

The new turn in modernist studies has done much to bring to the fore writers from the early to middle decades of the 20th century who languished on the sidelines while the dominant narrative was given over to those who self-consciously wrote modernism into being. But this chapter enters the debate from the other side, to argue that mainstreaming these writers should not translate into writing out of the script the resistant strand in their writing. Simon During (2015) in an article on Mansfield puts this argument into a theoretical frame when he talks of how "the consecration of a global canon has been organized from the old imperial centres" (35). The over-zealousness in making gestures of inclusion that this implies might mean subsuming the "ex-centricity" (both positional but also obdurately self-conscious as I have shown) of what those like Mansfield can bring to the discussion.

By choosing "Je ne parle pas français", a story that is almost completely steeped in her own literary ethos, this chapter has attempted to probe the critical and interrogative combativeness with which Mansfield engaged with the literary parameters being set and espoused by her metropolitan contemporaries. This is to put a slightly different spin on recent efforts to re-map modernism as a pluralized, de-homogenized body of writing. Rather than tracing correspondences between the established figureheads and the late entrants, identifying and foregrounding points of non-identity might be a more interesting way of opening up the canon. Trinh T. Minh-ha's (1991) theorization (in a different context) of the middle as "alert in-betweenness" (234) is one context within which Mansfield's interstitiality as developing into a contestatory reading of her times may be read. By probing how the chequered politics of the high modernists were being investigated and dissected by their contemporaries from the margins, the study of modernism can be opened up in crucial ways. The intersections between modernism and postcolonial thought in writers like Mansfield lead directly into this exercise. In the suspicious counter-readings of modernism's self-absorbed boundary crossings, the work of colonial parvenus such as Mansfield can be seen as a precursor to postcolonial self-writing.[2]

In a letter to Murry, wondering about the reception of one of her stories, Mansfield says, "Such a queer feeling—after one has dropped a pebble in. Will there be a ripple or not?" (*Letters* 4, 218). To stay with that image, I conclude by saying that the pebble was cast— in an eagerness to accord her work some higher place in the modernist canon, we might be in danger of killing off the ripples with which Mansfield set out to disturb and disrupt modernist formations. This chapter has tried to record those ripples as going a significant way to destabilize the "literary Greenwich meridian" (Casanova 2004, 4).

Bibliography

Begam, Richard and Michael Valdez Moses, eds. 2007. *Modernism and Colonialism: British and Irish Literature 1899–1939*. Durham, NC: Duke University Press.

---

[2] When Jamaican writer Michelle Cliff (quoted in Gerzina 2010, 82) asks "Is Woolf, the daughter of the tea table, who learned the racial attitudes of her time and class, able to see the African?", one finds a startling throwback to Raoul Duquette's reducing of the African laundress to a trope signifying otherness. To extend that point, one cannot but read the following statement from Mansfield as a part of the indirect, but suggestive and often acerbic (especially given the glance at the Woolfian trope of the room) cross-traffic between the two writers: "Confound my poverty! How I long to buy an exquisite room, absolute privacy, a devoted black woman, and some ravishing perfume" (*Letters* 1, 325).

Benzel, Kathryn N. and Ruth Hoberman. 2004. *Trespassing Boundaries; Virginia Woolf's Short Fiction.* New York: Palgrave Macmillan.

Brooker, Peter. 2007. *Bohemia in London: The Social Scene of Early Modernism.* Basingstoke: Palgrave Macmillan.

Brooker, Peter, Andrew Thacker, Andrzej Gasiorek and Deborah Longworth, eds. 2010. *The Oxford Handbook of Modernisms.* Oxford: Oxford University Press.

Carver, Beci. 2015. "What Women Want: The Modernist Kimono." *Modernism/ modernity* 22 (2): 303–14.

Casanova, Pascale. 2004. *The World Republic of Letters.* Translated by M.B. DeBevoise. Cambridge, MA: Harvard University Press.

Davison, Claire. 2015. "Introduction." In *Katherine Mansfield and Translation*, edited by Claire Davison, Gerri Kimber and Todd Martin, 1–11. Edinburgh: Edinburgh University Press.

During, Simon. 2015. "Katherine Mansfield's World." *Journal of New Zealand Literature* 33: 33–66.

Gerzina, Gretchen Holbrook. 2010. "Virginia Woolf, Performing Race." In *The Edinburgh Companion to Virginia Woolf and the Arts*, edited by Maggie Humm, 74–87. Edinburgh: Edinburgh University Press.

Gikandi, Simon. 2003. "Picasso, Africa and the Schemata of Difference." *Modernism/modernity* 10 (3): 455–80.

Hunter, Adrian. 2003. "Constance Garnett's Chekhov and the Modernist Short Story." *Translation and Literature* 12 (1): 69–87.

Liggins, Emma, Andrew Maunder and Ruth Robbins, eds. 2011. *The British Short Story.* Basingstoke: Palgrave Macmillan.

Mansfield, Katherine. 2007. *The Collected Stories.* London: Penguin.

Mao, Douglas and Rebecca L. Walkowitz. 2008. "The New Modernist Studies." *PMLA* 123 (3): 737–48.

March-Russell, Paul. 2009. *The Short Story: An Introduction.* Edinburgh: Edinburgh University Press.

Martin, Todd. 2017. "Introduction." In *Katherine Mansfield and the Bloomsbury Group*, edited by Todd Martin, 1–13. London: Bloomsbury Academic.

Marx, John. 2005. *The Modernist Novel and the Decline of Empire.* Cambridge: Cambridge University Press.

McDonnell, Jenny. 2010. *Katherine Mansfield and the Modernist Marketplace: At the Mercy of the Public.* Basingstoke: Palgrave Macmillan.

Murry, John Middleton, ed. 1984. *Journal of Katherine Mansfield: 1904–1922.* Hutchinson: Auckland.

McHale, Brian and Randall Stevenson, eds. 2006. *The Edinburgh Companion to Twentieth Century Literatures in English.* Edinburgh: Edinburgh University Press.

Moore-Gilbert, Bart, Gareth Stanton and Willy Maley, eds. 2013. *Postcolonial Criticism.* London: Routledge.

Minh-Ha, Trinh T. 1991. *When the Moon Waxes Red: Gender, Representation and Cultural Politics.* London: Routledge.

New, W, H. 1994. "Reading 'The Escape'." In *Katherine Mansfield: In From the Margins*, edited by Roger Robinson, 90–111. Baton Rouge, LA: Louisiana State University Press.

Rosner, Victoria, ed. 2014. *The Cambridge Companion to the Bloomsbury Group.* Cambridge: Cambridge University Press.

Said, Edward. 1979. *Orientalism.* New York: Vintage Books.

Seshagiri, Urmila. 2010. *Race and the Modernist Imagination.* Ithaca, NY: Cornell University Press.

Skrbic, Nena. 2004. *Wild Outbursts of Freedom: Reading Virginia Woolf's Short Fiction.* Westport, CT: Praeger.

Smith, Ali. 2007. "Introduction." In *Katherine Mansfield: The Collected Stories*, v–xxviii. London: Penguin.

Wilson, Janet, Cristina Sandru and Sarah Lawson Welsh, 2010. "General Introduction." In *Rerouting the Postcolonial: New Directions for the New Millennium*, edited by Janet Wilson, Cristina Sandru and Sarah Lawson Welsh, 1–13. London: Routledge.

Woolf, Virginia. 1975–1980. *The Letters of Virginia Woolf.* 6 vols, edited by Nigel Nicholson and Joanne Trautmann. London: Hogarth Press.

———. 2008. *Vintage Woolf: Selected Diaries*, edited by Anne Olivier Bell. London: Vintage Books.

The Art of Work: Katherine Mansfield's Servant and Perception

Maurizia Boscagli

The representation of the lower classes, and of the working class in particular, is not one of the major concerns of modernism. The topic seems to fade with the waning of the more socially *engagé* realism of the 19th century, and with the appearance of modernist aesthetic experimentation. Modernism is more concerned with individual consciousness and with the representation of new concepts of time and space than with class and collectivity. When the working class is represented by modernists it makes cameo appearances that only sanction the marginality of the lower class character—whether they be Sweeney, or toothless Lil' in T.S. Eliot's *The Waste Land*, or, as specimens of the lower-middle working class in the same text, the typist and the "young man carbuncular" (Eliot 2015, 63, l. 231). Alternatively, working class characters may be absent, simply because they do not interest the author, as in the case of Evelyn Waugh.[1] There are of course exceptions, which do nothing but confirm the rule: D.H. Lawrence is one of the few modernists who gives space and relevance to the lower classes, at least earlier in his career: *Sons and Lovers* is a working-class novel. Further, there are important 20th-century working class writers, for instance Hugh McDiarmid, Lewis Grassic Gibbon, or James Hanley, but they remain marginal to the modernist canon.

In the early 20th century, the time of the Russian revolution, of the industrial struggles of 1919 and 1926 in England, and of the Great Depression, when masses of working class people emerged on

---

[1] "I don't know them and I am not interested in them. No writer before the middle of the nineteenth century wrote about the working classes other than as grotesques or as pastoral decorations. Then when they were given the vote certain writers started to suck up to them" (Waugh 1963, 15).

the social and historical scene, the literary representation of the working classes appears to diminish, and writers turn, instead, to a more nostalgic and domesticated lower-class type, the servant. That is, the appearance of the working classes on the social and political scene seems to be inversely proportional to their presence in the literary text. Thus less attention is dedicated to the new industrial worker, no longer tied to his employer by a relation of tradition and deference, a figure who is all too realistically visible on the historical scene.

The servant is a vestigial social figure, reassuring to the bourgeois and upper class because his relation to his employer is not primarily, if at all, reliant on money. As Eric Hobsbawm (1968) affirms,

> the proletarian whose only link with his employer is a "cash nexus" must be distinguished from "the servant", a pre-industrial dependent, who has a much more complex human and social relationship with his "master" and one which implies duties on both sides, though very unequal ones. (85)

For Marx, servants are not proper workers, but "a case of luxurious, unproductive labour, not even an instance of exploitation [...]. Economically gratuitous, servants are mere signs of money, itself a sign" (quoted in Robbins 1986, 8). Thorstein Veblen (1957) adds that "the chief use of servants is the evidence they offered of the master's ability to pay".[2] Their relation to the master is therefore one of dependence, more post-feudal than modern, and as such more nostalgically reassuring to the middle-class writer. In narrative terms, at the modern end of a tradition that begins in the classical world, the literary servant is a subaltern who is not protesting his subalternity and is therefore pushed into the role of the eternal sidekick of the protagonist, the master (Robbins 1986, 6).

Katherine Mansfield was deeply interested in class and dedicated a significant amount of her production to the representation of lower and working class characters. "The Child Who Was Tired", "The Doll's House", "The Lady's Maid", and of course "Life of Ma Parker", as well as the end of "The Garden Party", all focus on a lower- or working-class figure. Mansfield distances herself from the modernist marginalization of the lower classes: the worker and the servant take centre stage in stories that are denunciatory not only of the character's condition but also, implicitly, of the structures that led to that condition in the first place.

I am interested in Mansfield's treatment of working class characters—who more often than not are women—because, through her stylistic choices, Mansfield suggests a new way of reclaiming experience and the emotions which is at odds both with the cool and distanced position of modernism, but also with realist objectivity. In the early 20th century the emotions, which had been so central to the sentimental novel of the 18th and 19th centuries, become a modernist taboo, and as such they signal a *passé* means of relating to reality. At the same time, the feeling subject, vis-à-vis a new type of subjectivity suspended between the machinic brutalism of the avant-garde and the detached and cynical attitude of high modernism, is no longer viable. In the 20th century, degraded to the level of low-brow culture, sentimentality is further discredited as popular, and therefore feminine. With the figure of the servant in Mansfield's fiction, however, sentimentality is again brought to the fore in modernist writing and, through a calibrated and innovative use of different stylistic registers, realist and experimental, it is turned into a means to access a new form of perception.

The emotions are deeply corporeal: they "move" the subject, make him or her lose control of him- or herself, restraining rationality. By denying the emotions and feeling, modernist literature retrenches into the hubristic position that, as Susan Buck-Morss (1992) affirms, characterizes the autotelic subject of modernity, the subject who claims to be self-generated, rather than dependent on the other, nature *in primis.* The claimed autonomy of *homo autotelus* is predicated upon a "narcissistic illusion of self-control" (6) and of his autogenesis. This autonomous subject relies on sensory alienation, being without a body, and therefore is, in Buck-Morss's term, "sense dead" (27). By turning to the by then disused narrative mode of realism, and, further, by queering realism with her own brand of sentimentality, Mansfield reaffirms precisely the corporeality of the subject and his or her permeability to sensations, emotions, and being part of nature. Further, by complicating the realistic portrayal of the working class with "feminine" sentimentality, Mansfield exposes and contradicts what modernist male chauvinism had made marginal and degraded: women and the popular.

My discussion of Mansfield's narrative technique focuses on one specific short story, "Life of Ma Parker". In the first part of the chapter I will examine the figure of the working character in realist fiction by considering Gustave Flaubert's novella "Un Coeur Simple" (1877). I will then analyze the same figure in modernist writing through the character of Mrs. MacNab in Virginia Woolf's *To the Lighthouse* ([1927] 1981). This part of my discussion will provide points of comparison with Mansfield's text. I will then focus on Mansfield's style: the way she complicates both realism and modernism through her strategic use of sentimentality. In the final section of the chapter I will interrogate the uneasy connection of modernism and sentimentality and what this connection produced in Mansfield's work: the possibility of a new mode of perception and a new way of recuperating what modernism laments as lost experience.

Gustave Flaubert

Flaubert's work was an important influence on Mansfield's writing. Her use of free indirect discourse and its participatory impersonality, and her deployment of subtle humour, and at times open sarcasm against the bourgeois are Flaubertian elements that Mansfield makes her own.

In "Un Coeur Simple", published in *Three Tales* (1877), the servant stands as the central figure. After a series of misfortunes when still very young, Félicité finds a place at Madame Aubain's, and becomes, almost, part of the family. Yet she is not allowed a human connection that can be her own. Her beloved nephew, who nonetheless exploits and takes advantage of her, and Madame Aubain's daughter, whom Félicité loves, both die. Soon the whole family disappears, and old and sick Felicité is allowed to live in the empty and decaying house until her death.

Felicité's affective and spiritual life hinges on the presence of a parrot, which she receives as a gift (it is in fact a discarded pet), from a neighbouring family. The bird is indexical of her lost nephew who died in Cuba, a place as exotic as the bird. As such, it stands as an affective presence, a compensation for her loss: "In her isolation the parrot was almost a son, a love" (Flaubert 1877, 6). At the same time the parrot, embalmed after its death, points to the efforts of an illiterate, lower-class woman, to make sense of religion:

> In church, she always gazed at the Holy Ghost, and noticed that there was something about it that resembled a parrot. The likeness appeared even more striking on a colored picture of Espinal, representing the baptism of our Saviour. With its scarlet wings and emerald body, it was really the image of Loulou. (Flaubert, 17)

In the end, the Holy Ghost, in Felicité's mind, is fully identified with the parrot.

In the best Flaubertian tradition, the narrative voice of the novella oscillates between the possibility of empathy with, and distance from, the character. When we are inside Felicité's consciousness, and follow her way of processing reality, the story is always on the verge of becoming sentimental. Nonetheless, thanks to Flaubert's objectivity, the narrative produces a defamiliarizing effect: we know more than Felicité does, and we can see what she cannot, her subalternity and exploitation. We know at all times that Felicité is not *like us* or like the narrator. We see more than she does. While pitying her, we look at Felicité as a spectacle, so that the mind of the servant becomes for the reader a titillating territory, similar to the visit of the 19th-century bourgeois to the Victorian slum. We are watching the life of the poor. How do we read her identification of the parrot with the Holy Ghost? Is this a moment of agency and self-affirmation for the character (in that she custom-makes religion and has it all figured out), or is her interest in the parrot nothing more than a sign of her lack of education, and, as the narrator points out more than once, of her lack of intelligence? This is also a comic moment, when the narrative voice affirms its own, and our difference from, and even superiority to, the character. "Un Coeur Simple": what do we make of Felicité's simplicity?

In answer to these questions another Flaubertian female working-class figure comes to mind. This is Catherine Elisabeth Nicaise Leroux, the peasant woman who wins an award at the Agricultural Fair in *Madame Bovary* (1857). After 50 years of work and service in a farm, Catherine receives a medal and 25 francs, which she plans to give to the *curé* so that he may pray for her. In a novel that centers on the opposition between work and leisure, duty and pleasure, production and consumption, the work ethic and escapist fantasies, Flaubert zeros in on the ruined, toil-worn hand of the peasant, to implicitly compare it to Emma's hands, "white like doves", caressed by Rodolphe, in the famous scene of Emma's seduction at the fair. Catherine Leroux represents work and duty, crucial bourgeois values. But while she is praised by her community, Flaubert describes the old peasant woman as being as "placid" as the animals she has taken care of for all those years. Through her work Catherine has become "animal like", inhuman. In this way she shares the "inhumanity" of Felicité, who becomes, after everybody's death, a fixture of the house, a thing, and is more than once described as an automaton, a machine: "When she was twenty-five, she looked forty. After she had passed fifty, nobody could tell her age; erect and silent always, she resembled a wooden figure working automatically" (Flaubert 1877, 3).

No longer the side-kick of the master, as had been the case for a very long time in the western literary tradition, in these two texts, "Un Coeur Simple" and *Madame Bovary*, the servant is visible and representable in her own right. At the same time, apart from the pain of Felicité's experiences:

> Then a weakness came over her: the misery of her childhood, the disappointment of her first love, the departure of her

nephew, the death of Virginia; all these things came back to her at once, and rising like a swelling tide in her throat, almost choked her. (Flaubert 1877, 16)

She does not recognize her exploitation and the real conditions of her existence, and rather remains an unself-aware victim.

Suspended between the spectatorial, the sentimental, and the comic, "Un Coeur Simple" walks the fine line between high realism and the popular, but it never lets the reader become too involved with the story to the point of identifying with the character. The novella ends with the description of Felicité's death: yet at this tragic moment we smile at her naiveté: "and when she exhaled her last breath, she thought she saw in the half-opened heavens a gigantic parrot hovering above her head" (Flaubert 1877, 20). It is thanks to Flaubert's comic, if not sardonic, tone that the story is saved from the dangers of sentimentality.

Virginia Woolf

In Virginia Woolf's ([1927] 1981) *To the Lighthouse*, Mrs. McNab, the caretaker of the Ramsays, is not a sentimental figure. Rather, she is introduced because she has a task to perform, practical and narrative: by cleaning and reorganizing the abandoned summer house, she brings back the light of "civilization" to the darkest point of the novel. Even more, Mrs. MacNab is a keeper of memory in a context completely stripped of human presence. Thus Woolf sets up an analogy between the servant and the woman artist, Lily Briscoe, whose work as a dilettante painter has an elegiac and mnemonic quality. Yet this is an analogy that the novel cannot sustain: after accomplishing her task, material and narrative, Mrs. MacNab disappears, while Lily remains to finish her painting and have her final vision.

Mrs. McNab makes only a cameo appearance in *To the Lighthouse*, but an important one. She lacks interiority as a character; all she tells us about herself is the physical pain she experiences when working (she is old; she suffers from arthritis). However, as the only human being alive in "Time Passes", Part Two of *To the Lighthouse*, she is the character who brings the house to order after ten years of abandonment, and brings unruly nature under the control of domesticity again through work. Just as the clothes left behind by the Ramsays and their guests retain the shape of the bodies of their owners, the caretaker is the keeper of memory: "What people had shed and left—a pair of shoes, a shooting cap, some faded skirts and coats in wardrobes—those alone kept the human shape and in the emptiness indicated where once they were filled and animated" (Woolf [1927] 1981, 129). To be aligned with objects is no natural prerogative or privilege of the humble. This representation of the subaltern is the product of Woolf's ambivalence towards "the servants"—an ambivalence, similar to that of Mrs. Ramsay, of the socially-minded upper-class liberal intellectual (see Williams 1996, 130). Mrs. McNab's presence, and above all, labour, proves again that civilization is sustained by the work of the subaltern. The end of the chaos of "Time Passes", and the restoration of the order of bourgeois domesticity and reason, is willed by the Ramsays but carried out by Mrs. MacNab, in the same way as Mrs. Ramsay had provided the recipe for the *boeuf en daube*, while the actual dish was cooked by Mildred, another servant. When, after ten years have gone by, Mrs. MacNab sets the house in order for the Ramsays, the split temporality of "Time Passes" is sutured by gendered human labour, the labour of the servant, a figure who is presented by Woolf as central and disposable at the same time.

While Lily Briscoe recaptures and re-settles this lost order through art, Mrs. McNab does so through her work, which is here ennobled by Woolf as the representation of the human agency that had disappeared in the nights and storms of "Time Passes". Both the servant and the woman artist seem to share the same "power of vision" and of memory: Mrs. Ramsey appears to both of them in their memories of the past. This unacknowledged symmetry between Lily and the subaltern culminates, paradoxically, in the moment when the artist, acknowledging the disinterestedness of her work, and her lack of interest in fame, anticipates the future of the picture: "It would be hung in the servants' bedrooms. It would be rolled up and stuffed under a sofa" (Woolf [1927] 1981, 158). But the addressee of Lily's painting will not be able to understand it: its non-representational, avant-garde quality will be wasted on an uneducated woman. Here Lily, and Woolf along with her, deny Mrs. MacNab the very visionary power which had been attributed to her earlier, to make her instead into a figure capable of reading only literally—that is, realistically.

The plot of *To the Lighthouse* poses a classed shift from one notion of production to another: while the female subaltern is handed the productivity of manual labour, the female artists (Lily and Mrs. Ramsay) are handed the conceptual, aesthetic, and affective productivity of the work of art. The prosaic reality of Mrs. MacNab, the materiality she helps produce through her work, is not occluded by Woolf, yet it does not amount to anything; it doesn't produce any development in the novel, and, after Part II, it disappears. The evanescence of time and experience that characterizes Woolf's narrative signals, but then erases, the presence of the time of manual production and of its subject. The servant leaves without a trace.

Katherine Mansfield

Things change radically in Katherine Mansfield's fiction: working-class characters are at the center of a number of her stories and the reader is made keenly aware of the way these figures fully perceive themselves and how they are oftentimes aware of their circumstances. In "The Child Who Was Tired", for example, the character reacts violently against her life as a servant and against her employer. In other stories, such as "The Lady's Maid", the character passively complies with the desires of her mistress, or, as in "The Tiredness of Rosabel", dreams of escaping her subalternity. Alternatively, when the character seems to passively suffer her condition of subalternity, this is made fully visible to the reader in an openly accusatory tone on the part of the narrative voice.

For some critics, Mansfield's working-class stories are not her most accomplished writing. Here she seems to abandon any modernist experimentation in order to represent the working characters in a more conventional way. Charles Ferrall (2014) notes: "Unlike Waugh, Mansfield *is* interested in the working class, but she is unable to represent this class except in ways that largely reproduce popular genres or the conventions of nineteenth-century realism" (117). It is precisely this stylistic "failure" that I find interesting and worth speculating about, because it leads us to a very productive and important aspect of Mansfield's writing as a modernist.

The double register of Mansfield's fiction, its simultaneous registration of modernist ambition and its realist tendencies, is acknowledged by most of her critics. As a modernist she does not always deploy the most experimental forms of modernist writing, but rather turns to realism or impressionism in order to affirm the primacy of individual perception, and to focus on the fragmentation of perceived reality in a complex and not fully knowable world: "Her impressionism is the epistemological record of sensory experience, to be accompanied by reflection, internalization, fantasies, and dreams. It is the ordinary, everyday life-speech that gives the sense of being real" (Van Gunsteren 1990, 9). Many of her contemporaries acknowledged her realist vein, among them the New Zealand poet A. D. Fairburn, who in 1928 called her "capable of sturdy realism", although her prose was unable to deliver "the power and virility" that New Zealand, now freeing itself from colonialism, needed to build its sense of nationalism (quoted in New 1990, 50). Her writerly perspective might also be included in critiques of her personality such as that of T.S. Eliot, who in a 1920 letter to Ezra Pound, and writing in a more vitriolic tone, highlights what he perceives as a sentimental quality of Mansfield's personality: "She's one of the most persistent and thick-skinned toadies and one of the vulgarest women I have ever met, and is also a sentimental crank" (Eliot and Haughton 2011, 329). Eliot may be referring to her personality, yet there is an implicit critique here as well of her 'sentimental' writerly perspective, associated with the vulgarity of mass culture.

Mansfield's sentimentality is undoubtedly an important quality of her writing. In "Life of Ma Parker" what we might call the double register of Mansfield's fiction, its use of modernist tropes in a realist register, is triangulated into a new stylistic constellation precisely by sentimentality. In turn, I suggest, this constellation opens the way to a new form of perception, and a new way of approaching the text for the reader. By welding together modernism, realism, and sentimentality, high and low culture, Mansfield manages to establish a terrain where, against the principle of realist detached objectivity, and of modernism's distrust of the emotions and its aloof aesthetic of distance, the experience of feeling, and experience at large can be restored. With "Ma Parker", as I will show, we are asked to be distant from *and* close to the story at the same time. Here Woolf's utilitarian use of the servant as a cog in her narrative machine, or the way in which Flaubert sets obstacles to the reader's emotional identification with the character, are overcome through the deployment of an innovative form of participatory detachment. Realist objectivity and modernism's distaste for the popular are mediated into a fresh perceptual mode that is newly made available to the reader.

Ma Parker is a charwoman, a domestic help to "the literary gentleman" (Mansfield 2010, 131). She comes to work the day after the funeral of her grandson Lennie, the light of her life, her only consolation. The callow employer can think of nothing better than to ask her whether the funeral went well:

> He could hardly go back to the warm sitting room without saying something—something more. Then because these people set such store by funerals he said kindly, "I hope the funeral went off all right." "Beg parding, sir?" said old Ma Parker huskily. Poor old bird! She did look dashed. "I hope the funeral was a-a—success," said he. Ma Parker gave no answer. (131)

In the literary gentleman's knowledgeable words ("Then because these people set such store by funerals") is contained Mansfield's sharp critique of the middle class and its sense of distance from, and indifference to, the working class, as well as the gentleman's lack of empathy, so degrading for the charwoman.

Ma Parker cleans and reflects on her "hard life" (Mansfield 2010, 133). We follow her flashbacks into the past, from her childhood in Stratford-upon-Avon (but she doesn't really know who Shakespeare was), to service in a family, where she is subjected to the cruelty of the cook, who tears up her letters from home so Ma Parker would not be dreaming instead of working. She marries a baker who dies of "white lung", of consumption (he dies literally from his work), and bears him 13 children, of which only six survive; all except one leave her. Her daughter Ethel, a single mother, and Ethel's son Lennie, are Ma Parker's only company, and now the little boy is dead. Ma Parker's thoughts and flashbacks are her way of facing trauma, the unspeakable, impossible-to-understand event of her grandchild's death.[3] She would like to cry, but she cannot do so: there is no place where she can express her feelings. It would be unprofessional to cry at work, and unsightly to do so on a bench in the street. The story ends, as so many of Katherine Mansfield's stories do, with a suspended and unresolved finale: having finished her cleaning at the literary gentleman's, Ma Parker leaves, hoping to find a place where she can cry, but there is no such place: "It was cold in the street. There was wind like ice. People were flitting by, very fast; the men walked like scissors; the women trod like cats". They move, that is, with the speed and indifference of objects or animals. And finally: "Ma Parker stood, looking up and down. The icy wind blew her apron into a balloon. And now it began to rain. There was nowhere" (137).

Ma Parker is a victim of her own life, of her circumstances, and class. This is perhaps one of the bleakest of Mansfield's stories, one where her proverbial humor, her irony (except perhaps when she makes visible the literary gentleman's inner thoughts), is absent. As the protagonist cannot emote, neither can the reader: this is a story without catharsis, or resolution, as are many of Mansfield's stories.
On the surface, the measured and apparently non-affective tone of "Life of Ma Parker" seems to invoke a purely modernist stance. Modernism is suspicious of the emotions, and rather favours an aesthetic of distance, irony, and cynicism: think of Evelyn Waugh, or

---

[3] For a discussion of trauma in "Life of Ma Parker" see Manenti (2015, 63–76).

James Joyce making fun of feminine sentimentality in "Nausicaa". However, to be able to feel is important, because it also means to be able to experience. As modernist intellectuals such as Walter Benjamin and Georg Simmel both affirm, experience (*Erfahrung*) is no longer possible in the 20th century, because it has been blocked by the individual's psyche as a response to the powerful shocks of modernity, from the trauma of war to the shocks of life in the metropolis. The subject has to distance him- or herself from these phenomena in order not to be affected by them. This distance is exemplified by the detached, blasé attitude of the city dweller, a form of self-defense against the damage brought about by a new, faster, and violent everyday reality. Yet, by shutting off to painful and shocking events, the subject also excludes and renounces many other types of experience, and comes to be alienated from life in its fullness.

Modernism places the character's interiority and consciousness at the centre of the text, but the emotions remain taboo. A case in point is Mrs. Ramsay refusing to say "I love you" to her husband, or the all-too-direct announcement of the parenthetical death of Andrew, Prue, and Mrs. Ramsay herself in *To the Lighthouse*. In modernism, feelings come to be associated with Victorian sentimentality, which pushes the reader to emotional peaks and the physical reactions of crying.[4] When the 18th-century sentimental novel, with Fielding, Sterne, Richardson, and Goldsmith, had exhausted its cultural task of educating the bourgeoisie into "human" and class refinement, sentiment was degraded to sentimentality and to an expression of popular culture; it was also, between the 18th and 19th centuries, redirected towards the melodramatic excess of the Gothic. The sentimentality that was acceptable in the 19th century had, by the early 20th century, come to be considered lowbrow and as such was refused by the modernists. Sentimentality and melodrama, with their turn to the emotions and to sensations, appeal to the body, and to the reader's capability to feel and react. This sentimentality, this excess of sentiment

---

4   On 19th-century sentimentality see, among others, Banfield (2007), Bell (2000), Kaplan (1987), and Tompkins (1986).

epitomized, for instance, by Dickens's Little Nell's death in *The Old Curiosity Shop*, is rejected first by the aesthetes and then more forcefully by the modernists: Oscar Wilde, Virginia Woolf, and Aldous Huxley in *Vulgarity and Literature* (1930), all disliked Dickens.

"Life of Ma Parker" evidently contains elements of sentimentality: the suffering heroine entrapped not in a physical space but in her own life, the cruelty of the male figure, the employer, the considerable burden of misfortunes to which she is subjected, and, above all, the death of the child. However, this sentimentality is made more complex by Mansfield's turn to both realism and modernism, and as such it has important implications for the scholar of modernism. On the one hand the story can be read as a social study of class, of the life of a working-class woman and its heartbreaking hardships. On the other, in a more modernist mode, we gain access to the heroine's life story only through her consciousness, memories, and reflections. Yet this is not all: Mansfield's simultaneously "objective" and "subjective" impressionistic style is undercut by the excess of Ma Parker's suffering, paradoxically amplified by the protagonist's inability to express it.

Life hurts; reading the story hurts: you cannot "just look"—the reader's gaze is complicated by the tactility of feeling—yet you cannot look away. The measured sentimentality of woman-as-victim, as both self-sacrificial and "beaten" by life (the Dickensian note), however, works in a double, contradictory manner: it does not allow a merely contemplative stance on the part of the reader, nor a fully participatory one. The sentimentality of the story affirms the impossibility of the spectacle, of a merely spectatorial position on our part, but at the same time, it prevents us from fully identifying with the character. The sentimental tone at work in "Life of Ma Parker" gestures towards melodrama without ever fully deploying its form. This aspect of Mansfield's style has two important consequences: first, it allows the reader to feel again, even though she might not emote. In other words, Mansfield's writing, when veering towards sentimentality, allows the reader a glimpse of experience, that which modernism bemoans as lost. Second, Mansfield affirms once again the corporeality of the modern subject, which in patriarchal modernity had been marginalized as feminine.

The return of sentimentality in the midst of a modernist text is not an exclusive prerogative of Mansfield's fiction: the same phenomenon is visible in another form of modernist textuality of the period: visual culture. Patrice Petro (1989) in her seminal book, *Joyless Street: Women and Melodramatic Representations in Weimar Germany*, studies the reappearance of melodrama and sentimentality in Weimar cinema and the popular press. Feminist theory and criticism have given much attention to sentimental and melodramatic forms. For Annette Kuhn (1992), melodrama is a feminine genre, "a narrative motivated by female desire and processes of spectator identification governed by the female point of view" (7). Petro considers cinematic melodrama as a form that addresses a female audience first of all, but also as one that makes available a new spectatorial position and a new form of perception to the modern subject. Her aim is to show how such a mass cultural form as cinema impacted upon changing modes of perceiving reality (see Doane 1991). In Petro's reading, Weimar melodrama disrupts the dualistic structure of perception that modernity sets in place. Beyond a simple opposition of contemplation (Heidegger), and distraction (Benjamin), Petro recognizes a third type of perceptual mode: "one that takes women as subjects of history and representation into account" (1989, 12). Thus she develops a different theory of the gaze associated with the female audience of melodrama: this time the contemplative gaze and its aesthetic distance that Heidegger (1962) reserves for high art, is appropriated by the female viewer, and thus merges with the women's absorbed, emotional, and highly concentrated gaze in the movie theatre (Petro 1989, 216–17). That is, a way of looking that for Heidegger can only be referred to the work of high art, becomes now the appropriate way of approaching a text of mass culture. Benjamin's non-committal distraction, which lets the text, and reality "hit" the viewer obliquely, thus excluding any absorbed contemplation and intentionality on the part of the subject, will not do for the female spectator. Rather, she is looking for proximity to the text, and for being affected and absorbed by it without losing her autonomy. Different from contemplation or distraction, the gaze of the female spectator in Petro's theorization of it, refuses to be categorized as modernist or popular: Weimar melodrama is "neither realist nor modernist, but a reinterpretation of both" (Petro 1989, 34).

Through her use of sentimentality, Mansfield, in writing her text, is neither fully realist nor fully modernist, but rather transforms both aesthetic modes. Mansfield's intentional deployment of a non-modern form is not a flaw. In fact this stylistic choice allows her to accomplish what modernist experimentation cannot. The undecidability and stylistic contamination of her writing, which combines modernism, realism, and melodrama, breaks the armor of the ironic and even caustic distance of the high modernists; in doing so, it breaches a modernist inability to really access or take in many aspects of reality. Mansfield's fiction, like Weimar melodrama, is neither realist nor modernist, but a reinterpretation of both styles. In "Life of Ma Parker" the reader is not locked into an either/or position of distance or participation, contemplation or distraction. This position of "engaged contemplation", of an involved gaze, that Mansfield makes available to her reader, and thanks to which she obtains our maximum affective engagement without making us cry, contributes, as I pointed out, to a new mode of perception. As readers of "Life of Ma Parker", we are not simply detached spectators, nor are we uncritical participants in the flow of the narrative: although we are deeply affected by the protagonist's predicament, we cannot cry. It is this participation without catharsis that makes the story so effective and so affecting: at the end, no liberatory cry, no open emoting is possible for the reader. We leave the last page carrying the same burden as Ma Parker, without being able to resolve or forget, or to overcome, the emotions we have experienced through the text. Our "involved" reading, like the involved gaze of Petro's Weimar female audience, allows us to assume the unique position of a participating gaze, the paradox of a 'close distance' from the story.

Confronted with "Life of Ma Parker", the reader's attitude is anything but distracted. In "The Work of Art at the Time of Mechanical Reproduction", Walter Benjamin (2003) embraces distraction as the mode of perception capable of antagonizing and defeating the contemplative attitude that the "sacredness" and unique aura of the work of art had demanded from its public for centuries. At the end of this essay, Benjamin replies to the critic George Duhamel, who believes that "film requires no kind of concentration and presupposes no intelligence", by affirming that while the concentrated connoisseur "is absorbed by the artwork [...] the distracted masses absorb the work of art in themselves" (Benjamin 2003 267). The cinema-going modern masses, therefore, assume a detached attitude to the filmic text that lets the image approach the viewer, and as such also redefines the idea of the subject's agency. Confronted with the narrative of "Life of Ma Parker", the reader's attitude stands midpoint between distraction and contemplation. As I explained, Mansfield overcomes, and yet engages with, the distance of both Heideggerian absorption into the work of art, and Benjamin's distraction, to create a new perceptual position for her reader. In this sense, Mansfield's art is suspended between two opposed perceptual attitudes, so that she is not aligned with either position. However, Mansfield's stylistic and generic choices show an important affinity with a different aspect of Benjamin's thought: her turn to the popular evokes precisely Benjamin's interest in the 'vulgar' commodity culture of modern capitalism.

For Walter Benjamin, as for the Surrealists, the encounter with mass culture and the commodity, albeit the *démodé* commodity he sees in the Parisian arcades, is precisely what will make experience possible again. Benjamin's modern subject is no longer in touch with himself and his feelings, is alienated from a no longer viable bourgeois interiority, and, as in the case of the enervated subject of his essay "Surrealism" (Benjamin 1999), is somewhat subjected to the nervous impulses and shocks of modernity. This citizen of modernity learns to emote again not by turning back to a romanticized notion of a pristine nature and shying away from the popular, but rather through an encounter with mass culture and technology. Benjamin (1985) gives an example when he writes in *One Way Street* of how: "people whom nothing moves or touches are taught to cry again by American films" (89). In another passage from the same text, the subject of modern consumer culture, fascinated, watches the return of experience in the reflection of a red neon sign in a puddle of water on the asphalt (90). The mesmerizing reflection of the red neon sign advertises an object for sale, of course: the magic is always that of the commodity itself. There's no outside to the world of capitalist reification for Benjamin. Modern enchantment can produce a new level of experience: one needs to find meaning, and a different understanding of value, from within the space of capital. While Benjamin, in order to make visible a different way of experiencing reality, turns to the dialectical image as a contradictory constellation of clashing elements drawn from different aspects of modern culture, Mansfield creates her own dialectical image at the level of style, through the uneasy and extremely productive juxtaposition of high modernism, realism, and sentimentality. She turns to what is discredited by high modernism in order to recuperate and make available what modernism is no longer capable of reaching: experience, and feelings as a path to experience. She gives up ironic distance in order to be, as Benjamin (2002) affirms in "Some Remarks on Folk Art", "in earnest" (278).

Benjamin is not afraid of the popular and of mass culture in his mission to find new possibilities for experience and perception. Neither is Mansfield. With the affective excess of "Life of Ma Parker" she disrupts literary genres, but also a traditional way of reading and of perceiving. By not letting the reader have a cathartic cry, so that the life of Ma Parker can be consumed, overcome and forgotten, Mansfield keeps the effects of the story lingering, suspended in a way that affects us deeply. Finally, thanks to Mansfield's stylistic *métissage*, her writing goes beyond the modern commonplace association of woman and mass culture, so central to Krakauer's and T.S. Eliot's thinking, for example, and instead demonstrates how a specific popular genre, melodrama and the sentimental story, centered on the figure of the servant, work to unmake the opposition of high and low that defines so much of male modernism.

Bibliography

Banfield, Marie. 2007. "From Sentiment to Sentimentality: A Nineteenth Century Lexicographical Research." *Interdisciplinary Studies in the Long Nineteenth Century* 4: 1–11.

Bell, Michael. 2000. *Sentimentalism, Ethics, and the Culture of Feeling*. Basingstoke: Palgrave Macmillan.

Benjamin, Walter. 1985. *One Way Street and Other Writings*. London: Verso.

———. 1999. "Surrealism." In *Walter Benjamin: Selected Writings*, Vol. 2, Part 1, *1927–1930*, edited by Howard Eiland, Michael W. Jennings and Gary Smith, 207–21. Cambridge, MA: Harvard University Press.

———. 2002. "Some Remarks on Folk Art." In *Walter Benjamin: Selected Writings*, Vol. 3, *1935–38*, edited by Howard Eiland and Michael W. Jennings, 278–80. Cambridge, MA: Harvard University Press.

———. 2003. "The Work of Art in the Age of Mechanical Reproduction." In *Walter Benjamin: Selected Writings*. Vol. 4, *1938–40*, edited by Howard Eiland and Michael W. Jennings, 251–83. Cambridge, MA: Harvard University Press.

Buck-Morss, Susan. 1992. "Aesthetics and Anaesthetics: Walter Benjamin's Art Work Essay Reconsidered." *October* 62 (Fall): 3–41.

Doane, Mary Ann, 1991. *Femmes Fatales: Feminism, Film, Psychoanalysis*. New York: Routledge.

Eliot, T.S. 2011. *The Letters of T.S. Eliot*. Edited by Valerie Eliot and Hugh Haughton. New Haven, CT: Yale University Press.

Eliot, T.S. 2015. *The Poems of T. S. Eliot*. Vol. I, *Collected and Uncollected Poems*. Edited by Christopher Ricks and Jim McCue. London: Faber and Faber.

Ferrall, Charles. 2014. "Katherine Mansfield and the Working Classes." *Journal of New Zealand Literature* 32(2): 106-20. Special issue, "Katherine Mansfield: Masked and Unmasked," edited by Charles Ferrall and Anna Jackson.

Flaubert, Gustave. 1877. *Un Coeur Simple [A Simple Soul]*. ebook, http://www.gutenberg.org/files/1253/1253-h/1253-h.htm.

Heidegger, Martin. 1962. *Being and Time*. Translated by John Macquarrie and Edward Robinson. New York: Harper and Row.

Hobsbawm, Eric. 1968. *Industry and Empire*. Harmondsworth: Penguin, 1968.

Kaplan, Fred. 1987. *Sacred Tears: Sentimentality in Victorian Literature*. Princeton, NJ: Princeton University Press

Kuhn, Annette. 1992. *Feminism and Cinema*. New York: Verso.

Manenti, David. 2015. "Unshed Tears: Meaning, Trauma, and Translation." In *Katherine Mansfield and Translation*, edited by Claire Davison, Gerri Kimber, and Todd Martin, 63–76. Edinburgh: Edinburgh University Press.

Mansfield, Katherine. 2010. *The Best Short Stories of Katherine Mansfield*. Edited and with an introduction by Enda Duffy. New York: Dover.

New, W. H. 1999. *Reading Mansfield and Metaphors of Form*. Montreal: McGill-Queen's University Press.

Petro, Patrice. 1989. *Joyless Streets: Women and Melodramatic Representation in Weimar Germany*. Princeton, NJ: Princeton University Press.

Robbins, Bruce. 1986. *The Servant's Hand: English Fiction from Below*. New York: Columbia University Press.

Tompkins, Jane. 1986. *Sensational Designs: The Cultural Work of American Fiction* 1790–1880. Oxford: Oxford University Press.

Van Gunsteren, Julia. 1990. *Katherine Mansfield and Literary Impressionism*. Amsterdam: Rodopi.

Veblen, Thorstein. [1890] 1957. *The Theory of the Leisure Class*. London: Allen and Unwin.

Waugh, Evelyn. 1963. "The Art of Fiction: Interview with Julian Jebb." *The Paris Review* 30 (Summer-Fall): 1–16. http://www.strakejesuit.org/s/103/images/editor_documents/4537_waugh.pdf?sessionid=b9f9c466-2592-4e41-81f4-e3e5c2a249c9&cc=1.

Williams, Raymond. 1996. "The Bloomsbury Fraction." In *Contemporary Marxist Literary Criticism*, edited by Francis Mulhern, 125–45. London: Longman.

Woolf, Virginia. [1927] 1981. *To the Lighthouse*. New York: Harcourt Brace Jovanovich.

UK and US Modernisms

"Slippery British":
Katherine Mansfield's Legacy in the UK

Ailsa Cox

In his Introduction to the hefty two volumes that are *The Penguin Book of the British Short Story* Philip Hensher (2015) explains his decision to exclude Katherine Mansfield as one of those writers "conferring merit on their place of birth rather than their residence" (xiii). In a brief correspondence with me on Twitter, Hensher remarked that she had been given quite enough attention by the New Zealanders. Some New Zealanders, as Vincent O'Sullivan (2004) comments in his Introduction to *The Oxford Book of New Zealand Short Stories*, may even feel that that there has been too much attention: he quotes Frank Sargeson writing to him in the 1970s about "paying too much attention to Mansfield, 'the Karori schoolgirl'" (x). On the other hand, Mansfield is often included in surveys of British short fiction, most recently the volume on *British Women Short Story Writers: The New Woman to Now* edited by Emma Young and James Bailey (2015). As I shall demonstrate, later in this chapter, Mansfield has been a formative influence on the British short story, especially for women writers, including many, if not most, selected by Hensher.

I am not suggesting that Hensher should have included Mansfield; it is the prerogative of the anthologist to select according to his own agenda. One thing that we can say with confidence, however, is that both the modern short story in general and Mansfield's work in particular are fundamentally transnational. This is a problem that editors of any short story anthology founded on region or nationality, as so many are, must all confront in one way or another. Hensher points out that notions of Britishness are especially "slippery and debatable" (2015, xi), not least because of post-imperial guilt, and even disavowal. If it is "not quite nice to think about being English", as A. S. Byatt says in her Introduction to *The Oxford Book of English Short Stories* (2009, xv), being "British" is even more *de trop*.

But if Hensher had chosen a story by Mansfield, which one might we recommend as her most representative, or her most startling, contribution to a "British" short story tradition, a tradition that he identifies with playfulness, subversion and performance? All of these qualities are abundant in her work; you could say that we were spoilt for choice. Out of so many, how do we select that "missing" story that might have appeared somewhere between D.H. Lawrence, Saki and Dorothy Edwards?

One approach might be simply to take one of those stories that reflect Mansfield's experience of Britishness and Britain, drawing on her life in London and her encounters with the British abroad. We might choose one of those character stories that champion the underdog, "Miss Brill" or "The Life of Ma Parker"; or those that satirize the intelligentsia, "Bliss", "Psychology" or "A Dill Pickle"; or how about "Two Tuppenny Ones, Please", presented as a script, documenting the kind of conversation you might overhear on a bus during wartime. Sydney Janet Kaplan's (1991) chapter on the city in *Katherine Mansfield and the Origins of Modernist Fiction* quotes from the journals and letters to explain how London was, in the early days, a place of inspiration, and how it was in London that she developed her most distinctive techniques, as a way of capturing the dynamic flow of experience: "I do not care at all for men, but *London*—it is life" (Murry 1954, 21). Many of the stories set in London, for instance "Pictures" and "The Tiredness of Rosabel", map its streets through topographical details, overlaid by both social observation and subjective impressions. This is the opening line of "The Tiredness of Rosabel":

> At the corner of Oxford Circus Rosabel bought a bunch of violets, and that was practically the reason why she had so little tea—for a scone and a boiled egg and a cup of cocoa at Lyons are not ample sufficiency after a hard day's work in a millinery establishment. (Mansfield 2007, 513)

Rosabel hops on a bus, thinking of a roast dinner followed by pudding with brandy sauce; she gazes through the wet windowpane, reading the advertisements, just as the girl next to her is reading the rain-spattered pages of a best-selling novel: "How many times had she read these advertisements—'Sapolio Saves Time, Saves Labour'—'Heinz's Tomato Sauce'—and the inane, annoying dialogue between doctor and judge concerning the superlative merits of 'Lamplough's Pyretic Saline'" (513).

The light falling on the rain-soaked streets turns the shop windows luminescent, and Westbourne Grove reminds her of a fantasy of Venice, the hansom cabs turning into gondolas, yet all of this is experienced simultaneously with the sweaty atmosphere on the bus and the banality of the hoardings and the tedium of managing life on a budget. Rosabel's room, up four flights of stairs on Richmond Road, resembles Ada Moss's "Bloomsbury top floor-back" in "Pictures" (Mansfield 2007, 119). In bed at eight in the morning, Ada is also dreaming of food. Like Rosabel, she feels the lack of a "good hot dinner in the evenings" (119).

"Pictures", even more than "Rosabel", is a collage of sense impressions. Ada's peregrination through theatre land in search of a job follows a linear narrative in that it is a journey through a clearly defined space and time towards her objective—paying her rent by eight o'clock that evening. But the linear sequence of cause and effect is punctured by random encounters and incidental details that seem straight from Lewis Carroll—the old brown cat without a tail; the "fair little baby thing about thirty" (Mansfield 2007, 125) who is trying her luck with the "*fil*-lums" (126). The journey is also disrupted by Ada's indecisiveness—"I'll go to Charing Cross. Yes, that's what I'll do. But I won't have a cup of tea. No, I'll have a coffee. [...] No, I won't go to Charing Cross. I'll go straight to Kig and Kadgit" (123). The narrative seems to be doubling back on itself, going round in circles.

Although the title is an obvious allusion to the visual and cinematic, all of the senses are evoked, and are mutually dependent. Mansfield orchestrates a polyphony, or rather a cacophony of voices, and you can hear in this sample from the rather camp theatrical agent how the visual is implicated within the auditory, through the interplay of "call", "see", "look" and the colloquial phrase "up to the eyebrows":

> Now I had a call for twenty-eight ladies today, but they had to be young and able to hop it a bit—see? And I had another call for sixteen—but they had to know something about sand-dancing. Look here, my dear, I'm up to the eyebrows this morning. (Mansfield 2007, 125)

The senses often seem overloaded, like the over-crowded and noisy spaces in the waiting rooms. The unsatisfied hunger of Ada Moss, and of Rosabel, stands in contrast to this saturation of sensory experience, an implosion so intense it is almost synesthetic. Throughout "Pictures" Ada's thoughts are presented as direct speech, a technique Mansfield uses in other stories, for instance "The Little Governess". Towards the end of the story, as she reaches the Café de Madrid, direct speech mingles with free indirect discourse in a more extended passage, drifting between conscious thought, external impressions and internal fantasy:

> My goodness, what a smack that little child came down! Poor little mite! Never mind–up again.... By eight o'clock tonight... Café de Madrid. "I could just go in there and have a coffee, that's all," thought Miss Moss. "It's such a place for artists too. I might just have a stroke of luck.... A dark handsome gentleman in a fur coat comes in with a friend, and sits at my table perhaps. 'No, old chap, I've searched London for a contralto and I can't find a soul. You see, the music is difficult; have a look at it.'" And Miss Moss heard herself saying: "Excuse me, I happen to be a contralto, and I have sung that part many times...." (Mansfield 2007, 127)

This passage is an echo chamber of voices: the authorial voice; the internal voice of Ada Moss and of the role she will assume in her internal fantasy; and the speech of the "dark handsome gentleman in a fur coat". Both Sydney Janet Kaplan and David Trotter (2007) have compared "Pictures" with Eliot's *The Waste Land;* Trotter's book, *Cinema and Modernism*, discusses what he calls a "will-to-automatism" in the modernist aesthetic, as writing becomes a medium for recording lived experience in all its heterogeneity (113ff.). Maurizio Ascari's *Cinema and the Imagination in Katherine Mansfield's Writing* provides a more detailed study of this aspect of Mansfield's writing. The fast intercutting and temporal fluidity of this story recalls silent film so strongly that it is easy to imagine this passage as silent film, the intertitle "By eight o'clock tonight. . . . " flashed over the sign for the Café de Madrid.

In its fascination with performance, its parodic elements and grotesque humour, "Pictures" could not be a clearer example of Mansfield in carnival mode. Carnival, as Bakhtin (1994) says, is "the true feast of time, the feast of becoming, change, and renewal" (199), defying death and subverting fixed categories of meaning. When I think about what is special and unique in Mansfield's writing it is this capacity for metamorphosis, and this permeability, not only of temporal and spatial boundaries, but also the interface between the self and the external world. The human subject is always embodied in Mansfield, represented through what Bakhtin calls "grotesque realism". Speaking of "the material bodily principle in grotesque realism", Bakhtin states: "The leading themes of these images of bodily life are fertility, growth, and a brimming-over abundance" (205). These are the qualities that are so pronounced in Mansfield's work.

"Something Childish But Very Natural" describes the coming of spring in London, a day when "city folks walked as though they carried real live bodies under their clothes with real live hearts pumping the stiff blood through" (Mansfield 2007, 596). Mansfield's characters inhabit flesh and blood bodies that are brought to life in the writing. They are tired, they are sweaty, and above all they are hungry. Food is so important in Mansfield's stories. Feasting and eating, Bakhtin says, are crucial aspects of carnival ambivalence, the act of eating absorbing the outer world into the human body. And the characters themselves are consumed by one another. What is it that is really on the menu in the Café de Madrid but the amply-fleshed Ada herself?

"Rosabel" or "Pictures" or even "Something Childish" might supply the "missing" story in Philip Hensher's anthology. What could be more British than sexual repression in a railway carriage? But our choices need not be restricted to the London stories. As Clare Hanson (1985) points out in her discussion of "The Doll's House", geographical settings in Mansfield's stories are often indeterminate (120–21); it would be possible to include "The Doll's House" without any reference to a New Zealand setting. In *My Katherine Mansfield Project,* Kirsty Gunn (2015) affirms, "what I loved about Mansfield was the way she was melding together a New Zealand and an England, a Wellington and a London" (62). Gunn realized that the act of writing constructs "a place of your own" (63) that is irreducible to a specific geographical location.

Philip Hensher's own choice for his anthology might have been "The Daughters of the Late Colonel", which he has cited in interview as one of the greatest stories ever written (Riekemann 2016). Produced two years before Mansfield's death, "The Daughters of the Late Colonel" is one of her best-known texts, and one she herself was most proud of. It is one of the two stories chosen by Hermione Lee (1995) for *The Secret Self* anthology of stories by women (the other is "The Man Without a Temperament"). It is also the starting point for Ali Smith's (2007) Introduction to the Penguin *Collected Stories*. In her essay for *Morphologies,* a collection of essays by contemporary British writers reflecting on their predecessors, Alison MacLeod (2013) begins with Mansfield's "queer tale", noting especially how, "in Mansfield the physical world is endlessly plastic. A head may also be a candle. A blancmange may exhibit fear. A dead father may be in a top drawer" (140). I have already referred to this capacity for metamorphosis; MacLeod's examples illustrate the hallucinatory properties of Mansfield's prose. In that almost stream-of-consciousness passage previously quoted from "Pictures", Ada observes the sparrows: "Cheep. Cheep. How close they come. I expect somebody feeds them" (Mansfield 2007, 127). In "The Daughters of the Late Colonel", the birds are not just observed, but also merge with the central consciousness: "Josephine felt they were not sparrows, not on the window-ledge. It was inside her, that queer little crying noise. *Yee-eyup–yeep.* Ah, what was it crying, so weak and forlorn?" (283)

As in dreams, Mansfield's characters float free in time and space, and are decoupled from any point of origin. This is how "The Daughters of the Late Colonel" begins:

> The week after was one of the busiest weeks of their lives. Even when they went to bed, it was only their bodies that lay down and rested; their minds went on, thinking things out, talking things over, wondering, deciding, trying to remember where.... (262)

Later, Constantia says, "Do you know what day it is? It's Saturday. It's a week to-day, a whole week" (282), but there is no sense at all, for the reader, of time as linear succession, despite the division of this elliptical narrative into twelve sections, reminiscent of the numbers on a watch. It is the decision that Cyril, the nephew, should inherit his grandfather's watch, that seems to anchor the story more firmly to a geographical location—"Cyril in London" (274), who squeezed in his previous visit between meeting a man in Victoria and hurrying back to meet another at Paddington "just after five" (276).

There are numerous signifiers of bourgeois British life in "The Daughters of the Late Colonel", notably the food—the plates of "mock something or other", that "white terrified blancmange" (265) that they are forced to eat with marmalade; the fruit cake and meringues. But there are also many images of India and the East—most notably the Buddha on the mantelpiece that seems to mesmerise Constantia, standing for an indefinable sense of loss and longing. The sisters are displaced colonials, whose mother died in Ceylon. You might say there were marginalized by British culture; but another way of looking at it would be to say that the colonial experience is intrinsic to British experience, and that Britishness itself is elusive, multiple, eccentric, paradoxical—"Slippery British". Perhaps that is why, if Hensher is right, the British short story is inclined towards parody and performance, the wearing of the mask.

Fortunately, I am not obliged to choose just one Mansfield story to serve as an example of her art and her legacy in Britain. Her contribution to the development of the form cannot be limited to any single country, but it is the "slippery" aspects that I especially want to foreground as I turn to the contemporary women writers in Hensher's anthology. I have discussed metamorphosis and indeterminacy mostly in terms of imagery, setting, ellipsis and the handling of time. But I also want to stress the importance of focalization and narrative voice. Reading "The Daughters of the Late Colonel" requires close attention, should you wish to differentiate between Josephine and Constantia's point of view, and, perhaps, a third state of consciousness, shared between the two. Free indirect discourse, the mingling of authorial speech with that of the characters within third-person narration, has become, one might say, the preferred mode for the modern short story. There are no better examples of its subtleties than in Mansfield's work. Her exploitation of double-voiced discourse and the dialogic properties of language are everywhere in her stories—not just in her use of free indirect speech, but also in the direct speech of her characters and her first-person narrators. The contemporary writers I shall now discuss—A.S. Byatt, Janice Galloway, Ali Smith and Tessa Hadley—have one thing in common; they are all included in Hensher's anthology. They also share Mansfield's interest in the short story as the interplay of competing voices. Looking at their work, I shall point to some themes and techniques that they have inherited, in some cases directly, from Mansfield.

A.S. Byatt

If any single writer should take the credit for A. S. Byatt's interest in short fiction then it is, as Byatt herself has testified, Alice Munro (Chevalier 2003, 230). But these footsteps lead, in an appropriately roundabout way, back to Mansfield, one of Munro's own influences (see Munro's explicit homage in "Jakarta"). "Racine and the Tablecloth" is taken from Byatt's (1987) first collection *Sugar*, which also includes "On the Day that E.M. Forster Died", a story that describes a novelist who is drawn to short fictions for the same reasons as Byatt herself. "On the Day that E.M. Forster Died" consists of an odyssey through the London streets, not unlike Ada Moss's journey and those of other modernist protagonists such as Mrs Dalloway. More importantly, Byatt says that, like her protagonist, she took up short fiction after a life-threatening illness:

> I suddenly realised that there were more and more and more things in the world that I noticed, and that I haven't got enough life to write already the novels I have thought of, without any more novels. And so I started seeing things in this very condensed clear way, as images, not necessarily to be strung together in a long narrative, but to be thought out from. (Chevalier, 2003, 230)

In other words, an acute awareness of mortality drives an urgency within the form itself. It is difficult not to think of Mansfield's illness and premature death when reading these words.

"Racine and the Tablecloth" is at first sight a more discursive story than Byatt's reflections on her practice might suggest, using a seemingly omniscient narrator, who addresses the reader directly and comments on events, in the manner of certain Victorian novelists. However the narrative is focalized through the character of the schoolgirl, Emily, and it is possible to read this apparently extradiegetic narrator as an adult version of Emily herself. When Emily becomes ill on the eve of an important examination, the self is fractured again:

> Emily was double. The feeling part had given up, defeated, abandoned to the bliss of dissolution. The thinking part chattered away toughly, tapping out pentameters and alexandrines with and against the soothing flow of the tears. (Byatt 1987, 616)

But this is not the only doubling of selves in the story. Emily's enemy throughout is the schoolmistress, Miss Crichton-Walker. Martha Crichton-Walker is a parodic figure; she tells the girls how much she enjoys sitting naked in her room, and rumour has it that she also swings naked in the school grounds at night. Despite their mutual antagonism, Emily knows that they share something in common, and that is their outsider status. Emily is far too clever to fit in with the other girls. Miss Crichton-Walker is a pantomime figure, despised and even vilified by the narrator, yet she is a shadow version of Emily herself. And like Constantia, who "crept out of bed in her night-gown when the moon was full, and [had] lain on the floor with her arms outstretched, as though she was crucified" (Mansfield 2007, 284) she has another nocturnal self.

If I were to make direct comparisons between an example of Mansfield's work and "Racine and the Tablecloth", it might be "A Married Man's Story", for the insistent voice of Mansfield's first person narrator, who also addresses the reader directly and invites judgement on his younger self: "Do you remember your childhood? [. . .] No wonder I was hated at school. Even the masters shrank from me" (Mansfield 2007, 432). Or, considering Byatt's exploration of adolescence as liminality I might compare it to "The Dove's Nest", which also uses shifts in focalization to expose the bizarre social rituals of the adults. In "The Dove's Nest", Millie Fawcett has "rare moods" and feverish nights; like Mansfield, Byatt evokes the heightened sensitivity of adolescence, especially when Emily defies medical advice and sits her exam:

> Between paragraphs, Emily saw, in the dark corners of the school hall, under dusty shields of honour, little hallucinatory scenes of tableaux, enacting in doorways or window embrasures a charade of the aimlessness of endeavor. She wrote a careful analysis of the clarity of the exposition of Phèdre's devious and confused passion and looked up to see creatures gesticulating on the fringed edge of her consciousness like the blown ghosts trying to pass over the Styx. She saw Miss Crichton-Walker, silvery-muddy as she had been in the underwater blind-light of the nursery, gravely indicating that failure had its purpose for her. She saw Aunt Florrie, grey and faded and resigned amongst the light thrown off the

white linen cloths and immaculate bridal satins of her work, another judge, upright in her chair. (619)

Reading this passage, I am reminded of the intermingling of memories, impressions and fantasies in Mansfield. Emily is answering a question on Racine's *Phèdre;* the imagery of the Graeco-Roman underworld combines with sense-impressions, such as the patterns of light that also recur in Mansfield's fiction as sunlight on the carpet or in this passage from "The Doves' Nest" when the young girl, Millie, is waiting for visitors with her mother and her hired companion:

> Everybody just waits for things to happen as they were waiting for the stranger who came walking towards them through the sun and shadow under the budding plane trees, or driving, perhaps, in one of the small, cotton-covered cabs.... An angel passed over the Villa Martin. In that moment of hovering silence something timid, something beseeching seemed to lift, seemed to offer itself, as the flowers in the salon, uplifted, gave themselves to the light. (Mansfield 2007, 450)

Janice Galloway

Janice Galloway (2015) is in some ways the closest of these writers to the modernist engagement with the passing moment and heightened states of consciousness, for instance in her best-known story, "Blood", which uses free indirect discourse to explore the interior consciousness of her adolescent protagonist, beginning with a traumatic visit to the dentist. As this might suggest, Galloway shares Mansfield's interest in the materiality of the body and grotesque realism. The "Scenes from a Life" stories in the *Blood* collection are hybrid texts, going even further than Mansfield's "Two Tuppenny Ones, Please", in their fusion of short story and theatrical convention. For his anthology, Hensher has chosen "Last Thing", a stream-of-consciousness account of the rape of a young girl. It is presented as a fragment of an ongoing experience:

> we were
> coming
>
> coming back from the pictures with half a packet of sweeties still coming round the corner at Meadowside with Mary saying she was feart to go up the road herself Mary is feart for everything but so I said I'll take you because I'm bigger than her the film thing we saw at the pictures that Halloween thing wasny really scary I don't think (Galloway 2015, 648)

I am forced to end the quotation arbitrarily because the narrative unfolds as a continuous sequence, rhythmic, repetitive and without punctuation. The speech of the other characters is integrated into the flow of the narrator's consciousness. Galloway's use of the demotic is reminiscent of the pronounced orality of Mansfield's writing; and as a sort of dramatic monologue we might compare "Last Thing" with "The Lady's Maid" or "The Canary". Both Mansfield stories combine an abrupt opening with a breathless syntax, suggesting the spontaneous outpouring of speech. "The Canary" opens with a single long, unspooling sentence:

> For instance, when I'd finished the house in the afternoon, and changed my blouse and brought my sewing on to the veranda here, he used to hop, hop, hop from one perch to another, tap against the bars as if to attract my attention, sip a little water just as a professional singer might, and then break into a song so exquisite that I had to put my needle down to listen to him. (Mansfield 2007, 419)

The extreme brutality of Galloway's story is extraordinary and devastating, and her protagonist seems a world away from the bourgeois indignation of Byatt's bookish schoolgirl. And yet both Byatt and Galloway show the subject splitting in two, in order to regain agency at a traumatic point in their lives. As Galloway describes it:

it was hard to keep breathing right with his hand pushing under my chin so all I could see was the sky a funny colour with the orange off the streetlight making wee grains in it like milk but right then right that minute something kind of turned in my head something kind of clicked and I wanted to look him right in the eye (2015, 649–50)

Galloway's closing lines form the ultimate open ending:

right into his eyes I looked right at him
keeping
  my sights
    clear
    and
    still
(650 51)

The precise layout is a reminder us of the affinity between the short story and poetry. Galloway's experiments with orality, voice and fragmentation exceed the possibilities available to Mansfield, and yet there is a discernible continuity between them.

Ali Smith

Ali Smith and Tessa Hadley share a well-documented interest in Mansfield's work; Smith's Introduction prefaces the Penguin *Collected Stories*, and Hadley cites Mansfield as a research interest at Bath Spa University, where she is Professor of Creative Writing. Smith (2011) quotes from Mansfield in the hybrid story/essay/lectures collected as *Artful*, and her story "The Ex-Wife", first published in the journal *Katherine Mansfield Studies*, is narrated by the anonymous partner of a modernist scholar whose relationship is infiltrated by the pervasive figure of Mansfield (95–106). Mansfield is initially nicknamed "the ex-wife" because the partner's obsessive research into biographical minutiae introduces a third, obtrusive presence into the relationship. As the relationship disintegrates, the narrator, in turn, is haunted by the figure of Mansfield herself, "a dead person stopping me on my path, young and wiry and alarmingly lively, alarmingly bright at the eyes" (Smith 2011, 99), and by her various utterances, echoing through the text in a seemingly random fashion.

"The Ex-Wife" problematises the atavistic power invested in the figure of Mansfield by many of her readers, a figure constructed from numerous sources within and beyond her own texts—and not least from our own emotional response to a writer whose stories, letters and journals are so marked by affect. Smith's own short fiction, including "The Ex-Wife" and other examples such as "True Short Story", reflects ironically on narrativity, genre and voice, maintaining a detached and rational authorial persona. For his anthology, Hensher has chosen one of her earlier stories, "Miracle Survivors", which consists of two separate narratives. In the first, an old man is discovered buried in the snow during a bad winter in the Scottish Highlands. In the second, two young girls break into a newsagent's on New Year's Eve. The tenuous link between them is the turning of the year, which is linked to the generation of yarns, speculation and gossip. Like Galloway, Smith mostly dispenses with speech marks. She weaves oral storytelling, newspaper headlines and conversations into a seamless whole:

> The nurse told the reporters what his first words had been when he came round: No Wonder. *No Wonder Says Miracle Survivor. He wanted to say something so I put my head to his ear to hear and he whispered the words 'no wonder' to me, said Nurse Margaret Gallagher* (22). Afterwards, when he was well enough to be photographed, the old man explained that it wasn't wonder he'd said, it was vinegar. (Smith 2015, 653)

In her Penguin Introduction, Smith places concepts of performance at the centre of Mansfield's aesthetic. The centrality of performance in her own work is evident in this story. All her characters are putting on a show; the old man for the media, the two girls making random phone calls, taking photographs and spelling out a message in sweet tubes and chewing gum packets. Breaking into a shop would be pointless without this kind of evidence. They have turned transgression into performance art.

Tessa Hadley

As Sue Vice (2015) has pointed out, Tessa Hadley is indebted stylistically to Katherine Mansfield, especially in her use of free indirect discourse and focalization (148-62).¹ For the Penguin anthology, Philip Hensher has chosen another story that, like Byatt's, reflects on teenage experience. "Buckets of Blood" is the first of two Hadley stories featuring the sisters, Hilary and Sheila, across her two collections *Sunstroke* and *Married Love*. Of course, Mansfield uses a set of recurring characters in "Prelude", "At the Bay" and "The Doll's House", the three stories Hadley recommended at a Royal Society of Literature masterclass in 2012. "Buckets of Blood" is focalized through the younger sister, Hilary, who is visiting Sheila at Bristol University in 1972.

Discussing the centrality of performance in Mansfield's work, Ali Smith refers to "the marked differences between theatre and 'reality'" (2007, xvii). In Hadley's story, too, those differences are delineated, in the contrast between outward display and the corporeal. Sheila "had always been braver about putting on a public show than Hilary was" (Hadley 2015, 659); she wears the flamboyant hippy-style clothes of the era. When Sheila's boyfriend, Neil, comes to meet Hilary at the coach station in Bristol, she notices his bare feet and black eye make-up. Neil is a performer in other ways too, notably the way he draws attention to his working class origins; the exploration of class difference is something else that Hadley shares with Mansfield.

Neil tells Hilary that her sister is "unwell"—"the word they had to use to the games mistress at school when they weren't having showers because they had a period. Hilary saved the joke up to amuse

---

1 Vice makes direct comparison between the moment of revelation in "Mouthful of Cut Glass" and "Miss Brill".

Sheila" (663–64). Hilary starts to panic as Neil leads her on a convoluted and exhausting journey through the dark city to the squat where he and Sheila are staying:

> She thought he might be taking her somewhere to kill her with a knife. She wouldn't say a word to save her life; she might swing at him with her grandfather's suitcase. Or she imagined drugs, which she didn't know anything about: perhaps drug addicts recruited new associates by bundling strangers into their den and injecting them with heroin. She didn't ever imagine rape or anything of that sort, because she thought that as a preliminary to that outrage there would have to be some trace of interest in her, some minimal sign of a response to her, however disgusted. (665–66)

In this reconstruction of the past, the immediate impressions of the younger Hilary are filtered through the comments of her older self, fused with the voice of the author. That tiny word "or" might imply alternatives; she might have thought she'd be killed or she thought she might have been drugged. Or it might suggest that her fears fluctuated between one possibility or another. Whatever the case, the specific nature of these terrors is almost unnameable, and barely recoverable through memory. That phrase "to save her life" may be read literally, but it is also a figure of speech—"I couldn't tell you to save my life"; "I can't remember to save my life".

Sheila is in fact having a miscarriage; when she finally arrives at the squat, Hilary's job is to nurse her sister through this ordeal, and dispose of the "buckets of blood" (667) that give the story its title. Once again, we are made acutely aware of the material body, through these graphic descriptions, more graphic than anything that might have been published in Mansfield's lifetime. And, as I have suggested, there is a contrast between this corporeal reality and the construction of an outer, social self. Neither Neil nor any of Sheila's university friends ever refer to what is going on, and Sheila herself underplays the whole experience. Indeed, it is because this experience is repressed that it continues to haunt Hilary's imagination.

Once again, adolescence is presented as a liminal condition, a heightened interior consciousness, uniquely suggestible and prone to altered states. Hilary is not plied with drugs after all, but she does drink on an empty stomach. Her consciousness distorted by drunkenness rather than illness, Hilary shares with Byatt's character, Emily, an ability to split herself in two:

> She didn't like the taste of beer but because the food was so salty she drank it in thirsty mouthfuls, and then was seized by a sensation as if she floated up to hang in some little way above her present situation, graciously indifferent, so that her first experience of drunkenness was a blessed one. (671)

(It is worth noting that Sheila is writing an essay on *The Oresteia*, an echo of the classical imagery in Emily's exam.)

And once again, like Mansfield's characters, Hilary is hungry; she has eaten nothing but a packet of crisps and some peanuts since she arrived in Bristol. Hunger is material, hunger is real, and it conditions altered states of consciousness. But hunger is also symbolic. It stands for the insatiable appetite for life, and this is made apparent in the closing lines of Hadley's story, as the coach taking Hilary home pulls out of the station. Like Rosabel, Hilary reads the world through a window, with mundane external reality mutating into the extraordinary:

> It desolated her to think that when she was dead she wouldn't be able to see it: cows, green hummocky fields, suburban cottages of weathered brick, a country factory with smashed windows, an excited spatter of birds thrown up from a tree. Then she started to see these things as if she was dead already, and they were persisting after her, and she had been allowed back, and must take in everything hungrily while she had the chance, every least tiny detail. (676)

There is so much that all these writers take from Mansfield; it is difficult to imagine the British short story without her. But above all it is the sharpness of this Dionysian hunger, this desire to absorb the world into the self, the self that records just a fraction of what may be seen or felt, knowing that the hunger is insatiable. That we can never get enough.

Bibliography

Ascari, Maurizio. 2014. *Cinema and the Imagination in Katherine Mansfield's Writing.* Basingstoke: Palgrave Macmillan.

Bakhtin, M. M. 1994. "Carnival Ambivalence." In *The Bakhtin Reader: Selected Writings of Bakhtin, Medvedev, Voloshinov,* edited by Pam Morris, 194–225. Translated by H. Iswolsky. London: Edward Arnold.

Byatt, A. S. 1987. *Sugar.* London: Penguin.

———. 2009. "Introduction." In *The Oxford Book of English Short Stories,* edited by A. S. Byatt, xv–xxx. Oxford: Oxford University Press.

———. 2015. "Racine and the Tablecloth." In *The Penguin Book of the British Short Story.* Vol. 2, edited by Philip Hensher, 596–622. London: Penguin.

Chevalier, Jean-Louis. 2003. "A. S. Byatt." *Journal of the Short Story in English* 41: 215–31.

Galloway, Janice. 1992. *Blood.* London: Vintage, 1992.

———. 2015. "Last Thing." In *The Penguin Book of the British Short Story.* Vol. 2, edited by Philip Hensher, 648–51. London: Penguin.

Gunn, Kirsty. 2015. *My Katherine Mansfield Project.* London: Notting Hill Editions.

Hadley, Tessa. 2008. *Sunstroke.* London: Vintage.

———. 2013. *Married Love.* London: Vintage.

———. 2015. "Buckets of Blood." In *The Penguin Book of the British Short Story.* Vol. 2, edited by Philip Hensher, 659–76. London: Penguin.

Hanson, Clare. 1985. *Short Stories and Short Fictions, 1880–1980.* Basingstoke: Macmillan.

Hensher, Philip. 2015. "General Introduction." In *The Penguin Book of the British Short Story*. Vol. 2, edited by Philip Hensher, xiii–xxxviii. London: Penguin.

Kaplan, Sydney Janet. 1991. *Katherine Mansfield and the Origins of Modernist Fiction*. Ithaca, NY and London: Cornell University Press.

Lee, Hermione, ed. 1995. *The Secret Self: A Century of Short Stories by Women*. London: Phoenix Giants.

MacLeod, Alison. 2013. "Katherine Mansfield." In *Morphologies: Short Story Writers on Short Story Writers*, edited by Ra Page, 137–53. Manchester: Comma.

Mansfield, Katherine. 2007. *The Collected Stories*. London: Penguin.

Munro, Alice. 1998. "Jakarta." In *The Love of a Good Woman*, 79–116. London: Chatto & Windus.

Murry, John Middleton, ed. 1954. *Journal of Katherine Mansfield*. London: Constable.

O'Sullivan, Vincent. 2004. "Introduction." In *The Oxford Book of New Zealand Short Stories*, edited by Vincent O'Sullivan, vii–xi. Melbourne: Oxford University Press.

Riekemann, Jane. 2016. "Interview with Philip Hensher." http://bath-shortstoryaward.co.uk/interview-with-philip-hensher/.

Smith, Ali. 2007. "Introduction." In Katherine Mansfield, *The Collected Stories*, v–xxviii. London: Penguin.

---. 2008. "True Short Story." In *The First Person and Other Stories*, 1–18. London: Penguin.

---. 2011. "The Ex-Wife." *Katherine Mansfield Studies* 3: 95–106.

---. 2013. *Artful*. London: Penguin.

---. 2015. "Miracle Survivors." In *The Penguin Book of the British Short Story*. Vol. 2, edited by Philip Hensher, 652–58. London: Penguin.

Trotter, David. 2007. *Cinema and Modernism*. Oxford: Blackwell.

Vice, Sue. 2015. "Class as Destiny in the Short Stories of Tessa Hadley." In *British Women Short Story Writers: The New Woman to Now*, edited by Emma Young and James Bailey, 148–62. Edinburgh: Edinburgh University Press.

Young, Emma, and James Bailey, eds. 2015. *British Women Short Story Writers: The New Woman to Now.* Edinburgh: Edinburgh University Press.

"Kew Gardens" and "Miss Brill": Virginia Woolf and Katherine Mansfield as Short Story Writers

Janet Wilson

This chapter considers the literary relationship between Katherine Mansfield and Virginia Woolf, whose complex friendship between 1916 and 1920 is well documented.[1] It suggests possible lines of influence between them, discernible in their experimentation with the short story genre during a formative period for both writers: when Woolf was writing short stories and before she had established her reputation as a novelist, and when Mansfield was approaching the mature style that would make her name as a short story writer par excellence. It will draw a comparison between two stories—Woolf's "Kew Gardens" (1917), and Mansfield's "Miss Brill" (1920)—both set in public gardens. As responses to similar settings that exhibit differences of modernist technique and approach the stories can also be read in relation to each other through the lens of Mansfield's and Woolf's inconstant friendship and literary rivalry.

Mansfield had earlier written of visiting the public gardens in Wellington in "In the Botanical Gardens" (1907), a sketch resembling a prose poem, now seen among other early pieces as seminal for her later modernism. Woolf's "Kew Gardens", it is believed, had its genesis in Mansfield's idea for a composition about gardens and flowerbeds outlined in a letter to Woolf (now believed to be lost) and another to Lady Ottoline Morrell (*Letters* I, 325), both written on the same day, August 15, 1917 (Alpers 1980, 249–51). These versions of "public garden" stories—that is, Mansfield's 1907 vignette, the flash of insight recorded in her letter of 1917, Woolf's "Kew Gardens" which it may have inspired, and Mansfield's "Miss Brill"—as well as other correspondence about their conversations, and Mansfield's review of

---

1   It is extensively discussed by Alpers (1980, 247–61, 410) and Tomalin (1988, 48–50, 197–205).

"Kew Gardens" in the *Athenaeum* of June 1919 (see Hanson 1987, 53–54), can be read as if in dialogue with each other. The early textual exchanges between Mansfield and Woolf through stories, letters and reviews, have been described as a "feminized sociology".[2] To them may belong Chapter 25 of *Night and Day*, Woolf's second novel, in which Kew Gardens are the setting for a tentative encounter between Ralph Denham and Katharine Hilbery. It is possible that the writers conversed about this as well as Woolf's story in August 1917, when Mansfield visited her at Asheham House in Surrey, as Woolf was probably writing this chapter then (Staveley 1997, 60). By November 1919, when Mansfield reviewed the novel in the *Athenaeum*, she would have read Woolf's chapter with its more extended treatment of Kew Gardens as a setting for courtship and declarations of affection. "Miss Brill", written the following year, is in many ways a contrast to the aesthetics and thematics of all these earlier "public garden" texts, and it reworks their oppositions—nature and culture, human and non-human, public and private, rationality and the unconscious—into a darker, more sinister vision. In addition, intertextual allusions to Woolf's "Kew Gardens" in "A Dill Pickle" (1917) in relation to memories of a past romance, and a possible link between the parasol, used by one of Woolf's characters in "Kew Gardens" (in *Night and Day* it is an umbrella) and a crucial accessory of the heroine of "The Escape" (1920), may be read as part of Mansfield's ongoing conversation with Woolf over issues of sexuality, betrayal and marriage.

That Mansfield introduced Woolf to modernist form during this time in her career when Woolf had only published one novel, *The Voyage Out* (1916), and had worked as a regular contributor to *Cornhill Magazine* is now a critical commonplace. Woolf began writing short fiction in 1906 in an apprenticeship style that was influenced by her early reviewing and experiments with biography, but a "major shift" in her fiction stems from the period when the writers were in regular contact professionally (Smith 1990, 156). These meetings,

---

2   I extend Staveley's (1997, 60) use of this term to describe the mix of conversation, correspondence and readings of texts in relation to "Kew Gardens" to include other texts by Mansfield and Woolf.

marking their fragile but often genuinely rewarding literary friendship, began after Woolf invited Mansfield to publish with the Hogarth Press her extended story about childhood, "The Aloe", which she had begun in 1915 and was revising in 1917; it was renamed as "Prelude" and published in 1918.[3] Woolf later claimed it was "much the best thing she's yet done" (Woolf, 1975–80, 2, 248), although in April 1917, when she asked Mansfield for a story to publish, she may only have read some of her *New Age* semi-satiric pieces like "Mr Reginald Peacock's Day". "Prelude", a long plotless story which explores family life and the seething tensions below its surface, has thematic affinities with *The Voyage Out*, and is considered a seminal influence on novels like *To the Lighthouse* and *The Waves* in that it provided Woolf with new topics, questions and techniques.

Both Mansfield's letter and Woolf's story belong to this early period of their friendship, when "Prelude" was being typeset and they were exploring innovative possibilities for fiction. It coincides with the new direction of two stories by Woolf representing a departure from her traditional mode of perception, and showing some affinity to Mansfield's work (Alpers 1980, 251; Smith 1999, 156–57): "The Mark on the Wall", written after Woolf had read "Prelude", "Kew Gardens", and possibly a third work, "An Unwritten Novel" (McLaughlin 1983, 155). Mansfield's inspiration for a story about gardens and flowers hints at the ongoing creative interaction of the two writers: the letter to Ottoline Morrell of August 15 1917 proposes a composition about the flower gardens at Garsington Manor, which she had just visited, in which several pairs of people walk and converse, and which would resemble a "kind of, musically speaking, conversation *set* to flowers". She opens by asking, as if in reference to a prior conversation: "Your glimpse of the garden [...] made me wonder again *who* is going to write about that flower garden" (*Letters* 1, 325; emphasis in original). Woolf alludes to this in writing to Ottoline (on the same day): "Katherine Mansfield describes your garden, the rose leaves drying in the sun, the

---

[3] It was the third of the Press's publications, the first two being the texts in *Two Stories* (1917): Virginia Woolf's "The Mark on the Wall" and Leonard Woolf's "Three Jews".

pool, and long conversations between people wandering up and down in the moonlight" (Woolf, 1975–80, 2, 174). Alpers (1980) speculates that, after receiving Mansfield's letter written on the Wednesday, Woolf wrote a draft of "Kew Gardens" before Mansfield's first visit to the Woolfs at Asheham House on August 17 to discuss the typesetting of "Prelude", possibly as a conversation piece in anticipation of this occasion, for Mansfield mentions the garden story in writing to Woolf subsequently (250–51; *Letters* I, 327; August 23, 2017; Woolf 1975–80, 2, 172).

At the time they met, Woolf, according to her own account, was writing experimental short fiction as a way of breaking through the constraints of Georgian literary form in order to find a new form for the novel (later realised in radical experiments like *Jacob's Room* and *The Waves*). In 1917 she wrote, for example, "it is easier to do a short thing all in one flight, than a novel. Novels are frightfully clumsy and overpowering" (Woolf, 1975–80, 2, 167). She was using her "tunnelling process, by which I tell the past by instalments" (1979–1985, 2, 272) as a way of foregrounding memory in the exploration of character, including the representation of states of consciousness. This vision of language, in which she sought depth of feeling while also representing the fragmentary, fleeting qualities of modernity through the break-up of narrative form, she discovered, was more achievable in short stories than the novel form. Stories like "The Mark on the Wall" and "An Unwritten Novel" (both published in *Monday or Tuesday* [1921]), are revisionary versions of the quest motif, being interrogative in orientation and containing metafictional comments on the art of writing, while also foregrounding her general critique of patriarchal ideologies.

Mansfield, by contrast, had moved away from the social satire of her stories published in *In a German Pension* (1911) and *The New Age*, and extended her writing talents in stories published in *Rhythm* that drew on the New Zealand outback like "The Woman at the Store" (1912), and in others about journeys in France like "The Little Governess" (1915) and "A Discreet Journey" (1915). Although her more mature style was still to develop, she showed new control over her subject matter in the innovative design of "Prelude", which along with "At the Bay" (1921) and "The Daughters of the Late Colonel" (1920) is as close to an achievement in the novel form that she came; while stories like "Feuille D'Album" and "A Dill Pickle", both written in late 1917, show some consolidation of her style. "Miss Brill" develops the *femme seule* thematic of these works further and can be linked to stories such as "Ma Parker", "Pictures", "The Daughters of the Late Colonel" and her last story "The Canary", about isolated and vulnerable elderly spinsters or widowers, whose psychological despair and longings are refracted through speech and movement. They demonstrate radical experimentation with voice, mood and setting in exploring the tensions between their public and private worlds and the different selves that inhabit these spaces, as her tragic heroines realise the impossibility of escape from the encroachment of age, loneliness, and death.

The writers had in common a quarrel with patriarchy and its ideology, which they saw as dominating conventional structure in art in terms of hierarchy, linearity, a privileging of order, unity and the rational. Woolf famously challenged the realism of John Galsworthy, H.G. Wells and Arnold Bennett in essays like "The Modern Novel" and "Mr Bennett and Mrs Brown" in 1924, but as Clare Hanson (1987) points out, such criticism of Bennett was circulating a decade earlier (148). Mansfield mocked and parodied the work of the realists, Arnold Bennett and H.G. Wells in her notebooks in 1912, and her parody of an epistolary novel, "Virginia's Journal", an attack on *The New Age* and its contributors, published in *Rhythm* in 1913, includes mockery of Bennett as the voice of modern literature (*CW*3, 407–10 and n.). In their resistance to these male-dominated literary models of realism, they shared a search for an alternative new form that would celebrate the fleeting, transient nature of modern life in ways that can be read gendered feminine. Their turn to literary impressionism was also inspired by the discoveries in visual art, evident in the paintings of Roger Fry's exhibition of 1910, "Manet and the Post-Impressionists", which suggested new ways of rendering perception, prompting Woolf to say that human character changed "in or about December, 1910"

(1988, 3, 384). Woolf draws upon visual Post-Impressionism for stylistic innovation in "Kew Gardens", for example, in the opening description of the flowerbed with its elaborate lyrical patterns and emphasis on the transformative interplay of colour, movement and light: "From the oval-shaped flower-bed there rose perhaps a hundred stalks spreading into heart-shaped or tongue-shaped leaves half way up and unfurling at the tip red or blue or yellow petals marked with spots of colour raised upon the surface" (Woolf 1985a, 84). For Mansfield, it was Van Gogh's paintings (especially his *Sunflowers*) that liberated her imagination. As she wrote to Dorothy Brett: "They taught me something about writing which was queer, a kind of freedom—or rather, a shaking free" (*Letters* 4, 333; Dec. 5, 1921). To both writers, then, Post-Impressionism stimulated further their interest in representing voice and subjectivity and alternative states like dream and reflection in fluid narrative forms such as free indirect discourse and stream of consciousness.

Glimpses of Mansfield's style and approach have been discerned in some of Woolf's subsequent novels, especially in the "high" modernism of *Jacob's Room* and *Orlando*; and intertextual links defined, such as between "At the Bay" with its poetic, musical framing, and *The Waves*, and between "The Garden Party", "Psychology" and *Mrs Dalloway*. There is little evidence of Woolf's direct influence on Mansfield, however, although Ann McLaughlin (1978) hints at affinities between the disordered mental processes in "The Mark on the Wall" (1917) and those of "A Married Man's Story" (1918) (372). The correspondence between Woolf, Mansfield and Ottoline Morrell in August 1917 is rare evidence of how new ideas about narrative were being received and were circulated in this circle. Mansfield confirms that "Kew Gardens" was discussed in her visit to Asheham in August in her thank-you letter to Woolf. Her allusion to the story's dynamic visual quality: "Yes, your Flower Bed is *very* good. Theres a still, quivering, changing light over it all", is followed by an ardent declaration of their shared aims: "We have got the same job, Virginia & it really is very curious and thrilling that we should both [...] be after so very nearly the same thing" (*Letters* 1, 327; 23 Aug 1917, emphasis in original).

"Miss Brill", written when the relationship had begun to founder after Mansfield's critical review of *Night and Day* in 1919, presents such a radical change in the mood and character of the "public garden" story that it suggests aloof detachment from this early excitement of shared literary discoveries.

*****

"Kew Gardens" is notable for its delicate counterpointing of human and natural worlds, and impressionistic rendering of light, colour and movement, qualities that may owe something to Mansfield's original vision. It also displays similar features to Woolf's earlier stories such as "The Mark on the Wall" that signalled Woolf's new direction in which, Angela Smith points out, objects (the mark on the wall, the flowers in Kew Gardens) take on the characteristics of a character, and external reality demarcates difference from the individual subjectivity rather than representing character (1999, 156, 157). In "The Mark on the Wall" the narrator's investigation (or "tunnelling") is marked by disintegration of the boundaries between reality and the fictional world, through manifestations of linguistic instability; the mysterious mark comes to have the status of an active presence as it becomes the subject of the narrator's questions and her puzzlement about what it represents introduces slippage between signs and signifiers. This allows her to move further into the fictional world and to inhabit other voices, making the enigmatic mark an axis around which different points of view are coordinated.

Likewise in "Kew Gardens" the narrative voice functions as a frame for the story, opening up the fictional world of the text with an intersubjective approach, and introducing different discourses with monotone and polyphonic voices. The cinematic close-up description of the profusion of flowers and their primary colours through intricate patterning means that external reality is registered as mood and impression rather than specific location. Mansfield's inspiration included "bright dazzle" (*Letters* 1, 325), and Woolf's gauzy rainbow mix of red, blue, and yellow tulip petals, when irradiated by light and animated by a breeze, means that "the colour was flashed into the air above, into the eyes of the men and women who walk in Kew Gardens"

(Woolf, 1985a, 84). The sudden flare is intensified by glancing illuminations of sunlight creating "a spot of the most intricate colour", striking disparate objects and causing a raindrop to swell almost to bursting point:

> The light fell either upon the smooth grey back of pebble, or the shell of a snail with its brown circular veins, or, falling into a raindrop, it expanded with such intensity of red, blue and yellow the thin walls of water that one expected them to burst and disappear. (Woolf 1985a, 84)

Juxtaposed with the description of the flower bed in the opening and concluding narrative frame, are the four couples strolling among the flower beds whose polyphonic voices and disparate points of view create the "musical" counterpoint, like a minuet, to the flowers. In keeping with Mansfield's suggestion that "the 'pairs' of people must be very different" (*Letters* 1, 325), Woolf provides a cross-section of social class, age and family type: a married couple with their children; two men of different generations, two lower middle class women, and a young couple in "the prime of youth" (1985a, 88). Mixing direct speech with reflection and comment the conversations are linked by references to the flower-beds, creating a layered, overlapping intersection between people and nature. Through the cinematic device of the slow dissolve Woolf effects a merging of people and flowers in the all-embracing, pulsing sunlight: "they wavered and sought shade beneath the trees, dissolving like drops of water in the yellow and green atmosphere, staining it faintly with red and blue" (Woolf 1985a, 89). Mansfield commented that she was "fascinated" by the "sense of those couples dissolving in the bright air" (*Letters* 1, 327).

The impressionist pointillist technique of showing the play of light on people as well as flowers yields to the transient and inconsequential: a passing snail moving around in the garden. As the narrator's alter ego, it signals Woolf's rewriting of the concept of the panoramic narrator into a modernist female-authored text, for its 'voice', rendered through free indirect discourse, conceals the narrator's presence in making transitions between the external speakers. In this impressionistic prose piece that moves back and forth between landscape and people, image and voice, lacking any storyline, this creature provides the only narrative component, linking the different couples through its agency and movement: "The snail had now considered every possible method of reaching his goal without going round the dead leaf or climbing over it" (Woolf 1985a, 87). The snail becomes one focus of activity in a story that is about anticipated action, about what has happened and what might happen, rather than action itself.

Mansfield's review of "Kew Gardens" in the *Athenaeum* of June 13, 1919 is both admiring and ambivalent, suggesting a certain critical distance. She registers the story's lyrical impressionism, its transience, as "poise [...] her world is on tiptoe", and she appreciates its "secret life" and "disturbing" beauty. Although "it belongs to another age", any hesitation about a lack of engagement with the present is passed over with her oblique comment that it is "love at second sight" (Hanson 1985, 53). Woolf noted Mansfield's approval that the story was the "right 'gesture': a turning point" (1977–84, 2, 44), and thought the story helped her to find her voice as a modernist. But Mansfield's critical review of *Night and Day*, that the novel "was unaware of what has been happening" (Hanson 1987, 59) concerning the impact of the war, anticipated her more negative response to Woolf's writing, including stories published in *Monday or Tuesday* (1921): "I didn't care for them. She's detached from life. [...] Nothing grows" (*Letters* 4, 285; Sept. 1921).

*****

Mansfield's impulse to bring her idea to creative fruition is stated in her 1917 letter: "I must have a fling at it as soon as I have time" (*Letters* 1, 327). Some of the "possibilities" that she saw in a "conversation *set* to flowers"—such as the "exquisite haunting scent", the need "to stoop & touch and make sure", and the shape of flowers as "formal and fine" as a "'flower of the mind'"[4]—can be traced to the

---

[4] Possibly a reference to *The Flower of the Mind* (1897), an anthology of English poetry selected by Alice Meynell. In 1908 Mansfield was a frequent dinner party guest of Meynell's daughter Monica, and her husband Caleb Saleeby, an amateur musician (Tomalin 1988, 59).

opening section of her 1907 vignette, "In the Botanical Gardens". These appear in the manicured, man-made garden with "spring flowers [that] are almost too beautiful", where the narrator bends over "a great stretch of foam-like cowslips", where "the air is heavy with their yellow scent, like hay and new milk and the kisses of children", and there is "laughter and movement and bright sunlight". The narrator's aesthetic eye lingers on the shapes of the flowers: rhododendron blossoms "rise, flamelike", pansies are "in clusters", forget-me-nots are "a mist", and anemones "a tangle" (*CW*1, 84–85).

But this rhapsodic response is either heavily mediated or absent altogether in subsequent public garden stories that feature distinctive characters. In "A Dill Pickle" (published October 4, 1917), the flower allusions seem to be in dialogue with Woolf's description of the flower beds in "Kew Gardens", published only two months earlier (and possibly to the Kew Gardens episode in *Night and Day*). Mansfield's heroine recalls the romantic aura of a public garden visit in turning to a nearly forgotten episode of some years earlier. Vera meets again, in a chance encounter, a man to whom she was once favourably inclined, and who reminds her of "that first afternoon spent together in Kew Gardens". He mimics Vera's voice telling him what he did not know then: "'Geranium, marigold and verbena'" (*CW*2, 99) (in ways reminiscent of Katherine Hilbery in *Night and Day* who upon meeting Ralph Denham in Kew Gardens is told the names of the flowers with which she was unfamiliar). With these flowers Mansfield introduces a parallel colour scheme to Woolf's red, yellow and blue tulips in "Kew Gardens" in a subtle intertextual play. But the thrill of romance is only a distant idealised memory in "A Dill Pickle": the man invokes Vera's incantation of the flowers' names as "some forgotten heavenly language", leading Vera to conclude that his was "the truer memory", and that it was a "wonderful afternoon" with flowers and gardens bathed in "warm sunshine" (*CW*2, 99). In the present-day encounter in the restaurant, however, which terminates abruptly with Vera's departure, such memories do little to assuage the bitter aftertaste of a failed relationship.

Published in the *Athenaeum* in November 1920, "Miss Brill" moves further away from the earlier sensuous descriptions of gardens that draw on Mansfield's love of flowers for their beauty and fleeting vitality as in "In the Botanical Gardens" and her use of them as metonymic of the female body and sexuality as in "A Dill Pickle". The story's relationship to her early vignette and to the intricate impressionism and delicate exploration of consciousness of Woolf's "Kew Gardens" may in fact be read in terms of contrast, juxtaposition and counterpoint rather than parallelism and continuity. Its setting in the "Jardins Publiques" (the exact location is not given), and focus on an elderly woman, suggest Mansfield was returning to her earlier exploration of individual subjectivity in a garden setting, whether this be the metropolitan public gardens of Wellington in "In the Botanical Gardens", or the domestic gardens of the Burnell family in "Prelude", with their contrasting manicured and wild spaces that recall those of the earlier vignette. But "Miss Brill" shows that Mansfield's art had moved into a different phase, one undoubtedly conditioned by the advance of her illness and the problems of her marriage to John Middleton Murry who earlier in the year had started a relationship with her friend Dorothy Brett. In August of that year she had cut off her relationship with Virginia Woolf without explanation, leaving the older writer hurt and puzzled.

At one level "Miss Brill" might be seen, like the 1907 vignette, as a pure experiment in form and sound in representing the subjectivity of Miss Brill, a teacher of English pupils in France. Unlike Woolf's vibrant synaesthesia of colour, movement and light in "Kew Gardens", the narrator's observation of different species in "In the Botanical Gardens", and Mansfield's imagined "conversation *set* to flowers" *(Letters* 1, 325; emphasis in original), the focus is not on the visual spectacle of garden beds and flowers. Indeed, flowers are now detached from their settings in flower-beds and seen as accoutrements to the human spectacle that Miss Brill witnesses rather than as signs of nature's abundant riches. Nor is conversation between couples reported to the reader as in "Kew Gardens" but overheard by Miss Brill who considers herself "quite expert [...] at listening as though she didn't listen, at sitting in other people's lives just for a minute while they talked round her" (*CW*2, 251). Instead of the snail of "Kew Gardens", a distinct entity with its own trajectory, there is the semi-animate fox fur, both an object and a pet, with which Miss Brill has "uncanny exchanges" (Hanson 2011, 120).

No longer a space to explore or to marvel at nature's wonders, but a backdrop for Miss Brill's day-dreams, the Jardins Publiques are filled with strolling couples, visitors and onlookers, who act out their little personal dramas to the sounds of the band. Its rhythms and music become synchronised with Miss Brill's thought processes: the drum beat, heard as "'The Brute! The Brute!'" (*CW*2, 253), is her comment on a gentleman's abrupt dismissal of a young lady's advances, witnessed from her vantage point near the band rotunda. Like other incidents that she interprets, it leads her to believe that she is an actress on stage. The style also suggests the artifice of performance. Brightness and light are imaged in terms of contrivance, painting and cosmetic makeup: the "blue sky" is "powdered with gold" and later Miss Brill wonders if it might have been painted (*CW*2, 253). A chill in the air hints at the late spring season, unlike the "sunlit wonder" of spring flowers in "In the Botanical Gardens" and the perfect July weather of "Kew Gardens" that anticipates its crowning vision of organic unity.

But on another level, "Miss Brill's" more artificial world with its hints of darkness and images of coffin-like confinement, suggests a death-in-life immobility and sense of foreboding that exceed the character's consciousness. Confinement to a claustrophobic narrow enclosure was not only a metaphor of her own encroaching illness, but reflects obliquely Mansfield's own fears of the dark and of small spaces, imaged, for example, in exchanges with Murry in which she sees herself as "a tiny girl whom someone has locked up in the dark cupboard", and whom he will let out with a key he has made himself (*Letters* 2, 81; Feb. 20, 1918). Later, Murry writes reassuringly to Mansfield in response to a dream she has had about physical disintegration, redeploying the same image and offering himself as safeguard against dissolution and internment: "Now I intend to put you in a box and keep you there. Don't be frightened. I'll never shut the lid" (October 12, 1919; cited by Smith 1999, 71). These disturbing images of their private play are reincarnated in Miss Brill's "little dark room", and the story's dramatic prop: the fox fur that lives in a box, which is an aspect of Miss Brill's subjectivity, expressing her unconscious, buried feelings. Her dependence on this inanimate object is represented grammatically by the terminal location of the noun in the opening sentence, which concludes with Miss Brill's decision to wear the necklet:

> Although it was so brilliantly fine—the blue sky powdered with gold and the great spots of light like white wine splashed over the Jardins Publiques—Miss Brill was glad that she had decided on her fur. (*CW*2, 250)

Mansfield's presentation of events hinges on the role of the fox fur. Its anthropomorphism—associated with Miss Brill rubbing its "dim little eyes" in order to restore it to life, and feeling it "biting its tail just by her left ear"—displays an intense self-other interconnectedness. The fox fur's helplessness and lack of agency elicit her tender response; its feelings on being taken out of its box are ventriloquized: "'What has been happening to me?' said the sad little eyes" (*CW*2, 251). The rhetorical trope of *prosopopeia*, of giving voice to an inanimate object, dramatizes Miss Brill's fetishisation of this creature or necklet which, when returned to its box in the story's conclusion, expresses inner distress, although whether the sounds of crying she hears are her own or the fox-fur's is deliberately ambiguous. These noises, projecting a painfully fractured subjectivity at a semi-conscious level, illustrate Mansfield's technique of unmediated representation—implying feelings through gesture, voice, action—as she explores the human/non-human boundary more radically than Woolf does in her experimentation with the snail in "Kew Gardens".

Familiar tropes, motifs and images for representing flowers and people in a public space are also redeployed with sinister effect in

"Miss Brill". The letter's recommendation of "peculiarity" in the pairs of people—"some [...] seeming so extraordinarily 'odd' and separate from the flowers" (*Letters* 1, 325)—as if out of touch with organic sources of life, was followed through by Woolf in "Kew Gardens". It appears in a disconnected conversation between the two men, in particular the elderly war veteran who rambles incoherently causing the two working class women who follow them, to wonder whether they were "merely eccentric or genuinely mad" (Woolf 1985a, 87). Mansfield may have recalled either her original vision or Woolf's representation in "Kew Gardens" in writing "Miss Brill", in which oddness evokes the borderline state of life in death, linked to the burial of the fox fur in its cupboard each year. It is vividly imaged in the "odd, silent, nearly all old" people who come routinely to the Gardens "Sunday after Sunday", and her own confinement is imaged in their appearance "as though they'd just come from dark little rooms or even cupboards" (*CW*2, 332). Seated to listen to the band play they are part of the human spectacle, a still point amidst the bustle of the new Season, and families, children, courting couples, all with their outfits—such as the band conductor's new coat—and accessories on display. There are no flower beds to stoop over to catch the scent of in the Jardins Publiques as the letter recommends and "In the Botanical Gardens" illustrates; instead flowers are commodified for human use, but associated with poverty, betrayal and poison, not beauty. An old beggar who, like the elderly listeners and the fox fur, is confined to a single space "with his tray fixed to the railings" (*CW*2, 252) sells them in bunches. A "beautiful woman" drops a bunch of violets but when they are handed back to her she throws them away "as if they had been poisoned" (*CW*2, 252), evoking Mansfield's symbolism of violets as images of betrayal in love in another early sketch "In a Café" (1907), or in "Psychology" (1920), where a "dead bunch" (*CW*2 198) is a sign of devotion on the part of the narrator's female companion.

Mansfield's aim to represent her story as both narrative and dramatic performance, capturing character through rhythm, tone and sound effect, inspired one of her rare comments about her artistic practice. She wrote to her brother-in-law, Richard Murry:

I chose not only the length of every sentence, but even the sound of every sentence—I chose the rise and fall of every paragraph to fit her—and to fit her on that day at that very moment. After Id written it I read it aloud—numbers of times—just as one would *play over* a musical composition trying to get it nearer and nearer to the expression of Miss Brill—until it fitted her. (*Letters* 4, 165; January 17 1921; reprinted in *CW*2, emphasis in original)

This recalls her recommendation that the story about the gardens at Garsington should be "musically speaking, a conversation *set to flowers*" (*Letters* 1, 325); for the "musical composition" of "Miss Brill" consists of overheard conversations and sights, which when linked to music evoke a subjectivity comprising reflection, vision and fantasy. These techniques of characterisation contribute to the story's representation of the life force as waxing and waning, and Miss Brill's performance as a puppeteer in taking the fox fur out and putting it back into its box. But in the story's ending, she does not know how to close down: the ambiguity of "she thought she heard something crying" (*CW*2, 254) suggests uncertainty now about who she is.

Through implying her heroine's shock at the insults, "that stupid old thing" with a "silly old mug", wearing a fox fur that looked "exactly like a fried whiting", Mansfield develops satire into a darker vision. In the deflation of Miss Brill's jaunty self-image, and exposure of her afternoon's enjoyment as partly delusional, her story contrasts most radically with "Kew Gardens". Woolf's story concludes with an inclusive, harmonious vision of the gardens expanding into a contrasting panorama of the city, animated by mechanisation, one that has been widely praised by reviewers including Mansfield herself.[5] Her *Athenaeum* review comments of Woolf's final paragraph that

---

5   Harold Child in the *Times Literary Supplement* review of May 1919, writes of the "full expression [of its voices] and unity in a 'common life'" (Majumdar and McLaurin 1997, 66–67), and John Oakland acclaims its "harmonious, organic optimism", and the "universality of voices in the final paragraph" (1987, 264; both cited by Staveley, 2004, 44–45).

"suddenly with a gesture she shows us the flower bed growing, expanding in the heat and light, filling whole world" (Hanson 1987, 54). Here, as Kaplan points out, she discovers Woolf's "epiphanic moment" (1991, 151), so that readers experience both Woolf's epiphany and Mansfield's simultaneously. The dazzling vision that occurs in a privileged moment through an intense communion with nature appears in several Mansfield stories in which the garden is a locus of revelation: for example, the aloe in "Prelude", the pear-tree in "Bliss", the flowers in "Taking the Veil". The moment of reversal in "Miss Brill", the non-revelation and shock of humiliation leading to a fracturing of selfhood, make it a study in dissonance in relation to Mansfield's other garden stories as well as to "Kew Gardens".

*****

Both "Kew Gardens" and "Miss Brill" reinterpret the romance plot of conventional fiction in terms of courtship, sexuality and propriety in a public space in ways that emphasise the writers' different ideas of feminism due to their education, class and upbringing. As Kaplan and Hanson point out, Mansfield's bisexuality in her early years gave her the view that gender was more a construction than a biological given, allowing her to develop a stronger feminism than Woolf and a sharper critique of heterosexual relations (Hanson 1987, 19; Kaplan 1991, 12). The satire on her ageing spinster with her dreams of love and courtship conveys a jaded view of romance that might reflect her own problems with Murry then. Heterosexual relations are either fraught or unfulfilled in "Miss Brill", as the discarded bunch of violets symbolises, undermining her curiosity about romance and its values. The rejection by the "gentleman in grey" of the soliciting "ermine toque" she witnesses as if on the edge of her seat. The young couple who denounce her she romanticises as the "hero and heroine [...] just arrived from his father's yacht". But in fact, the young man is frustrated by sexual urges, and their unwittingly cruel remarks about Miss Brill are a distraction from their furtive exchange: "'No, not here,' said the girl. 'Not yet'" (*CW*2, 335).

Mansfield's lovers and their brash, destructive comments are in pointed contrast to Woolf's young couple in "Kew Gardens" who speak in "toneless and monotonous voices" (88), and whose actions reflect a more optimistic view of courtship, sexual desire and matrimony. The justification for their visit to the gardens, which is also an act of courtship, is expressed elliptically, because the young woman is unable to broach or put into words the question of her personal worth when reckoned in terms of sexual desire. Her challenge to the man's costing of their visit (and hence of her worth): "'Isn't it worth sixpence??'" (the entry price to the gardens on Fridays), and his query, "'What do you mean by 'it'?", yield a non-committal "'O anything—I mean—you know what I mean'" (Woolf 1985a, 88). This inconclusive exchange culminates in a gesture that, according to Alice Staveley "codes the sexual implication of courtship" (2004, 50). The couple come together by pressing

> the end of the parasol deep down into the soft earth. The action and the fact that his hand rested on the top of hers expressed their feeling in a strange way, as though those short insignificant words also expressed something (Woolf 1985a, 88).

Woolf transforms the parasol as prop into a sign of togetherness, so giving credibility to semi-articulated feelings and desires that otherwise could only be realised in marriage. It becomes a symbol of trust, a protection against potential disruption of their relationship through misunderstanding. By contrast to Mansfield's juxtaposition of sexual desire with verbal impropriety and the collapse of Miss Brill's romantic illusions, Woolf probes relationships and endorses normative gender identifications: the concern of the young woman, Trissie, about his intentions, the man's sense of possession signified by the coins he fingers in his pocket to pay for the tea, and the masculine power implied in his gesture of removing the parasol and then heading towards the tea rooms.

In what might be considered coded intertextual allusions in two stories, Mansfield seems to intervene in and rewrite Woolf's narrative of heterosexual love in "Kew Gardens". The Kew Gardens encounter between Vera and her lover recalled in "A Dill Pickle" can be further connected to Woolf's brief narrative through her figure of Trissie, who wishes to explore, "forgetting her tea", and "remembering orchids and cranes, among wild flowers, a Chinese pagoda, and a crimson-crested bird"; but she is overtaken, because "he bore her on" (Woolf 1985a, 89). Mansfield's protagonist reflects on her failed romance and the day in Kew Gardens when she and her lover drank tea in the same Chinese pagoda (*CW2*, 99) mentioned in Woolf's story. Mansfield may be indirectly challenging the traditional male assertiveness of Trissie's lover implied in the phrase "he bore her on", for her protagonist is recalled in a way that matches the ambiguous impression he conveys to Vera as she sits across from him in the restaurant some years later: instead of sweeping her away as Woolf's hero does, he "behaved like a maniac" (*CW2*, 99) in trying to beat off the wasps.

A later story, "The Escape" (1920), can also be read in relation to "Kew Gardens" as a possibly deliberate reversal of Woolf's image of the parasol to signify the sexuality of courtship. Mansfield introduces this prop, transformed into a narrative device that is also a figure of the woman's vulnerability—similar to the fox fur in "Miss Brill". The pampered, self-obsessed heroine is overwrought because she believes her husband has deliberately caused them to miss their train. Her vengeful fury mounts as they set out in a carriage to catch another train and his suggestion that she raise her parasol as a protection against the swirling dust, drives her to further heights of dramatic self-pity. When her parasol falls out of the carriage onto the road, she feels this too is due to his malevolence against her, and hysterically declares its sentimental value: it belonged to her mother. "'The parasol that I prize more than—more than ...'" (*CW2*, 220). The image of the airborne parasol can be contrasted to the parasol that "earths" Woolf's lovers and imparts a deeper meaning to their "short insignificant words". An artificial prop that provides the illusion of self-autonomy, it has been read as a protective shell between the woman and others (Hanson 1985, 79–80), a vehicle for her anger as well as a thematic pointer, and as a narrative ploy (New 1999, 163–64). In "The Escape"'s portrait of a collapse in marital relations, the woman's heightened crisis over losing her parasol closes down any chance of reasonable or civil communication between the couple, by contrast to Woolf's implication that the parasol might compensate for the limits of words in a nonverbal union suggestive of marriage. In these intertextual allusions Mansfield seems to be sending a contradictory message to Woolf's assertion about the viability of heterosexual relations in "Kew Gardens".

****

The differences in representational mode between Mansfield's writing, which Woolf acclaimed for its "transparent quality" and for being "—all clear as glass—refined spiritual" (1989, 127–28, 13 Feb. 1921) and Woolf's more, interrogative, reflective style, also relates to the different philosophical and artistic views they held of the self/other relationship. "Miss Brill" foregrounds character by representation through voice, speech and rhythm, using ventriloquism of the fox fur to present plural versions of voice corresponding to Miss Brill's private and public notions of selfhood. This story, one of her most affective, illustrates how Mansfield plays on the boundaries between human and non-human in delineating reciprocal relations. In other stories, however, the individual is shown as rooted in the natural world through connections to flowers, birds, animals, insects in relationships of heightened transitivity: for example, Laura's nascent burgeoning sexuality in "The Garden Party" where she sees the canna lilies as "almost frighteningly alive on bright crimson stems [...] she felt they were in her fingers, on her lips, growing in her breast" (*CW2*, 404). The perception of heightened transference between subject and object underpins the guiding aesthetic principle of her literary modernism, namely that art and life are inseparable. It also informs her ideas about the artist's impersonality as she says on several occasions: "The artist must give himself so utterly to life that no self qua personal self remains"; and "when I am writing of another—I want to lose myself in the soul of the other, that I am not" (*Letters* 4, 180–81).

Woolf also represents transitions between the human and non-human: not only is the snail humanised in "Kew Gardens", but the perceiving and recording narrative eye uses the cinematic techniques of dissolve and condensation to dissolve the two into each other. Such human immersion and participation in the natural world is registered through the perspective of the individual who is subordinated to life itself, which Woolf saw as a work of art, rather than through Mansfield's self/other fusion due to the artist's necessary dedication to life. In contrast to Mansfield's Fauvist aesthetic of the bounding outline into which art makes "that divine *spring*" after it has passed through "the process of trying to *become* these things before recreating them" (*Letters* 1, 330; italics in original), Woolf represents difficulties in distinguishing the "real" from the unreal. In "Kew Gardens" the young man suffers a passing moment of unreality after uprooting the parasol, as the mist lifts from the tearooms: "it was real, all real [...] real to everyone except to him and to her" (Woolf 1985a, 88). As the ebb and flow of experience makes recognition of any definitive moment impossible, objects remain caught in the flux of time rather than acquiring a distinctive life force. The larger pattern eludes definition because of our participation in the flow, for "behind the cotton wool is hidden a pattern; that we [...] are connected with this; that the whole world is a work of art; that we are part of the work of art" (Woolf 1985b, 72).

For Woolf, there is uncertainty about the role of life and her question, "is life very solid, or very shifting? I am haunted by the two contradictions" (1977–84, 3, 218), informed her preferred idea of reality as combining "the solidity of granite and the evanescence of rainbow" (Whitworth 2000, 150), making objects appear both solidly anchored and near invisible as the prismatic raindrop in the midst of the luxuriant gardens at Kew illustrates. The distinctive moment that springs out like a shock or revelation is one of the defining features of the short story with its emphasis on slices of life, but Woolf's difficulty in defining or fixing such a moment suggests that the more leisurely pace of the novel, which can convey it as emerging from the flux of time, rather than the brevity of the short story which foregrounds and shapes it, was more suitable as her creative mode (Olsen 2009, 63). Mansfield who preferred "sharp lines" in a story, and wished that the outline not be blurred (*Letters* 3, 273), complained about this aspect of Woolf's aesthetics, imaging her stories as "flower heads in flat dishes" not "cut flowers" *(Letters* 4, 285).

*****

Both Mansfield and Woolf introduced structural fragmentation, disunity and indeterminacy into the short story, while also achieving a more fluid expression of subjectivity as they rewrote literary conventions into a feminist modernism. "Kew Gardens" with its brilliant descriptions, impressionist technique, and lack of story line suggests the possibility rather than the realisation of action (Skrbic 2004, 19); it introduces comment on the war and rationing and it images urban mechanisation with an airplane overhead and omnibuses "turning their wheels and changing their gear" (Woolf 1985a, 89). Mansfield offers an art of revelation or showing that aims for immediacy of effect through a traditional format of the single episode and change in character implied by symbol. Yet, given what is known about "the motives and interactions" involved with the composition, transmission and reception of these texts (McKenzie 1985, 6–7; cited by Staveley 1997, 59), the vicissitudes of the friendship between Mansfield and Woolf, and the stylistic choices that Mansfield makes, it is possible to read "Miss Brill" in complementary juxtaposition to "Kew Gardens", a black to its white, a yin to its yang. Their endings stand out in stark contrast: "Kew Gardens" juxtaposes its pastoral opening scenes with a macrocosmic view of the city in the throes of modernization. "Miss Brill" demarcates a retreat from the public domain to the private world of the spinster's cupboard-like room, in shock at the betrayal of language and an uncaring society that undermines and even—it is implied—excludes her.

The stylistic innovativeness of "Kew Gardens", evident in the use of cinematographic techniques such as the close up, the time lapse shot and dissolve (Banks 2004, 22), suggests that Woolf and Mansfield were sharing a cinematic aesthetics in approaching narrative, one that Mansfield had used in her work since 1915 (Sandley 2011, 78). "Kew Gardens" is now appreciated as "arguably Woolf's most widely read short story" (Staveley 2004, 42). Its popularity, evident in publication by the Hogarth Press twice in 1919, and again in 1927, suggests that it advanced Woolf's name for avant garde writing in artistic, intellectual circles as she shaped the modernism that she would develop further in novels such as *Jacob's Room* (1922), *To the Lighthouse* (1927), *Orlando* (1928), and *The Waves* (1931). This reception, suggesting a fashion for storylessness, exploration of subjectivity and lack of authorial presence, no doubt informed Mansfield's decision not to have her plot-driven story "The Woman at the Store" republished in *Bliss and Other Stories* in 1921. Instead she recommended "When the Wind Blows" (1915), an atmospheric piece praised by Bertrand Russell, Virginia Woolf, Lytton Strachey and others *(Letters* 3, 273–74), perhaps because it was stylistically closer to the vivid impressionism and "poise" that she admired in "Kew Gardens".

Despite some agreement on style and aesthetics in their valuing of what was new, the writers never resolved their differences at the level of conception and execution. Woolf's comment, made in 1931, that Mansfield "can't put any thoughts, or feelings or subtleties of any kind into her characters" (1975–80, 3, 59) suggests an indifference to, or unawareness of the radicalness of her experimentation in voice, image and symbol in the short story genre, while Mansfield's criticism of Woolf's stories, that "one can't scrap 'form' like that. [...] I suspect novelty as novelty" (*Letters* 4, 285), suggests she could not see how far into new directions Woolf's experimentation in the novel would take her. Her early death that left her with a much smaller legacy than Woolf prevented any such development in her own work or in her appreciation of Woolf's endeavours. Woolf looked upon Mansfield as a rival, saying "I was jealous of her writing, the only writing I have been jealous of" (Woolf 1977–84, 2, 227). Yet she also recognised that Mansfield's views on writing complemented her own, that she was not always in direct competition with her, and she praised her gift as "that direct flick at the thing seen" (1977–84, 4, 315). The loss of a competitor who was in some ways a kindred spirit, led to feelings of loneliness after Mansfield's death and to being haunted by her in dreams (1975–80, 4, 366). As she confessed to her diary: "But though I can do this better than she could where's she who could do what I can't?" (1977–84, 2, 226).

Bibliography

Alpers, Antony. 1980. *The Life of Katherine Mansfield*. London: Jonathan Cape.

Ascari, Maurizio. 2010. "Katherine Mansfield and the Gardens of the Soul." *Katherine Mansfield Studies* 2: 39–55.

Banks, Joanne Trautmann. 2004. "Through a Glass, Longingly." In *Trespassing Boundaries: Virginia Woolf's Short Fiction*, edited by Kathryn N. Benzel and Ruth Hoberman, 17–24. London: Palgrave Macmillan.

Benzel, Kathryn N and Ruth Hoberman. 2004. "Introduction." In *Trespassing Boundaries: Virginia Woolf's Short Fiction*, edited by Kathryn N. Benzel and Ruth Hoberman, 1–14. London: Palgrave Macmillan.

———. eds. 2004. *Trespassing Boundaries: Virginia Woolf's Short Fiction*. London: Palgrave Macmillan.

Dick, Susan. 2004. "Foreword." In *Trespassing Boundaries: Virginia Woolf's Short Fiction*, edited by Kathryn N. Benzel and Ruth Hoberman, xv–xx. London: Palgrave Macmillan.

Hanson, Clare. 1985. *Short Stories and Short Fictions, 1880–1980*. London: Macmillan.

———. ed. 1987. *The Critical Writings of Katherine Mansfield*. London: Macmillan.

———. 2011. "Katherine Mansfield's Uncanniness." In *Celebrating Katherine Mansfield: A Centenary Volume of Essays*, edited by Gerri Kimber and Janet Wilson, 115–30. London: Palgrave Macmillan.

Kaplan, Sydney Janet. 1991. *Katherine Mansfield and the Origins of Modernist Fiction*. Ithaca, NY and London: Cornell University Press.

McKenzie, D.F. 1985. *Bibliography and the Sociology of Texts*. London: The British Library.

McLaughlin, Ann L. 1978. "The Same Job: The Shared Writing Aims of Katherine Mansfield and Virginia Woolf." *Modern Fiction Studies* 24 (3): 369–82.

---. 1983. "An Uneasy Sisterhood: Virginia Woolf and Katherine Mansfield." In *Virginia Woolf: A Feminist Slant*, edited by Jane Marcus, 152–61. London and Lincoln, NE: University of Nebraska Press.

Majumdar, Robin and Allen McLaurin, eds. 1997. *Virginia Woolf: The Critical Heritage*. London and New York, Garland.

New, W.H. 1999. *Reading Mansfield: Metaphors of Form*. Montreal and Kingston: McGill-Queens University Press.

Oakland, John. 1987. "Virginia Woolf's 'Kew Gardens'." *English Studies: A Journal of English Language and Literature* 68: 264–73.

Roe, Sue. 2000. "The Impact of Post-Impressionism." In *The Cambridge Companion to Virginia Woolf*, edited by Sue Roe and Susan Sellers, 164–90. Cambridge; Cambridge University Press.

Sandley, Sarah. 2011. "Leaping into the Eyes: Mansfield as a Cinematic Writer." In *Celebrating Katherine Mansfield: A Centenary Volume of Essays*, edited by Gerri Kimber and Janet Wilson, 72–83. London: Palgrave, 2011.

Skrbic, Nena. 2004. *Wild Outbursts of Freedom. Reading Virginia Woolf's Short Fiction*. Westport, CT and London: Praeger.

Smith, Angela. 1999. *Katherine Mansfield and Virginia Woolf: A Public of Two*. Oxford: Clarendon Press.

---. 2000. *Katherine Mansfield: A Literary Life*. London: Palgrave.

Staveley, Alice. 1997. "'Kew Will Do': Cultivating Fictions of Kew Gardens." In *Virginia Woolf and the Arts: Selected Papers from the Sixth Annual Conference of Virginia Woolf*, edited by Diane F. Gillespie and Leslie K. Hankin, 57–65. New York: Pace University Press.

---. 2004. "Conversations at Kew: Reading Woolf's Feminist Narratology." In *Trespassing Boundaries: Virginia Woolf's Short Fiction*, edited by Kathryn N. Benzel and Ruth Hoberman, 39–62. London: Palgrave Macmillan.

Tomalin, Claire. [1987] 1988. *Katherine Mansfield: A Secret Life*. London: Penguin.

Whitworth, Michael. 2000. "Virginia Woolf and Modernism." In *The Cambridge Companion to Virginia Woolf*, edited by Sue Roe and Susan Sellers, 146–63. Cambridge: Cambridge University Press.

Woolf, Virginia. 1975–1980. *Letters of Virginia Woolf*, edited by Nigel Nicholson and Joanne Trautmann, 6 vols. London: Hogarth Press.

---. [1919] 1976. *Night and Day*. Harmondsworth: Penguin.

---. 1977–1984. *The Diary of Virginia Woolf*, edited by Anne Oliver Bell, assisted by Andrew McNeillie, 5 vols. London; Hogarth Press.

---. 1985a. "Kew Gardens." In *The Complete Shorter Fiction*, edited by Susan Dick, 84–89. London: The Hogarth Press.

---. 1985b. "A Sketch of the Past." In *Moments of Being: unpublished autobiographical writings*. 2nd ed., edited by Jeanne Schulkind, 61–160. London: Hogarth.

---. 1988. "Mr Bennett and Mrs Brown." In *The Collected Essays of Virginia Woolf*, 6 vols (1986-2011). Vol. 3. *1919–24*, edited by Andrew McNeillie, 384–89. London: Hogarth.

---. 1989. *Congenial Spirits: The Selected Letters of Virginia Woolf*, edited by Joannne Trautmann Banks. London: Hogarth.

Katherine Mansfield's American Legacy: The Case of Margery Latimer

Sydney Janet Kaplan

Part One

Katherine Mansfield's American legacy is a surprisingly under-explored topic in Mansfield studies. I had casually assumed that so much had been written about her influence on the American short story that nothing more needed to be examined. I was greatly mistaken. Although I had long believed that nearly every modernist short story writer in the United States had read Mansfield, I was surprised to discover that there is a virtual absence of critical studies documenting that influence. Recent work, such as *Katherine Mansfield and Literary Influence*, edited by Sarah Ailwood and Melinda Harvey (2015), contributes greatly to remedying the paucity of work on Mansfield's New Zealand and Australian legacy, and adds to an increasing body of studies of Mansfield and her British contemporaries, but it does not address Mansfield's influence on any American writers. My cursory search through the list of hundreds of books and articles related to Mansfield in the MLA Bibliography uncovered only *two* articles specifically linking her to American writers of fiction. The most recent is Emily Ridge's (2015) fine essay on Mansfield and Edith Wharton in *Katherine Mansfield and the Postcolonial*. The second one turned up only when I nearly came to the end of the MLA list, where I discovered an essay linking Mansfield's stories and those of Jean Toomer, the African-American author of *Cane*, whom I will discuss later (see Rankin 1976). It is true that important 20th-century American short-story writers, such as Willa Cather, Dorothy Parker, Katherine Anne Porter, and Conrad Aiken wrote appreciative reviews and essays about Mansfield. Eudora Welty discussed her enthusiastically during an interview; and Ernest Hemingway (1964) did so slightingly in *A Moveable Feast* (133).

Yet, Influence is itself an amorphous concept. It is important to remember that Mansfield's legacy was double-sided: her revolution of the short story genre *and* her life story. That combination is particularly apparent in the reactions to Mansfield amongst the American writers of fiction in the decade immediately following her death. Of her generation of British modernists, she was the first to become an iconic figure: sadly, because her death preceded that of the others. (Of course Lawrence too achieved celebrity, but much of that was while he was still alive—and notorious. Virginia Woolf only became iconic during the latter part of the 20th century, through a combination of second wave feminism and academic revisionism.)[1] In contrast, Mansfield's image was constructed and quickly recirculated by her husband, John Middleton Murry in *The Adelphi*, and then by the publication of his version of her journal. Mansfield's American legacy was later further enhanced by Murry's lecture tours in the United States during 1935 and 1936, where he spoke about her to enthusiastic audiences.[2] Such marketing of Mansfield—which coincided with the rise of celebrity worship during the 1920s—intersected with the development of American modernist fiction. Mansfield's importance in relation to that development is a project I am presently undertaking, but it is too large to fully explore here. Instead, this chapter focuses on one particular—if unusual—case of influence and intertextuality in life and fiction, that of the American modernist, Margery Latimer (1899–1932).

Latimer's short stories appeared in many avant-garde magazines, such as *transition*, in which her story, "Grotesque", is in the same

---

[1] Mansfield also became an iconic figure in France after her death. See Gerri Kimber (2008) and Christiane Mortelier (1970) for discussions of Mansfield's reception in France.
[2] See F.A. Lea (1960) on Murry's trips to the United States in 1935 (219–20, 225–29). Lea quotes one of Murry's remarks about Chicago: "full of nice people, but then I suppose so is Hell" (219).

issue as Gertrude Stein's "As a Wife Has a Cow", and sections from James Joyce's *Finnegans Wake*. She published two books of short fiction: *Nelly Bloom and Other Stories* (1929) and *Guardian Angel and Other Stories* (1932); also two novels: *We Are Incredible* (1928) and *This Is My Body* (1930), all to critical acclaim. The modernist poet and critic, Horace Gregory (1971), remarks in his memoir how "New York critics and editors at cocktail parties began to speak of her as a Midwestern Katherine Mansfield" (119).

More recently, Joy Castro (herself a prominent writer of fiction and memoir), whose 1997 dissertation on Latimer still remains the most comprehensive study of her life and work, precisely describes in words that could easily be transferred to Mansfield, Latimer's "sensuous lyricism", "clever biting satire", and "striking metaphors":

> Modernist to the core, Latimer was brilliant, innovative, passionate, revolutionary, and self-conscious in the best sense of the word. Her genius is for transmitting a certain immediacy of experience—transcendent moments, small epiphanies—by means of the carefully rendered physical detail. (1997, 15)

Yet, can we really determine the exact nature of a connection between two writers who never met, who lived on different continents, were of different nationalities? Nonetheless, once we accept our intuitions about connection, see the possibilities of expansion from seemingly irrelevant details, something happens, perhaps similar to what happened to me when I first read the following description of Latimer's death by one of her closest friends, the noted feminist writer, Meridel LeSuer (1984): "at thirty-three years, dead of hemorrhaging in childbirth, on Division Street, at the center of the Gurdjieff group under Jean Toomer, in Chicago" (230). Struck by the coincidences of Latimer dying almost at the same age as Mansfield, of bleeding to death in a place associated with Gurdjieff, my curiosity was ignited. Furthermore, LeSuer boldly stated Latimer's significance for future generations of women, emphasizing her courage in telling the truth of women's experiences, in exposing the secrets that had been impermissible in fiction, such as her depiction of a horrifying abortion in *This Is My Body*:

> Margery's stories, seized from women's prisons of the past, like messages left on a wilderness trail, warn us, guide us, and certainly give us a sharing in the pain of women between the centuries of struggle. The great span of years between 1880 and 1930 are anguished, mute years of women's struggle out of the torturous cocoon of dead structures. They went far to the edge of their blind exploitation and died there on the rim, leaving strange messages for us to decipher. (231)

When I read LeSuer's words, more than 30 years ago, I was immersed in writing *Katherine Mansfield and the Origins of Modernist Fiction*. I then began reading Latimer's *Guardian Angel and Other Stories* and was immediately intrigued by them, but did not have the time to further develop my intuition about her connections with Mansfield. That intuition was further enhanced by reading Horace Gregory's blurb on the back cover of the 1984 Feminist Press reprinting of the book:

> Margery Latimer belongs to the tradition [...] of Katherine Mansfield and D.H. Lawrence. The genius in all three cases is unmistakable—but is intensely personalized, and in her case, as well as in Katherine Mansfield's, cut short by death. Less exquisite, less frail, less delicately formed than Katherine Mansfield's prose is hers, but the emotion behind the words cuts deeper.[3]

---

[3] Gregory's remarks were taken from a review he published in the *New York Herald Tribune Books* on November 6, 1932 (2) following Latimer's death.

Note that Gregory's definition of a "tradition" linking Mansfield and Lawrence suggests that she was already canonized in the United States less than a decade after her death. I wondered then about how much of Mansfield's writing Latimer had read.

Although Latimer's letters do not mention any specific stories, her familiarity with Mansfield is clearly apparent in the following remark about her reaction to reading Mansfield's letters (which were published in the United States in 1929): "Not nearly as good as the journal though. Mr Husband must have left a lot out" (quoted in Castro 1997, 160). Murry had written in his "Introductory Note" to *The Letters of Katherine Mansfield* that some of them, "notably in the three weeks [...] during which she was detained, seriously ill, in Paris during the bombardment, and again while she was isolated in Ospedaletti in January 1920, are too painful for publication" (Murry 1929, viii). He also suggested that he had intended to make the letters, "taken together with her Journal [...] an intimate and complete autobiography for the last ten years of her life" (vii). These would have had to serve as such for Latimer, who died a year before the publication of Ruth Mantz's biography of Mansfield.[4] Murry's introduction to his highly edited version of her notebooks, *Journal of Katherine Mansfield* (which had been published in the United States in 1927), constructed a portrait of Mansfield that should have resonated with Margery Latimer, who would have identified with his descriptions of Mansfield's youthful revolt against provincialism, her desire to escape to London, and the interconnection between her passionate devotion to the art of writing and her personal suffering.

Murry's emphasis upon Mansfield's "fairly constant rebellion against what she then considered the narrowness and provincialism of a remote colonial city" (1927, viii), could easily be applied to Margery Latimer, who grew up in the small Midwestern town of Portage,

---

4   Gerri Kimber's comprehensive biography (2016) of Mansfield's youth contains numerous facts about her family background, childhood, and adolescence, which, had they been available to Latimer, would have further bolstered her intuitive sense of likeness.

Wisconsin, and who also strained against her home town's conventionality and closed-mindedness. If Mansfield had envisioned London "as the living centre of all artistic and intellectual life" (Murry 1927, viii), Latimer in turn, yearned towards New York for similar reasons. Mansfield's preliminary exposure to the cultural richness of London during her stay at Queen's College ignited her restless imagination and fuelled her desire to return. Latimer's first forays away from Portage, however, were much closer to home: a small college and then to the University of Wisconsin, where she would sophisticate a talent for writing already apparent in adolescence. She had a brief tentative first exposure to New York during a break in her college years, when she took a summer writing course at Columbia University and then worked briefly for the magazine, the *Woman's Home Companion* (see Loughridge 1984; Castro 1997).

She returned to the university during the autumn of 1922—that banner year for modernist literature when *The Waste Land*, *Ulysses*, *Jacob's Room,* and *The Garden Party* were all published. Exactly at the same time that Katherine Mansfield was spending the last weeks of her life in Fontainebleau, Marjorie Latimer was busily engaged in the production of the university's literary magazine, contributing essays and reviews to it, all the while working on a novel. She was blossoming as a writer and discovering people who shared her passion for the art. She had become part of a cohort of budding modernists at the university, some of whom were already publishing in notable avant-garde literary journals, such as *Poetry* (which had been founded in Chicago by Harriet Monroe in 1912). Most of those new friends would go on to make significant contributions to American literary modernism. Included among them were Horace Gregory; Marya Zaturenska, who later married Gregory and would go on to win the Pulitzer Prize in poetry in 1938; Carl Rakosi, one of the original group of Objectivist poets influenced by Ezra Pound and William Carlos Williams; and Kenneth Fearing, later called "the chief poet of the American Depression", who became Latimer's on-and-off-again lover for the next five years.

By the end of the academic year, Latimer decided to leave the university and return home to Portage to complete her novel. Like Mansfield during the period of her return from Queen's College to the Beauchamp home in Wellington, Latimer strained at the constrictions of family and societal conventions. She too would need to escape to the metropolis in order to pursue her career as a writer and to reclaim the personal independence she had experienced during her first foray to New York. This second foray to New York in 1923, would not be financially supported by her parents (unlike Mansfield, who was given an allowance of £100 a year), and Latimer needed to work at clerical jobs and write book reviews for New York newspapers to earn her living. Her room at the Old Chelsea on West 16th Street quickly became a gathering place for both her visiting friends from the university and a new set of avant-garde writers and artists (including Georgia O'Keeffe, Alfred Stieglitz, Walter Kuhn, Anita Loos, and Carl Van Vechten). Horace Gregory honoured the times he spent there by entitling his first book of poetry *Chelsea Rooming House* (1930).

Part Two

Janet Wilson (2011) has argued that Mansfield's "colonial modernism entailed a reconfiguring of the dialectic of home and away, due to an oscillation between belonging and yet not belonging" (176), and that her "adolescent wish to distance herself from family and nation, then her later urge to recover belonging, are paradigmatic of subjects from the white settler colonies of New Zealand, Australia, South Africa and Canada" (178). But Latimer's experiences do not completely conform to this pattern. In a sense, they are reversed. Rather than loneliness and alienation in the city, Latimer's travels would have a different trajectory. They brought her to new kinds of "belonging"; she found herself in communities: first of college rebels, then artist colonies, bohemian enclaves, Gurdjieffian communes. "Home" had been the place of loneliness and alienation. Not the city. She would never approach her memories of small town life in Wisconsin with the underpinning of nostalgia that marks such stories as "Prelude" and "At the Bay", so well expressed in Mansfield's letter to Dorothy Brett, on October 11, 1917:

> You know, if the truth were known I have a perfect passion for the island where I was born. [...] I tried to catch that moment—with something of its sparkle and its flavor. [...] I tried to lift that mist from my people and let them be seen and then to hide them again. (*Letters* 1, 331)

For Latimer, the division between province and city did not depend upon the kind of physical distance that Mansfield's exile entailed. Instead, there was a continual "oscillation" between the two. Portage, Wisconsin, was but a day's train ride from New York. Each trip home only reinforced her sense of alienation there. Moreover, Margery Latimer's experiences in New York also counter the mystique of the American expatriate, which is the focus of much critical work on Stein, Hemingway, Pound, and Eliot. Aspiring American writers and artists did not really have to go abroad to be at the heart of modernism. This was particularly true of those like Latimer and other women from families of modest means.[5] New York in the 1920s had become a major center of modernism, a truly cosmopolitan city that was a magnet for legions of artists, writers, and performers from around the globe.

Yet, as with Mansfield, much of Latimer's fiction continues to return to the provincial setting, but her depiction of it is more overtly ideological. As Joy Castro notes, she "uses the experimental language and narrative structures of the avant-garde to render rural small town life in middle America. [...] She has been called a feminist Sherwood Anderson" (2001, 153). And Louis Kampf (1984) astutely remarks that Latimer's "stories reveal the sensibility of modernism rendering 'local color' into a theater of the absurd". He recognizes that "Latimer is not a local colorist trying to evoke the charm of small town America", but a writer who conveys "the sense that the sharply etched

---

[5] See Malcolm Cowley (1935) for a first-hand study of the American expatriates in the 1920s.

surfaces, the well ordered exteriors, are about to burst apart" (236–37). Latimer's imaginative return to the provincial world of her childhood contains a profound critique of how it was blighted by the internalization of the ideology of American exceptionalism. Its inhabitants are mired in disappointment over what they see as the loss of the American dream. This emphasis on disillusionment is in keeping with what Michael North (2006) has described as "a kind of crisis in the social and aesthetic influence of American modernisation", which is manifest in American modernist fiction of the 1920s, and "which seem to feature crisis and collapse and not the heady optimism of the European avant-garde" (51).

Clearly, a sense of "crisis and collapse" marks Latimer's 1929 story, "The Family", which can be read alongside Mansfield's "Prelude" and "At the Bay" as excursions into the consciousness of family members that reveal the selves that they keep hidden. She goes further than Mansfield, however, in linking a family's dysfunction to the extent by which it is dominated by a seemingly inescapable "political unconscious".[6] For example, here is Mr Beale, the head of the family, reacting to a dinner-table quarrel and then rushing outside into the garden:

> The wind raised up his hat and he reflected that the winds and storms of God could lay waste to the land and the fury of waters could wash everything away, all traces of homes and gardens and miserable lives. He felt as if he had been struck over the head with a mallet and as if the shock went down to his toes. Now a deep murmur of thankfulness went all through him and he heard himself thanking God for his child, his wife, for his home that he loved and the safety and warmth inside. He rushed in. "The fact of the matter is, with all our faults the United States is the greatest nation the world has ever seen. We stand above them all. We stand for

---

[6] For a comprehensive analysis of the psychological, cultural, and political history of this term, see Fredric Jameson (1981).

democracy, right thinking, for right living, decent living and we live for the next generation, that's our religion, that's our whole life, the next generation that is to make humanity better, leave it with higher ideals and hopes, a bigger conception of life than we have ever known." (Latimer 1984, 31–32).

He finishes his speech with the comment: "There's good in all religion. But the important thing is to live up to the constitution of the United States" (32). Yet it is only the housekeeper who pays attention to his oration. Mrs. Beale ignores it, and while he looks at her "face stiff and remote as if she were far away" he silently reflects how she

could have anything he had, he would save her in a fire or a wreck, he would always take care of her and he had already given his life to her, first to his mother and sisters and then to his wife, he had sacrificed himself from the time he could remember to a pack of ungrateful women who were always at his heels. He took the whetstone out and spit on it. Then he began sharpening his knife blade. (Latimer 1984, 32)

In contrast to Stanley Burnell in "Prelude", who happily "ran his eye along the edge of the carving knife", and "prided himself very much upon his carving, upon making a first-class job of it", Mr Beale takes up his knife in a state of impotent resignation. Stanley basks in the glow of being able to outshine women: "He hated seeing a woman carve; they were always too slow" (Mansfield *CW*2, 85). The argument that had preceded Mr. Beale's oration reveals how much he lacked this kind of self-satisfaction and confidence that radiates from Stanley Burnell. Instead, Latimer draws a portrait of a man who has been thwarted in his pursuit of worldly success. Although he devotes himself entirely to working to support his family, he believes that they do not appreciate his sacrifices for them:

Mr. Beale look straight ahead of him, as if his eyes were seeing something far, far off, as far away as the Baltic Sea or the Indian Ocean, and he held up his knife and fork dripping with gravy. "I try to make everyone happy," he said gruffly, "I try to do good to everyone. I try to think right and talk right and do right. Who ever does anything for me?"

"Please, you're dripping," said Mrs. Beale gently.

"I haven't got a friend anywhere." He couldn't help but remember his mother and the way she held him on her lap once after his brothers had chased him. (Latimer 1984, 23–24)

Latimer's decision not to give first names to either the husband or wife suggests that they are meant to stand for a generic married couple, both of them entrapped by their given roles. Mrs. Beale uses silence and avoidance techniques such as focusing on trivial household details to cover up her dissatisfaction with her marriage. She also reveals symptoms of hysteria, needing her husband to calm her down and put her to bed. Latimer makes it quite clear that Mrs. Beale's condition is the product of a clash between ideology (the socially constructed definition of a "good woman") and individuation (the realization of selfhood):

In all the dark houses all over the world, she thought, are people who once were happy, who knew a day that was above all days, and now they can't remember how they felt or what it meant or what it was for. I am Mrs. Beale, a wife and mother, respected by the doctor, the dentist, our butcher. [...] No one needs to know what I think or feel about anything. That is my own. I can nod, no matter what is said, whether I believe or not, and know in myself what I really believe and I don't care what anyone in the world believes just so I can have peace and quiet and no one drips on the clean cloth. (Latimer 1984, 37–38)

Her secret life, like that of Linda Burnell in "Prelude", is interior, and also like Linda's, deeply infused with imagery from the natural world. Her reveries, also like Linda's, fuse present and past in a struggle to maintain a sense of self-worth.

In the night Mrs. Beale got up and went to the open window. She leaned out and smelled the cool dark air, she felt as if she were wandering under the trees down there in the dark garden with face lifted and head empty, heart empty, all young and happy. Tears started to her eyes and she said to herself sternly, "I am not unhappy. I am a wife and mother. I am respected in town wherever I go."

But she saw the Mrs. Beale who had stood by the open window thinking of her baby that was not born yet, she saw that Mrs. Beale as clear as day. She had on a wrapper with pansies in it and her hair was in a bang just above her brows and done in a knot at the back. [. . .] She saw it all, the sun on everything, the dog licking her puppies all over, and she saw the warmth and understanding that had streamed out of her to the dog, the garden, as if it had been something tangible. She could see it streaming from her eyes, her arms, her whole body. It went into the small fruit trees just coming into bloom, it seemed to blaze down on the ground and fertilize it and make it thick and sharp with green sprouts, and it seemed to be making the blossoms on the trees open out. (Latimer 1984, 33–34)

The association here between the fertility of the natural world and a woman's epiphanic absorption into it resembles, but reverses, Linda Burnell's responses in "Prelude" and "At the Bay". Linda struggles to separate herself from the generative process; she bemoans her "three great lumps of children" (Mansfield *CW*2, 87), and enjoys identifying herself with the aloe that blooms only once in a hundred years (73). Instead, Mrs. Beale remembers her pregnancy as the pinnacle of her emotional life. Her conflict is not with an amorous husband whose sexual demands she fears, but with her own sense of guilt that she has married a man whom she does not desire, and that her youthful dreams of "the face and body of the ideal man who was to love her" were never realized. She helplessly regrets that she had once decided that "it would be better" to take "a man who was good and honest and had a fair business than to live wildly in the flesh" (Latimer 1984, 37).

In juxtaposing the interaction between Mr. and Mrs. Beale, Latimer uses their memories of animals to underscore the sources of their present disappointments. Mrs. Beale feels a connection between herself and the dog with her puppies, but Mr. Beale remembers how his father had once taken him to see a "sick bull. He could see the mud, the flies stuck in it and circling above, singing like hornets" (33). Her father's rant during dinner so affects the little girl, Dorrit,[7] that she stops eating, and that infuriates him:

> Now what are we going to do with you? You're a coward, you haven't got any digestion, and I don't know what's to become of you. [. . .] I suppose we'll have to let you grow up into an invalid [. . .] always hanging to your mother, weak livered and not worth anything at all to humanity. (24)

It is Dorrit who plays the "Kezia" role in Latimer's story. She represents the emerging artist who must break free both from the mind-sets of her parents and the constraints of social convention. By the end of the story, Dorrit's modernist paintings have been displayed at the Art Institute of Chicago and she has become an expatriate in Paris, estranged from her family. A visiting neighbor from home spies her in a Left Bank café, drunkenly laughing with her bohemian friends, and overhears her parodying her father, puffing out her cheeks and declaiming in a pompous voice:

> America is the greatest nation the world has ever seen. [. . .] Indeed America is teaching the world how to live, she is showing the dirty foreigners how to respect womanhood, how to make homes, how to live always for the glorious next generation and how to turn it into honest, God fearing men and women. (67)

---

[7] Like Mansfield, Latimer was enamoured with/of Charles Dickens.

Part Three

Margery Latimer's recognition of an emotional and aesthetic affinity with Katherine Mansfield is most fully revealed in the similarity of their spiritual quests. She would have appreciated Murry's insistence on the "peculiar quality" of Mansfield's writing "as a kind of *purity*" that "corresponds to a quality in her life" (1927, xi). His emphasis upon how she "accepted life completely, and she had the right to accept it, for she had endured in herself all the suffering which life can lavish upon a single soul" (xv–xvi), would have been words that catalyzed Latimer's devotion to Mansfield. Yet by the time she had read those words, she was already attempting to live her life through the philosophical framework propounded by Gurdjieff, whose teachings she had discovered in 1924, when she was living at the Old Chelsea in New York. Her involvement in his movement was—ironically—initiated by none other than A. R. Orage, the former editor of the *New Age*, who had set Mansfield off on her literary career and later was instrumental in her decision to move to the Institute for the Harmonious Development of Man in Fontainebleau. He had recently been appointed by Gurdjieff to head the New York branch of his Institute.

According to Nancy Loughridge (1984) in her short biographical essay for the 1984 publication of Latimer's *Guardian Angel and Other Stories*:

> No matter how hectic her schedule, Margery [. . .] tried not to miss A. R. Orage's Monday night lectures on the Gurdjieff philosophy. [. . .] Gurdjieff's movement had become famous (or infamous) in 1923 when writer Katherine Mansfield, a recent convert, had died at his Institute for the Harmonious Development of Man in Fontainebleau. [. . .] Margery [. . .] found Gurdjieff's teachings impenetrable but she was drawn to the charismatic Orage who soon became her friend and literary mentor.
>
> Margery needed all of Orage's support and encouragement (he predicted that she would one day surpass

Katherine Mansfield) as the new version of her novel had met with a cold reception. [...] Margery concluded that it wasn't publishable in any color and scrapped it. At the same time, she followed Kenneth's [Fearing] advice—or perhaps a nudge from Orage—and abandoned her highly romantic, almost inflated style [...] and employed sharp, minimal, effective prose for the short stories she was now writing. (220–21)

Thus it seems clear to me that Latimer's link to Mansfield was deeply indebted to Orage. How many conversations between them were about Mansfield? How I wish we could know! Latimer's own words in a 1925 letter do suggest the power of Orage's impact on her development as a writer, and they are strikingly similar to some of Mansfield's thinking expressed in her own letters and notebooks during her last days: Latimer wrote:

I discovered one thing from writing my book and it seems hideous—I had heard it said, I suppose, a million times but it never came to me really until we began to write. That we make our bondage with all our deliberate, unconscious nature, we seek our thralldom and they try to destroy it intellectually when all the time that is what we want, the suffering, the actual physical pain of it, everything. I believe Orage now when he told me that I was in love with my subconscious and would always woo it. It seems the most terrible bondage in the world. And yet isn't it nearly every one's? (Latimer, "Letters", University of Wisconsin)

Another letter, written the same year, describes Latimer's reaction to reading Orage's "Talks with Katherine Mansfield at Fontainebleau", which had appeared in *The Century Magazine* in November, 1924:

What has changed me? I went to the library one day and hunted and hunted for ages to find Orage's talk with Katherine Mansfield in the Century, published some time ago. I remembered reading it when it came out, and then having your note telling me not to miss it, and writing you that I didn't care much for it. That it was old stuff and not there.

I found it and as I read again I had that terrific thing that happened when I saw Avinoff's picture.[8] I trembled all over. I knew I was crying but it was so deep it was only partly conscious, I knew that something deeper was pushing, and crowding and trying to say in different words from any I knew—"You are asleep! You are ASLEEP! And the time is so short!" I went outside into a snow—conscious of what I was not and this tremendous pounding going on and on in and through me. Just the memory of it does such vital things to me. It was a different current, like nothing before,—how lifeless those words are for it. But the dullness, the bluntness of the mechanism when faced by such a flame, the thickness of the tongue, the weight of inarticulacy—a mountain, a world.

[. . .] I almost *know* what I want to be. That moment in the library! With Orage's article, the one with Avinoff's picture—they must come faster and faster and I must make them come. I think I am not quite the same now—am I? (Latimer, "Letters", University of Wisconsin)

The letter combines elements of Gurdjieff's method (self-awakening) and Mansfield's prescience about the shortness of life. The epiphanic intensity of Latimer's description resembles moments in some of Mansfield's stories, such as "Bliss" and "The Escape". Yet Latimer's self-awareness that she will need to "make them come" also

---

[8] Andrej Avinoff (1886–1949) was a Russian entomologist (famous for his collections of butterflies) and artist who fled during the Revolution and eventually settled in the United States, where he became the director of the Carnegie Museum of Natural History.

recalls Mansfield's parodic depiction of Raoul Duquette's exclamation of his "moment—the *geste*!" in "Je ne parle pas francais" (*CW*2, 114).

Latimer provoked scandal when she married Jean Toomer, the already famous author of *Cane* ([1923] 1975), an experimental novel (or prose-poem, as it has been called), about African American life in the South. Toomer had become a follower of Gurdjieff soon after the publication of *Cane*. Before he met Latimer, he had travelled several times to Fontainebleau to study directly under Gurdjieff. Latimer's relationship with Toomer was initiated through their joint involvement in trying to establish a Gurdjieffian center in the outskirts of Latimer's home town, Portage, Wisconsin. The irony of this vision of a mini-Institute situated in the same conventional, puritanical environment that Latimer dissected in her stories cannot be overstated. Loughridge mentions that to the townspeople, "The Portage Experiment", as it was called, "was widely misconstrued at the time (outsiders thought it a haven for Communism, free love and nudism)" (1984, 225). (Such terms would be eerily replicated when they were used again to attack the "Hippie" communes that arose during the 1960s.) After the news media circulated the gossip about the purported behaviour of the Portage participants, it then expanded its range to publicize the marriage between Latimer and Toomer, which took place on October 30, 1931. Loughridge explains how a Hearst reporter linked the commune and the marriage together

> to produce an outrageously malevolent story which made headlines from coast to coast. The Portage Experiment was portrayed as the first step, with Margery as the first recruit, of a sinister conspiracy to "mongrelize" the white race. *Time* magazine professed to be shocked that the Toomer's marriage was actually legal. Reporters and photographers besieged their house [...] the Toomer's [*sic*] mailbox was flooded with hate mail and threats. (1984, 227–28)[9]

---

9   The *Time* article, "Just Americans", appeared on March 28, 1932.

The failure of the Portage Experiment set off a search for a more receptive home for the Gurdjieffian center. Not surprisingly, their travels brought them to locations which had already developed the reputation of receptivity to non-conformity that they still hold today: Taos, New Mexico; the Big Sur in Northern California; and the Los Angeles area, including Pasadena and Hollywood. Latimer was especially eager to go to Taos, after they had received an invitation from Mable Dodge Luhan (D. H. Lawrence's great patron), who had become a devotee of Gurdjieff and had suggested that she might consider establishing a Gurdjieff center on her ranch. Loughridge comments that Latimer "had looked forward to meeting Frieda Lawrence and Dorothy Brett because of their connection to Katherine Mansfield" (1984, 226). (Such a meeting, however, did not take place, neither did the establishment of the center.) Throughout the nearly nine months of continual travelling, Margery Latimer was pregnant, and often ill. (Her physical and emotional struggles because of this constant moving are reminiscent of those of Mansfield in her sojourns in France.) Disappointed by their lack of success in attracting donors for the center—not surprising, since it was now the middle of the Great Depression—Latimer and Toomer returned to the mid-west, to Chicago. There Margery Latimer died, giving birth to a daughter whom Toomer named Margery, on August 16, 1932, less than a year after their wedding.

Bibliography

Ailwood, Sarah, and Melinda Harvey, eds. 2015. *Katherine Mansfield and Literary Influence*. Edinburgh: Edinburgh University Press.

Castro, Joy. 1997. "Splitting Open the World: Modernism, Feminism and the Work of Margery Latimer." Dissertation, Texas A & M University. Ann Arbor: UMI.

---. 2001. "Margery Latimer." *Review of Contemporary Fiction* 21 (3): 151-95.

Cowley, Malcolm. 1956. *Exile's Return: A Literary Odyssey of the 1920s*. New York: The Viking Press.

Gregory, Horace. 1930. *Chelsea Rooming House*. New York: Covici, Friede.

———. 1971. *The House on Jefferson Street: A Cycle of Memories*. New York: Holt, Rinehart and Winston.

Hemingway, Ernest. 1964. *A Moveable Feast*. New York: Charles Scribner's Sons.

Jameson, Fredric. 1981. *The Political Unconscious: Narrative as a Socially Symbolic Act*. Ithaca, NY: Cornell University Press.

Kampf, Louis. 1984. "Afterword: The Work." In *Guardian Angel and Other Stories* by Margery Latimer, 236–46. Old Westbury, NY: The Feminist Press.

Kimber, Gerri. 2008. *Katherine Mansfield: The View from France*. Bern: Peter Lang.

———. 2016. *Katherine Mansfield: The Early Years*. Edinburgh: Edinburgh University Press.

Latimer, Margery. 1928. *We Are Incredible*. New York: J. H. Sears.

———. 1929. *Nellie Bloom and Other Stories*. New York: J. H. Sears.

———. 1930. *This Is My Body*. New York: Jonathan Cape and Harrison Smith.

———. 1984. *Guardian Angel and Other Stories*. Old Westbury, NY: The Feminist Press.

———. "Letters to Blanche C. Matthias from Margery Latimer and Jean Toomer." University of Wisconsin Library, Department of Special Collections.

Lea, F.A. 1959. *The Life of John Middleton Murry*. New York: Oxford University Press.

Le Sueur, Meridel. 1984. "Afterword: A Memoir." In *Guardian Angel and Other Stories* by Margery Latimer, 230–35. Old Westbury, NY: The Feminist Press.

Loughridge, Nancy. 1984. "Afterword: The Life." In *Guardian Angel and Other Stories*, by Margery Latimer, 215–29. Old Westbury, NY: The Feminist Press.

Mortelier, Christiane. 1970. "The Genesis and Development of the Katherine Mansfield Legend in France." *Journal of the Australasian Universities Language and Literature Association* 34 (November): 252–63.

Murry, John Middleton, ed. 1927. *Journal of Katherine Mansfield*. New York: Alfred A. Knopf.

---. ed. 1929. *The Letters of Katherine Mansfield*. New York: Alfred A. Knopf.

North, Michael. 2006. "1922, Paris, New York, London: The Modernist as International Hero." In *The Edinburgh Companion to Twentieth-Century Literatures in English*, edited by Brian McHale and Randall Stevenson, 48–57. Edinburgh: Edinburgh University Press.

Orage, A.R. 1924. "Talks with Katherine Mansfield at Fontainebleau." *The Century Magazine* 109 (November 1924): 36–40.

Rankin, William. 1976. "Ineffability in the Fiction of Jean Toomer and Katherine Mansfield." In *Renaissance and Modern: Essays in Honor of Edwin M. Moseley*, edited by Murry J. Levith, 160–71. Saratoga Springs, NY: Skidmore College.

Ridge, Emily. 2015. "Workmanship and Wildness: Katherine Mansfield on Edith Wharton's *The Age of Innocence*." In *Katherine Mansfield and the (Post)colonial*, edited by Janet Wilson, Gerri Kimber, and Delia da Sousa Correa. Edinburgh: Edinburgh University Press.

Toomer, Jean. [1923] 1975. *Cane*. New York: Liveright.

Wilson, Janet. 2011. "'Where is Katherine?' Longing and (Un)belonging in the Works of Katherine Mansfield." In *Celebrating Katherine Mansfield*, edited by Gerri Kimber and Janet Wilson, 175–88. Basingstoke: Palgrave Macmillan.

Poetry, Suffering and the Self

On First Looking into Mansfield's Heine: Dislocative Lyric and the Sound of Music

Claire Davison

Katherine Mansfield's "Heine" is a burgundy-bound, 250-page volume of Heinrich Heine's *Buch der Lieder* [*Book of Songs*] that looks rather like a hymnbook, edited by German scholar Ernst Elster in the 1880s. It was a present from Thomas Trowell, inscribed: "To dear Kass, wishing you the most prosperous of New Years from Tom. Xmas. 1903".[1] It is now in the Mansfield archive of the Alexander Turnbull Library, where the accompanying leaflet ends with the following observations:

> It is evident, from the way she annotated it over a number of years, that this book was of particular importance to Mansfield. It is not surprising that these lyrics of romantic despair appealed to her, particularly at that period of her life and having been given to her by the young man who was the object of her first heterosexual romantic passion but who failed to reciprocate her feelings for him.

Although quite dated now, and intended for a broad readership, this conclusion inspires a certain critical reserve today. The book was clearly well-read, as hand-written markings attest; meanwhile Mansfield's various references to, and quotes from the volume at various points of her life suggest that it accompanied her on many subsequent travels, once the object of her unrequited passions had long since faded into a distant memory. But should the volume only be

---

[1] ATL–MSX-5218. I would like to thank the Alexander Turnbull Library for permission to consult and quote from the book and accompanying library notes, and research librarian Linda McGregor for her assistance. All quotes from the volume will henceforth be referenced KMH immediately after quotations.

indexed to pathos and intimate biography? Or to reassuringly heteronormative stirrings of desire? Was the young Kathleen Beauchamp reading Heine's "lyrics of romantic despair" merely as a convenient outlet for the outpourings of the soul, by proxy?

This chapter will be proposing a rather different take on Mansfield's volume of Heine. I shall be suggesting that it mattered less as a memento, or relic, of young love spurned, and more as an inspirational mode of translation and transposition. This will entail looking closely at a number of the poems marked up in the volume, and listening to Heine within his own subtly double-voiced lyricism, and against the established lyrical mode of the late 19th century. Setting key verses in parallel with some of Mansfield's early writings opens up new approaches to some of the compositional forms the apprentice writer was exploring, and points to modes of expression that she would make her own creative idiom. From this angle, some of her earliest encounters with foreign voices and dislocated literary heritages find their place in the evolution of the writer to come: Heine's "short forms" offer a formative stepping-stone towards the condensed flashes of emotion, tone and reversal that were soon to be the hallmark of the slightly longer format of the vignette and sketch that Mansfield explored, before expanding these into what is now the more familiar form of the short story.

First, it is essential to contextualise Heine's presence as reference or intertextual echo in Mansfield's development as a writer, and in terms of her own textual production. To date, critics charting her European literary heritage have paid less attention to German Romanticism than to French or even East European romantic influences—which is doubtless in part a reflection of the sad decline in German studies over the past few decades.[2] It can also be explained by the fact that, at least at the height of her career, Mansfield appears

---

[2] See Da Sousa Correa 2013 and 2015 for rare and highly illuminating studies of Mansfield's connections with German culture and German romantic music in particular.

better versed in French.³ This was arguably not the case during her school years, however; furthermore, a supposed lack of linguistic finesse is certainly no reason to preclude exciting transliterary and translinguistic encounters, especially in the nascent, formative years of a future modernist. As Woolf would insist in several essays from the 1910s and 1920s, not knowing languages, and thereby reading them outside their familiar orbit, can be the key to their radical strangeness, their contrapuntal resonances and unexpected rhythms—features that the "specialist" or native takes for granted: "Foreigners, to whom the tongue is strange, have us at a disadvantage" (Woolf 2010, 202).⁴

So when, and in what contexts, was Mansfield encountering Heine? Either the poet himself or allusions to his verses occur most in three distinct periods: 1903–04, 1908–09 and 1917.⁵ Even from a purely biographical perspective, these time spans are revealing. They are her years of intense traveling, prompting imaginative investment in new worlds, and a recurrent sense of "unbelonging"—the immense voyages from New Zealand to London and back (1903–04), travels from Britain to continental Europe (1908–09), and dreams of warm solace on the French Riviera that turned into intense solitude, crippling ill health, arduous train journeys and precarious refuge in wartime Paris (1917). The two later periods are indeed crux years in terms of

---

3   Her attachment to the language and culture of Germany was lifelong, however. Even in 1921, Mansfield was revelling in a rare opportunity to speak German again (*CW*4, 363). See also Davison and Spooner (2016, 18–21).
4   See in particular Woolf's essays "On Not Knowing Greek", "The Russian Point of View" and "On Not Knowing French" (Woolf 1994, 38–52, 181–89; and Woolf 2010, 3–9). For further explorations of the political and ethical repercussions of Woolf's transpositional approach to foreign languages read "unknowingly", see Davison 2016.
5   For reasons of length and also thematic unity, this chapter only focuses on Mansfield's reception of Heine in her formative years, pre-1910. Her 1917 return to Heine was part of a collaborative translation and reading venture undertaken with Murry, in very different conditions. See *CP*, 120 and 180, plus references throughout the volume to Mansfield's Heine resonances.

alienation, and the experience of a body taken up by, and betrayed by, medical science. Even if Mansfield was not conversant with Heine's biography, his poems vividly conjure up a poetic persona's experience of vast wanderings, sea travels, loneliness, and debilitating physical decline, and it is indeed likely that these high romantic themes and first-person testimonies would have struck a chord. For these reasons, the first section of the *Buch der Lieder*, entitled "The Sorrows of Youth", along with many poem titles or first lines, might seem to bear out the emotional identification signalled by the Turnbull library leaflet. However, a quick read through Heine's poems themselves tells a different story: an initial expression of grief for lost love is rarely the sign of a sentimental love poem to come, as two short verses (pencil-marked, like all those mentioned here, by Mansfield) illustrate:[6]

> Du liebst mich nicht, du liebst mich nicht,
> Das kümmert mich gar wenig;
> Schau' ich dir nur ins Angesicht,
> So bin ich froh wie'n König.
>
> Du hassest, hassest mich sogar,
> So spricht dein rotes Mündchen;
> Reich mir es nur zum Küssen dar,
> So tröst' ich mich, mein Kindchen (KMH, 78).
>
> You love me not, you love me not,
> That irks me not a tittle;
> To look on you such joy has bought
> I envy kings but little.
>
> You hate me—hate me, well I wis,
> Your rosy lips declare it;
> Give me those charming lips to kiss,
> For comfort I can bear it (Heine 1907, 89).

---

[6] Published translations of Heine's verse into English used here all date from the 1880s to the 1910s.

Overall, the annotated poems prove not to be the more markedly sentimental verses (the sections entitled "Dream Pictures" and "Sonnets"). Mansfield's pencil-marked preferences are concentrated in the major poetry cycles: "Lyrical Intermezzo", "The Homecoming", "The North Sea" and "The Harz Journey", where the dominant mode is dialogic and enchanting rather than sorrowful and self-focused, and where the key themes are enchantment, reversal or wayfaring.

A non-exhaustive list of the poems in the *Buch der Lieder* that she highlights proves eloquent—"Der arme Peter", for example, is marked "One of my favourites" (KMH 38), and reads like a succinct folk tale in verse form, telling of a waif-like, poverty-stricken child watching a happier couple live out their cosy, romantic idyll. Resonances of Mansfield's "Thoughtful Child", "Shadow Children" and even little Else in "The Doll's House", as well as various fairy-tale figures she favoured in early poetry and prose,[7] lend weight to the idea that many of Heine's characteristic themes would also become Mansfield's—as becomes apparent to any reader who opens Heine's *Buch der Lieder* alongside Mansfield's *Collected Poems*:

> (Poems listed in ink by Mansfield on the inside cover of the volume, also pencil-marked on the individual pages)
> Der Hirtenknabe [The Herd-boy]
> Die Heimkehr [The Homecoming]
> Nachts in der Kajüte [Night in the Cabin]
> Frieden [Peace]
> Wahrhaftig [In Truth]
> An Eine Sängerin [To A Singer, As she sang an old romance]
>
> (Examples of poems pencil-marked next to the first line)
> Die Fensterschau [A Glance from the Window]
> Die Heimführung [The Homeward Way]
> Der Herbstwind rüttelt die Baume [The Wind in the Trees]

---

7   Mansfield's vivid interest in the Germanic and High Romantic fairy-tale tradition also extends to Goethe and Andersen. See in particular Gerri Kimber's essay in this volume.

Ein Fichtembaum staht einsam [A Pinetree Stood Alone]
Die alten, bösen Lieder [Those Bitter, Bad Dreams]
Die Nacht am Strande [The Night on the Shore]
Mein Kind, wir waren Kinder [My Child, We Were Children]

Another interesting formal characteristic in *Buch der Lieder* and all Heine's other poetry collections is his careful organisation of apparently stand-alone poems into sequences or cycles linked by an overriding sense of quest, or the phases of love, or revisited memory and desire. This keen attention to how the formal arrangement of poems can contribute to a sketchy but linear narrative framework provides an interesting way to approach Mansfield's own experiments with poetry cycles—notably "The Earth Child" sequence for which she sought a publisher in 1910.[8]

Echoes from Heine, however, are certainly not restricted to Mansfield's own specifically poetic output of these years. There are "Heinesque" resonances, and wide-ranging examples of German intertextuality, throughout her writings from the years 1903–04 and 1908–09, in far greater quantity than any French or Francophone traces. Heine's compact narrative style in verse and his scenic evocativeness, for example, recall Mansfield's sketches, fairy tales and prose poems, to be found, sometimes as fragments or partly completed sketches, in her early letters, notebooks and creative fiction. In many cases, these gain from being read—at least in part—as imaginative unleashings or expansions of scenes first met in Heine—fine examples being her "Die Einsame" (*CW*1, 20–22), or "Evening. By the sea" (*CW*4, 88–89). In both cases, the type of resonance to be found is different to what might be labelled "intertextuality", "pastiche" or "influence", which imply a more conscious anchoring in another author's textuality or style. The impression one gets when looking from Mansfield's scenes to Heine's is that the apprentice writer is learning to read, feel and decipher her world through a bioptic device that

---

[8] "The Earth Child" cycle arguably reflects the high point of Mansfield's formative readings of Heine. See more extended coverage in *CW*4, 459–487 and *CP*, 76–94.

combines both what she sees around her, and what she sees through Heine's eyes. Take Heine's powerfully atmospheric seascapes in poems 2–7 of "The North Sea" cycle, for instance (KMH 194–207), which constantly merge into a more intimate mode of mindscape; this entails using the sea and sunlight as dramatic devices to stage feelings or figures of enchantment—earth children, sea-children, changelings and variations of the self, caught midway in the course of magical metamorphosis:

"Evening Twilight"

> On the pale strip of seashore
> I sat, lost among fugitive thoughts, and alone ["einsam"]
> The sun was sinking lower and threw
> Glowing, red beams upon the water.
> And the white, widening line of waves,
> Pulled by the urging tide,
> Rolled in and rumbled nearer and nearer—
> A curious mingling of wailing and whistling,
> Of laughing and murmuring, sighing and shouting;
> And, under it all, the strange croon of the ocean.
> It was as though I heard forgotten stories,
> Ancient and lovely legends,
> That once I had heard as a child. (Heine 1907, 236)

In the same way, Mansfield's own scenes of the same years begin as what appear to be records of experience, only to shift into a more transfigured, fairy-tale world:

> Evening. By the sea. Lying thus on the sand, the foam almost washing over my hands, I feel the magic of the sea. Behind the golden hills the sun is going down, a ruby jewel in a lurid setting, and there is a faint flush everywhere over sea & land. To my right the sky has blossomed into vivid rose but to my left the land is hidden by a grey blue mist lightened now here now there by a suggestion of the sun—colour—it is like land

seen from a ship a very long way away—dreamland, mirage, enchanted country. [...]

And there are exquisite golden brown sprays & garlands of seaweed set about with berries, white and brown. Are they flowers blown from the garden of the sea-King's daughter—does she wander through the delicate coral forest seeking them, her long hair floating behind her, playing upon a little silver shell? And near me I see a light upon the blue coast—steadily tenderly it beams—a little candle set upon the great altar of the world. The glow pales in the sky, on the land, but the voice of the sea grows stronger. Oh, to sail & sail into the heart of the sea. Is it darkness and silence there or is it—a Great Light. So the grey sand slips—sifts through my fingers. (*CW*4, 89–90)

Heine's "Evening Twilight", "Night by the Strand" and "Declaration" explore similar transfigurations or dislocations of setting, and provide fascinating bridges to certain prose vignettes by Mansfield, such as her "Die Einsame":

Yes, it was true. All night she spent by the ocean, by the great tall rocks. Her hair hung loose and streamed out behind her like a veil. Her face was white, white as her dress, and her eyes were like misty stars. She sang with her arms outstretched to the sea. Sang with a passionate longing, a wild, mad entreaty. Sometimes she knelt upon the sand, the tears streaming down her face, and ever she sang the same song. (*CW*1, 20).

This intimate form of "reading alongside" suggests that the scenes Mansfield evokes in her vignettes are in part inspired by pictures conjured up in her mind when reading Heine, as she imagines and beholds her world in mid-transformation, just as he invites his reader to do. In such cases, the lingering appeal of his poetry would have been heightened by her *not* entirely "understanding German"— the very unfamiliarity of the language obliges the reader to advance slowly, alert to the strange sounds and figures that emerge hesitantly from the page. Slow reading is the privilege of the non-proficient, attentive learner.

All the poems that Mansfield flagged up in her *Buch der Lieder* play with changeling forms, using disconcerting doppelgängers, masks, outcasts and outsiders, who feel their displacement and dispossession intensely, and yet cultivate it too—in other words, features which are highly characteristic of Mansfield's earliest poems and prose pieces too. Likewise in tone, there are striking resonances between her writings and Heine's in the way they tread a tentative path between high romantic exaltation and sly wit. They can conjure up bitterness and humour within expressions of tender effusiveness, which will constantly tremble on the brink of sincerity. Take Heine's "Am fernen Horizonte", for instance. In a manner highly suggestive of Mansfield's later predilection for staged scenes, partly misconstrued or curtained off, both onlooker and reader perceive the beauty of a moment which remains partly veiled in obscurity:

> Am fernen Horizonte
> Erscheint, wie ein Nebelbild,
> Die Stadt mit ihren Türmen
> In Abenddämmerung gehüllt.
>
> Ein feuchter Windzug kräuselt
> Die graue Wasserbahn;
> Mit traurigem Takte rudert
> Der Schiffer in meinem Kahn.
>
> Die Sonne hebt sich noch einmal
> Leuchtend vom Boden empor,
> Und zeigte mir jene Stelle,
> Wo ich das Liebste verlor (KMH, 119–20).
>
> On the dim and far horizon
> Appeareth, misty and pale
> The city with all its towers
> In evening twilight's veil.

> A humid gust is ruffling
> The path o'er the waters dark;
> With mournful measure the oarsman
> Is rowing my tiny bark.
>
> The sun once more ariseth
> And over the earth gleams he,
> And shows me the spot out yonder
> Where my loved one was lost to me. (Heine 1866, 203)

Even in the archaising style of the mid-Victorian translator, this is a fine illustration of Heine's mastery of indeterminacy and lingering strangeness, a skill Mansfield would later make her own: he paints scenes but withholds or defers full meaning; he promises a narrative yet decentres the tale, leaving a bewildering sense of elusiveness. These are key characteristics of what, once rendered in prose form, was poised to become the modernist short story, when the compact conclusiveness of mid to late-19th-century precursors (in its Gothic or detective mode for example), gave way to scenes and sketches that eschew narrative precision or plot in favour of evocative atmosphere, and leave any sense of an ending to the mind of the reader.

The myriad thematic or atmospheric resonances between Mansfield and Heine's poetic worlds inevitably invites the question of what Mansfield might have known of the poet: if studied at school, how might he have been presented? As readers familiar with Heine's biography today know, his prestige as one of the figureheads of German Romanticism was long contested, in part on account of his lifelong status as an outsider (which he at once spurned and embraced): his Jewish origins, his social inferiority, his tendentious conversion to Christianity, his years abroad, and his sometimes unveiled contempt for the mediocrity and smugness of the German middle classes—especially the commercial and financial bourgeoisie—which might have appealed to the rebellious schoolgirl. But were such features foregrounded in the early 20th century? Questions of cultural contextualisation are of course essential if we are to avoid the traps of critical anachronism—such as presuming that a mutual sense of liminality transformed into a creative dynamic might draw Mansfield to Heine. Late 19th-century teaching manuals, literary companions and poetry readers, however, reveal a different biographical approach, where "outsiderness", if mentioned, is only regretted in terms merely of personal misfortune or as markers of inconsistent talent.[9] In fact, Heine himself is decidedly underrated—Bowring deems him a "minstrel" rather than a poet (Heine 1866, xi). The few poems the anthologies favour tend to be those linked to German mythology (especially "The Loreley"), and the longer, mythological epics from *Romanzero* rather than the *Buch der Lieder*. The quest to resituate Heine within the social, cultural and pedagogical worlds of the turn of the century, however, did reveal what is probably a far more reliable indicator of Mansfield's familiarity with the poet and his works, both within the colonial environment of Wellington, and in mid-Edwardian Britain. The turning-point was the two poems evoked above, "Evening Twilight" and "Am fernen Horizonte".

It is the German language that provides the key here, rather than similarities in theme and tone. The German title of "Evening Twilight" is "Abenddämmerung". The same word occurs on line 4 of the first stanza of "Am fernen Horizonte": "In Abenddämmerung gehüllt" [Veiled in twilight]. The dense, sonorous word clearly appealed to Mansfield, for it figures in a 1907 notebook, after an evocation of a cello lesson with Mr Trowell: "Then in the Abenddammerung I went out in to the streets. It was so beautiful—the full moon was like a strain of music heard through a closed door" (*CW*4, 51). Of course it is no surprise to find numerous references to twilight in Mansfield's

---

[9] The pedagogical *Thesaurus of German Poetry* for example notes: "His writings display a strange medley of refined feeling, unrestrained wantonness, and unsparing satire. He often begins a poem in a tone of pleasing gracefulness or deep melancholy and closes with the cutting dissonance of startling raillery. His good points are often thrown into the shade by his shameless scoffing at all that is good and great. One of the peculiarities of this poet is the little attention which he pays to poetic form" (Graeser 1860, xxxviii).

work in these years—including a poem with the same title (1903). The same might be said for nearly every writer's works at the time—the romantic beauty and wistfulness of dusk, the symbolic associations with fading love, beauty, and indeed the fin-de-siècle are archly conventional poetic tropes. "Abenddämmerung" was not only familiar in semantic terms, however. It was an evocative musical reference, as a list of all the compositions bearing that title would confirm, and these "sounds of music" can point to Heine's abiding importance for Mansfield, and his arrival in her life and book collection, via Trowell.

"Am fernen Horizonte" is poem XVI from Heine's "The Homecoming" cycle in *Book of Songs*. The poem was in no anthology of German poetry in English translation from the 1860s–1910s that I consulted. It was, however, highly familiar to the lyrically- and literary-minded publics of the late 19th century as song lyrics.[10] While volumes of Heine's poetry (in translation and in German) were reprinted in the English-speaking world approximately each decade in the years 1880–1910, his shorter poems were among the most familiar classical song repertoire in home and chamber recitals in the same years. Reprinted in a host of different editions, they circulated as inexpensive sheet music and graced many a private home. Heine's Lieder had been set to music by all the foremost German composers of the day—Brahms, Schubert, Mendelssohn, Schumann, Liszt, to name but the most familiar—and were particularly appreciated in the collection "Six Songs", which form parts 8–13 of Schubert's *Schwanengesang* cycle [Swan Songs], D. 597. Their titles as song lyrics sometimes obscure their origin in Heine's own oeuvre, where they figure merely as numbered sets of verses within a larger series. "Am fernen Horizonte", for example, bore the title "Die Stadt" [The Town] in Schubert's *Schwanengesang*. The other titles were "Ihr Bild", "Das Fischermädchen", "Der Doppelgänger", "Der Atlas" and "Am Meer" [Your Picture,

---

10 Another popular salon song with the title "Abenddämmerung", with lyrics from a poem by Schack, was Brahms's Op 49, n° 5, a work that also includes his famous "lullaby" (n° 4). A slightly less familiar version of Heine's lyrics now, which was highly popular in the 1890s, was by Max von Schillings, Opus 1a (1891).

The Fishermaiden, The Double, Atlas, and By the Sea]. In Mansfield's *Buch der Lieder*, these were: "Du schönes Fischermädchen" (114), "Das Meer erglänzte weit hinaus" (118), "Still ist die Nacht" (121), "Ich stand in dunkeln Träumen" (123) and "Ich unglücksel'ger Atlas!" (124).

The likelihood of Heine's poems as salon lyrics being familiar to the apprentice writer relies not only on their great popularity at the time, although this argument itself is substantial. Newspaper archives show they were regularly performed at concerts in Wellington.[11] They were inevitably familiar to the key musical mentors in Mansfield's life: New Zealand-based choirmaster and conductor Robert Parker, who was music teacher at the Beauchamp children's school in Wellington, and Mansfield's piano teacher,[12] and Mr Trowell senior, a close friend of Parker's, whose versatile musical talents also included teaching singing.[13] Meanwhile, some of Thomas Trowell's earliest compositions are explicitly influenced by the 19th-century Lied tradition, including Opus 50 (1912) which sets two Heine poems from the same *Buch der Lieder* to music.[14] Mansfield's familiarity with the Heine-inspired Lieder becomes even more plausible when we consult her volume of Heine, where every pencil-marked poem proves to have been set to music, often many times, by the turn of the century. These include settings by composer Macdowell, whom she appreciated in the same years, as letters and diary attest. In fact, Heine's appeal as a lyricist is perhaps the key to one of the first poetry entries in Mansfield's diary, dating from 1903: a transcription of Heine's "Der Tod, das ist die kühle Nacht", number 87 in "Die Heimkehr" in her *Buch der Lieder*. It was one of Heine's poems most frequently set to music, the most popular version being by Brahms (Op. 46). It is also regularly cited,

---

11 https://natlib.govt.nz/items?i%5Bprimary_collection%5D=Papers+Past&text=Schubert+Heine; last accessed January 14, 2017.
12 For Parker's role in Mansfield's life, see Kimber (2016, 86); for Trowell's participation in Parker's annual concerts, see Griffiths (2012, 18–30). For programmes of his annual concerts, see ATL-Eph-B-MUSIC-Parker-1890.
13 See Kimber (2016, 94); Griffiths (2012, 11–21); and Davison and Spooner (2016, 11–14).
14 See Thomas Trowell, *Two Songs for Madame Blanche Marchesi*, Opus 50.

with "Die Lorelei" and "Du bist wie eine Blume", as the best known of Heine in song-form in those years (Youens 2007, 312–18). It is certainly in song-form that it makes most sense in the schoolgirl world of the Beauchamp sisters—it features in a great many song collections and school song books, as well as circulating as sheet music, while the poem was rarely anthologised.

While the light such links may shed on the musical environment of the apprentice writer are certainly fascinating from a biographical perspective, it proves problematic for the literary critic now. How are we to make sense of these examples of High German romanticism in the evolution of the modernist short story technique of Katherine Mansfield, and the more general mappings of European modernism that contemporary scholars are so skilfully illuminating? The same question holds for all Mansfield's literary contemporaries: while their characteristic stylistic and formal experimentation has invited parallels with the experimental composers of the era—Schoenberg, Stravinsky and Debussy being the most frequently cited as the modernists' musical counterparts—the literary modernists' listening habits or musical familiarity proves decidedly classical. They show little awareness of contemporaneous musical experimentation, but were all conversant with the 19th-century giants, Beethoven, Brahms, Wagner, Schubert and Chopin, an acoustic environment that appears much less amenable to literary pioneering.

The answer, surely, is to be found in "the unexpected handling of the well-known" (Parsons 2004, 86), as they borrowed, pastiched, and recycled the artworks of the past. In the case of Mansfield and Heine, the rich source of inspiration that his poetry and poetic output in performance could provide can be seen first by comparing Mansfield's response to the poetry, and the conventional reception of the times. In fact, by the end of the century, Heine's lyrics had become entirely synonymous with the auditory rapture, tender effusions and sentimental outpourings favoured by the late Victorians. Youens (2007) spares no irony when summarising the appropriations of his verses to fit prevalent performance tastes: "chocolate-box terminology, [and] settings sickly sweet full of overblown pathos common to the parlour songs of the era and the saccharine devotional music heard in Victorian churches" (285). The lachrymose, self-indulgently lyrical mode was also reproduced in the illustrations and script favoured by the publishers of sheet music, centring on whimsical cosiness, pastoral uplift or sentimental romance. However, this constituted a resolute misreading of the early Romantic dynamic in general, and of Heine's own, decidedly more uncomfortable poetic and narrative stance in particular—his "untrustworthy surfaces", biting irony (especially at the expense of the more gushing, middle class emotional indulgences of the time), and his often "mischievous delight" (Youens 2007, 273). Mansfield, however, who also had a sharp ear for hearing against the conventional grain, may have perceived, while reading, singing or listening to Heine, ways to reinvest the sentimental tropes of the time and ironically subvert them. Her own ventures into this vein in exactly the same years certainly invite parallels of this sort.

To weigh up between mere coincidence and actual creative resonance would require a far broader investigation than the present chapter can aspire to, but a few eloquent examples may point the way to promising fields of future research. One feature is their highly slippery use of the first person. Both Heine and Mansfield excel in the art of adopting the lyrical "I", only to redeploy it in a series of duplicitous selves that are, and are not, about the speaking self. In fact, the musico-literary critic Stein's (1996) definition of Heine's poetics could apply, word for word, to Mansfield, as acknowledged by contemporary criticism:

> Heine's poems are not in the Goethean tradition of *Erlebnisgedichte*, confessional poems, drawn from life, each triggered by an individual experience. They are brilliant exercises in permutation and variation on a highly sophisticated theme. They abound in theatrical gesture, paradox, word play, irony, destruction of illusion and atmosphere, the surprise ending, self-ironizing hyperbole; they are in essence rational and epigrammatic. Heine was by no means the naive poet he seems to be in poems like "Du bist wie eine Blume"

[...] he is the brilliant inventor, the cynic, the destroyer of illusion, and with it all, a poet of deep feeling. (559)

Just as the Lied recasts poetry as dramatic monologue (Parsons 2004, 174), so revisiting Heine's musical poems—musical in theme, or musicalized as lyrics, and with elusive musician-figures—side-by-side with Mansfield's poetry or prose vignettes reveals a comparable art of theatricalised selves and masks emerging from "image, paradox, pun, epigram, surprise" (Stein 1966, 561).[15] Take Heine's "To a Singer", for example, that figures in Mansfield's list of favourite verses. Stanzas one and five read as follows:

That fair Enchantress I remember—
As first her now I see!
How her blithe notes, the charmed air winging,
Set in my heart strange echoes ringing!
Fast fell my tears at her sweet singing
I knew not what hapt to me [...]

It was a loud discordant clamour
That called me back from dreamland so.
The ballad sung, the people clapping
And on the benches madly rapping,
With cries of "Brava" broke my napping
There was the Singer, curtseying low. (Heine 1907, 64)

The way Heine stages the singer and the song performance, and deliberately subverts the romantic musings that the listener indulges in while the music lasts, provides a tempting approach to Mansfield's similar staging and subverting of song: prime examples being her early poems "My Lady Sits and Sings", or "Child of the Sea",

---

[15] Another possible bridge from Mansfield to Heine would be via Symons, whom she was reading avidly in the same years. Symons' works resituate Heine in the poetics of the fin-de-siècle; he also translates Heine's verse and travel-writing.

but also the sorts of reverie and cold-shower awakenings used for wickedly comic effect in her stories to come—"The Modern Soul" or "Mr Reginald Peacock's Day". In other words, Mansfield was perhaps hearing through Heine ways to weave dissonance into emotional compactness and even surface sentimentality—registering high romantic outpouring, and then wickedly chuckling about it. The same mood is captured in one of her fragments noted on loose paper presumably acquired during a voyage, which might be real life overheard, and might be Mansfield commenting in a theatrical aside on the poem written overleaf, or might again be a fictional imagining, noted down in case it can be used later:

> I do not know why things touch me so, she said—Home Sweet Home. You know I think of all the maudlin—piteously inane—foolishly insipid songs—and its pauses are perpetually punctuated with vociferous nose blowing—people are fools. (*CP*, 159)

Even in this briefest of sketches, it is the performance of song in a maudlin, hyper-conventional manner that is the trigger of the distinctly wicked irony—a fine illustration of the emerging writer learning the art of extracting shafts of comic effect by homing into the underlying dissonance of insincerity. One only needs to recall the huge presence of songs and singers in Heine's and Mansfield's oeuvre, and the often unexpected or disruptive performative power of song, to appreciate how enduring this insight could be.

To return to the concept of "not understanding" in some of Woolf's key essays, we thus find Mansfield embarking on a new apprehension of the world opened up by reading Heine—not as a skilled student perfecting her German, but as an avid, language-and-music sensitive apprentice. Because she does not fully understand Heine's language, she can linger over the richness of the sounds and lilt of words or turns of phrase, which are defamiliarised by being acoustically reminiscent of English, yet with radical changes of intonation and rhythm when spoken or sung, and frequently defamiliarised anew by

Gothic script in published poetry volumes.[16] Here too, in this defamiliarization of conventional forms, is the nascent modernist impulse emerging from revisiting the classics and romantics. It is surely no coincidence that she composes some of her early poetry to be set to music by Tom Trowell (*Letters* 1, 83), or that when she evokes new poems dedicated to Garnet Trowell, she focuses on how they are to be performed, construing her poetry as music. She insists the poetry be read not as lyrical, but as lyrics, how the music should accompany and enhance the underlying pulse and mood of the words, and how the voice even standing alone can seek to emulate the musical inflections and intonations of phrasing:

> For instance that one "In the Church" almost recitative at the beginning with a strange organ like passage—then the ivy, rough, cruel, horrible, and then the first verse in a dream—you hear it?—And then "By the Sea Shore", with strange Macdowell, Debussy chords—and the lilac tree full or [sic] a rythmic grace. (*Letters* 1, 80)[17]

She was thus defining a new form of composition and performance, somewhere between declamation, recitative and song, taking literature further from the mimetic and the printed word, and closer to sound art and pictorial art. This too she would have encountered in Heine's transposition from poetry to Lied (Parsons 2004, 93), and from print to performance. He could thus prove the ideal guide "into life's strangeness" (Sammons 1984, 1254), into a world of transitions and displacements, that was in part assembled from snatches of lines overheard, which in Mansfield's works and in the modernist context, could reappear as forms of riff and collage, unfamiliar sounds, roughly understood. One final Heine poem, although less familiar as song

---

[16] Mansfield's *Buch der Lieder* does not use Gothic script, but many contemporary poetry collections do—including the Graeser *Thesaurus of German Poetry*, "especially adapted for the use of schools" as the subtitle indicates.

[17] For further discussion of these passages, and the composers evoked, see Davison and Spooner (2016, 15–18).

lyrics, can point to common resonances of this sort, waiting to be explored.[18] This (untitled) poem offers a similar assemblage of unlikely voices—children, lovers, animals, past and present, real and fantasied—welling up like an unseen choir from a single speaking voice. Like all the other poems explored here, the text bears Mansfield's pencil marks in the margin:

> My child, we two were children,
> Two children small and gay;
> We crept into the hen-house,
> And hid ourselves under the hay.
>
> We crowed like cocks, and often,
> As grown-up folk went by—
> Cock-a-doodle-doo! They thought it
> The cock's own real cry.
>
> [. . .] Our neighbour's ancient tabby
> Came often to pay a call;
> We met her with bows and curtsies,
> And compliments none too small.
>
> [. . .] And often we sat there talking
> Like old folk seriously
> Complaining how all went better
> In the good old times gone by (Heine 1907, 160)

Here, Heine's children playing at being animals and grown-ups, and aping their voices, offers a scene that prefigures, in more restrained form, Mansfield's dazzling fictional craftsmanship in part 9 of '"At the Bay" (*CW*2, 361–62).

Heine's poetic art and its 19th-century afterlife as lyrics thus provide a rich means to reassess Mansfield's own musical stories,

---

[18] Musical adaptations include Johann Vesque von Püttlingen's 1851 "Die Heimkehr" cycle, and his Opus 38 *Humoristica from Heine's Poetry*.

where fantasies of "charming", "heavenly", "enchanting" melody and auditory rapture prove to be but a fragile gloss over music that discomfits and disturbs. It is also one of the finest means to reassess the lyric in her early work, where the "I" is always already in part a construct, or a mask. The musical component is prerequisite, and not merely secondary or complementary. Unlike conventionally construed poetic lyric, traditionally presumed to be synonymous with intimate and sincere emotional spontaneity, musical lyric has always been intentionally indirect, dislocated from any source or origin. It is a second-hand mode, designed for performance, where poetry as song lyrics is neither the poet's "I", nor the composer's, nor the singer's, nor the listener's. Yet all these interpreters and listeners will feed off the lyrical invitation, empathizing and identifying with the lyric appeal, sharing an experience of musical feeling as a public mode of intimacy.

Mansfield's volume of Heine perhaps began as a memento of love, but the flurry of emotion soon passed.[19] In fact, a letter drafted even when she was supposedly smitten already suggests that the would-be romance with Tom Trowell served more to explore the tropes of romantic convention than stoke the fires of passion (*Letters* 1, 24–25). The volume's transformative effect on her literary apprenticeship was of this order. A close reading of Mansfield and Heine side-by-side, and a detailed scrutiny of the pages of her volume of one of the greatest, but also longest misunderstood and reappropriated German Romantics, offers today's scholar a new vision of the young Kathleen Beauchamp, gazing, like Keats on first looking into Chapman's Homer, upon a new reading of the world. Revisiting romance through the double veil of what are quite literally Heine's songs, and Mansfield's reinvestment of the German Lied, incites us to retrieve Heine from the genteel salon conventions of the late 19th century, listen to music against the safe, cosy vein of the salon, and perceive the original, dislocative dynamics of his early romantic innovation. In either place, we rediscover the essential tension and strangeness of the lyric—

---

[19] See her thoroughly down-to-earth rationale on the day the romantic bubble bursts (*CW4*, 554–55).

which in turn lends itself splendidly to the dynamics of nascent modernism. The lyric recovers its force as a disruptive, halfway figure, telling of exile, displacement, and transposition. It is the place where voices are willingly lent and borrowed, staging distinctly modern souls and selves speaking in a language which, like music, can be felt and shared, but can never be entirely translated.

Bibliography

Bradley, Carol June. 2003. *An Index to Poetry in Song*. London: Routledge, 2003.

Buchheim, C. A. 1885. *German Poetry for Repetition*. London: Longmans & Green.

Da Sousa Correa, Delia. 2013. "Katherine Mansfield and Nineteenth-Century Musicality." In *Words and Notes in the Long Nineteenth Century*, edited by Phyllis Weliver and Katharine Ellis, 103–18. Woodbridge: Boydell Press.

---. 2015. "Katherine Mansfield's Germany: 'these pine-trees provide most suitable accompaniment for a trombone!'." In *Katherine Mansfield and Continental Europe*, edited by Gerri Kimber and Janka Kascokova, 99–116. Basingstoke: Palgrave Macmillan.

Davison, Claire. 2016. "Bilinguals and Bioptics. Virginia Woolf and the Outlandishness of Translation." In *Virginia Woolf: Twenty-First Century Perspectives,* edited by Jeanne Dubino, Gillian Lowe, Vera Neverow and Kathryn Simpson, 72–90. Edinburgh: Edinburgh University Press.

Davison, Claire, and Joseph Spooner. 2016. *The Musical World of Katherine Mansfield*. Katherine Mansfield Birthday Lectures, No. 7, edited by Gerri Kimber. Bath: Katherine Mansfield Society Publications.

Gelber, Mark H., ed. 2004. *Confrontations / Accommodations: German-Jewish Literary and Cultural Relations*. Tübingen: Max Niemeyer Verlag.

Gibbs, Christopher H., ed. 1997. *The Cambridge Companion to Schubert*. Cambridge: Cambridge University Press.

Graeser, John. 1890. *A Thesaurus of German Poetry*. London and Berlin: Nutt and Asher.

Griffiths, Martin. 2012. "Arnold Trowell: Violoncellist, Composer and Pedagogue" (unpublished). PhD thesis, University of Waikato, NZ.

F. H. Hedley. 1876. *Masterpieces of German Poetry*. London: Trübner & Co.

Heine, Heinrich. 1866. *The Poems of Heine*. Translated by Edgar A. Bowring. London: Bell and Daldy.

---. 1907. *Book of Songs*. Translated by J. Todhunter. Oxford: Oxford University Press, 1907.

---. Undated. *Buch der Lieder*, edited by Ernst Elster. Berlin: Fischer—Verlag. With hand annotations by Thomas Trowell (dedication) and Katherine Mansfield. Alexander Turnbull Library—Manuscripts. MSX–5218.

Kimber, Gerri. 2016. *Katherine Mansfield: The Early Years*. Edinburgh: Edinburgh University Press.

Manners, Lady John, ed. and trans. 1865. *Gems of German Poetry*. London: Blackwood.

Osbourne, Charles. 1974. *The Concert Song Companion: A Guide to the Classical Repertoire*. London: Gollancz.

Parker, Louis Napoleon (composer and translator). 1891. *Twelve Songs by Heine*. London: Peters.

Parsons, James. 2004. *The Cambridge Companion to the Lied*. Cambridge: Cambridge University Press.

Perloff, Marjorie. 2010. *Unoriginal Genius: Poetry by Other Means in the New Century*. London and Chicago: University of Chicago Press.

Prawer, Siegbert S. 1960. *Heine: Buch der Lieder*. London: Arnold.

Rasula, Jed. 1998. "Understanding the Sound of Not Understanding." In *Close Listening: Poetry and the Performed Word*, edited by Charles Bernstein, 233–61. Oxford: Oxford University Press.

Sammons, Jeffrey L. 1979. *Heinrich Heine. A Modern Biography*. Princeton, NJ: Princeton University Press.

---. 1984. "Heinrich Heine. Reception in the World's Strangeness." In *Literary Theory and Criticism. Festschrift in Honour of René Wellek*, edited by J. P. Strelka, 1245–64. Bern: Peter Lang.

Stein, Jack M. 1966. "Schubert's Heine Songs." *Journal of Aesthetics and Art Criticism* 24 (4): 559–66.
Woolf, Virginia. 1994. *The Essays of Virginia Woolf,* Vol. 4, edited by Andrew McNeillie. New York and London: Harvest–Harcourt.
———. 2010. *The Essays of Virginia Woolf.* Vol. 5, edited by Stuart N. Clarke. New York: Houghton Mifflin Harcourt.
Youens, Susan. 2007. *Heinrich Heine and the Lied.* Cambridge: Cambridge University Press.

Constructing Jealousy, Exacting Revenge: Katherine Mansfield's "Poison" and Robert Browning's "My Last Duchess"

Todd Martin

In a recent special issue of *PMLA* entitled "Literature in the World", several theorists take aim at recent trends toward normalizing world literature, most notably David Damrosch's (2009) *How to Read World Literature*. The critics' concerns are centered around the idea that such approaches tend to dehistoricize world literature, taking it out of its local contexts. Their apprehensions appear to be summarized in S. Sankar's (2016) statement that "As an area of critical endeavor, world literature—with its implied coherence, stability, and emerging or achieved global homogeneity—is a problematic rubric under which to organize critical study of literatures in the world" (1411). Such homogeneity—or attempts to universalize literature—they contend, oversimplify both the production and consumption of literature.

Pascale Casanova (2004), however, implies that rather than ignoring the local context of a work, proponents of a critical view of world literature merely foreground another layer of context by considering "the totality of texts and literary and aesthetic debates with which a particular work of literature enters into relation and resonance" (3); she argues that the "world republic of letters has its own mode of operation: its own economy, which produces hierarchies and various forms of violence; and, above all, its own history" (11). Casanova, then, is interested in how an author responds to her situation within both her national and world contexts, including her artistic choices and even the language in which she chooses to write. And, while allegations of Eurocentrism may have some purchase in critiques of such an approach to world literature, Robert Young (2013) insists that judgment and taste—which necessitate a hierarchy—are a key component of the aesthetic approach which he and Casanova advocate, something lacking in postcolonialism which he suggests prioritizes political readings over artistic value (213–23).

David Damrosch takes a somewhat different approach. From his statement that "works of art refract their cultures rather than simply reflecting them" (2), one can infer that the literary choices an author makes may attempt to establish the literary capital Casanova discusses, but Damrosch seems more interested in understanding an author's artistic choices within a broader, world tradition. He suggests that "a great deal is conveyed through literature's kaleidoscopes and convex mirrors, and our appreciation of a work can be enormously increased if we learn more about the things it refers to and the artist's and audience's assumptions" (2–3). Staving off critiques like Sankar's of oversimplification and universalism, however, he notes that one must "beware the perils of exoticism and assimilation, the two extremes on the spectrum of difference and similarity" (13). Thus, approaches such as those promoted by Young, Casanova, and Damrosch do not necessarily limit the work's historical context, but rather expand it from the more localized historical-political into a broader literary tradition, whether that is studying how an author manoeuvers to find her place within that tradition or how a particular text fits within and reacts to a global literary tradition.

Nevertheless, reservations about world literature as the term is currently being employed cannot be ignored. Reacting in particular to Robert Young's contention that world literature and postcolonial literature are opposed, Jane Hiddleston (2016) offers an appealing balance, suggesting their respective goals are not mutually exclusive. She borrows from Edward Said's notion of worldliness to argue for a more nuanced approach to world literature. Hiddleston explains that "*Worldliness*, as I use it here, connotes connectedness but not fusion, an awareness of how global history shapes national history but at the same time a commitment to challenging inequalities produced by these histories" (1389, italics in original). This reappraisal of worldliness, she suggests, "might [...] challenge the false universalism of world literature, since worldliness suggests a way of thinking, an alertness to different cultures but also a worldly wisdom about the text's limits that attenuates the utopianism of some theories of world literature" (1388). In so doing, she aims for something broader than postcolonial national boundaries while insisting on unsettling the hegemonic tendencies she perceives in Young. She understands a literary work as "multidirectional", that is, as having a dialogical structure in which the author speaks to both cultures (1391). The author finds commonality between both the local and global, but such an approach still recognizes the tension that exists between the two cultures. What she proposes as "multidirectional", however, does not seem altogether dissimilar to Damrosch's concept of "refraction" which likewise purports to recognize the local origin of a text while examining its place in the broader world tradition, identifying the dialogical tensions between them. The difference is that Hiddleston's emphasis is on the political and Damrosch's on the aesthetic tensions.

Taking care not to ignore the complex interrelationship between the local and the global, then, an aesthetic approach such as that endorsed by critics of world literature can open up new perspectives on Katherine Mansfield. Rather than simply understanding her as a colonial outsider, a more worldly approach allows one to explore how Mansfield's agency is demonstrated in her use of the dominant culture of the metropole—specifically her choice to appropriate the dramatic monologue in her story "Poison" (1920)—not merely as a means of "writing back", but as a wilful participation in a much broader literary tradition. As I hope to demonstrate, if we can look beyond her position as an outsider—neither ignoring nor privileging it—we can see that Mansfield's use of Robert Browning's (1842) "My Last Duchess" in "Poison" is not just a gendered statement on male possessiveness, but also an artistic choice that reveals her thinking about her craft.

Biographical and Bibliographical Contexts

Gerri Kimber and Vincent O'Sullivan, in their edition of *The Collected Fiction of Katherine Mansfield*, provide valuable notes and contextual details for "Poison", indicating that the story is "enmeshed in the biographical details of [John Middleton Murry's] flirtation in

London with Princess Elizabeth Bibesco, and [Mansfield's] bitterness and loneliness as she waited for mail to arrive at Menton" (see *CW2*, 260 n. 1). Such intersections between life and art are not uncommon for Mansfield. However, despite the apparent relevance of her notebook entry dated December 27, 1920, in which she writes, "No, I've been poisoned by these 'letters'" (*CW4*, 339), referring to the letters which Bibesco continued to send to Murry even during his visit to Mansfield in Menton that month, the dates don't quite mesh. Mansfield's correspondence suggests that "Poison" was composed sometime in mid-November 1920, and Mansfield most likely enclosed it with a letter she sent to Murry on November 18. Murry, though, didn't pursue Bibesco until November 29 of that year,[1] when he first kissed her, an event that apparently sparked the affair. And certainly nothing was confirmed until Murry sent his confessional letter, composed on December 10, in which he details several of his transgressions, including that with the Princess, to Mansfield's vexation (Hankin 1991, 332–34). Mansfield sent a biting reply: "What happens in your personal life, does NOT affect me" (*Letters* 4, 149). I am not convinced, however, that Mansfield is quite as stoical as she makes out.

But while it is unlikely that Murry's affair with Bibesco was the main source of "Poison", the fact is that Mansfield already had doubts about Murry's faithfulness during this time. According to Jeffrey Meyers (2002), during the fall of 1920, Mansfield's "greatest source of anxiety [...] was the infidelity of her handsome husband, who inspired affection in women, was starved for physical love, and was thoroughly weary of Katherine's emotional onslaughts" (206). As Meyers points out, Mansfield had recently returned to Menton having spent the summer in London with Murry, during which time she expressed concern that he was having an affair with Dorothy Brett, the more likely source of Mansfield's resentment. On July 19, 1920 she wrote in her notebook:

---

1 I have arrived at this date by tracing Murry's account back from December 10 (a Friday in 1920), when Hankin (1991) indicates he probably wrote the letter.

Murry let fall this morning the fact that he had considered taking rooms with Brett at Thurlow Road this Winter. Good. Was their relationship friendship? Oh, no! He kissed her and held her arm and they were certainly conscious of a dash of something far more dangerous than l'amitié pure. [...]

I suppose one always thinks the latest shock is the worst shock. This is quite unlike any other I've ever suffered. The lack of sensitiveness as far as I am concerned—the <u>selfishness</u> of this staggers me. (*CW*4, 316; emphasis in original)

The acerbity of her feelings during the last half of 1920, despite her brave front, certainly must have fed into her story "Poison", with Murry philandering back in London and she ruminating on her isolation, alone in Menton. From these feelings, I contend, she found an affinity with Browning's "My Last Duchess" in which an overly jealous Duke has his duchess killed because he believes her too promiscuous, though there are no direct references to Browning's poem within the story itself.

Mansfield's exposure to Browning's verse dates at least from her first years at Queen's College in London, for the Newberry Library holds the 1903 edition of his poems that Mansfield presented to Ida Baker in May 1905 with the inscription, "To my friend Ida, From Kass 19-5-05". The first mention of Browning in Mansfield's writings, however, occurs in a brief, disparaging description of him that she copied out in 1907 from John Davidson's *The Rosary* (*CW*4, 41). A year later, in 1908, very likely spurred on by her reading of Arthur Symons's *Studies in Prose and Verse*,[2] she wrote to her sister, Vera: "I have had too, quite a mania for Walter Pater—and Nathaniel Hawthorne—and also Robert Browning—and Flaubert—Oh, many others" (*Letters* 1, 46). What is perhaps more significant, though, is that references to Browning after these early instances tend to coalesce around the time Mansfield was writing "Poison" in 1920. Mansfield alludes to Browning in letters to Murry at the end of 1919, at the beginning of 1920,

---

2   See Kaplan (1991, 57 n.7). Significantly, Symons had also written *An Introduction to Robert Browning* (1886).

and then again in mid 1921. Further, her notes for a book review of *The Lost Love* by Ashford Owen refer to the book's opening, which describes Owen's interactions with Browning as well as Tennyson, Swinburne, and Carlyle (*CW4*, 293). The review itself appeared in the *Athenaeum* in May 1920 under the title "Pressed Flowers" (*CW3*, 595–96). The concentration of these Browning references, while not conclusive, provides compelling evidence that Mansfield was reading and certainly channeling Browning into her writing around the time that she was writing "Poison". Something more concrete in the story itself is the narration and its potential borrowing from the dramatic monologue genre.

Dramatic Monologue

In *The World Republic of Letters*, Pascale Casanova promotes readings which, instead of dwelling on historical-political contexts, focus on the literary-political context, emphasizing the literary tradition that an author contends with. According to Casanova:

> [T]he writer stands in a particular relation to world literary space by virtue of the place occupied in it by the national space into which he has been born. But his position also depends on the way in which he deals with this unavoidable inheritance: on the aesthetic, linguistic, and formal choices he is led to make, which determine his position in this larger space. He may reject his national heritage, forsaking his homeland for a country that is more richly endowed in literary resources than his own, as Beckett and Michaux did; he may acknowledge his patrimony while trying at the same time to transform it and, in this way, to give it greater autonomy, like Joyce [...]; or he may affirm the difference and importance of a national literature, like Kafka [...] but also like Yeats and Kateb Yacine. All these examples show that, in trying to characterize a writer's work, one must situate it with respect to two things: the place occupied by his native literary space within world literature and his own position within this space. (2004, 11)

Over the course of Mansfield's writing career, one sees elements of several of these manifestations. When she first returned to England in 1908, she was happy to leave New Zealand behind and embrace the metropolis, claiming its literary tradition. Of course, she never fully escaped New Zealand as a subject in her fiction, and her oft-quoted manifesto to "make our undiscovered country leap into the eyes of the old world" in 1916 signals a desire to acknowledge her patrimony (*CW*4, 191); but if Virginia Woolf found few forebears in her appeal for a room of her own, Mansfield feels she must forge her own tradition, a poetic prose:

> Then I want to write poetry. I feel always trembling on the brink of poetry. [...] But especially I want to write a kind of long elegy to you perhaps not in poetry. No, perhaps in Prose—almost certainly in a kind of special prose. (*CW*4, 192)

The result of this is manifest in her mature work in which she not only incorporates lyrical descriptions, but also relies upon dramatic techniques which employ the slice of life—"glimpses into the lives of individuals, family, captured at a certain moment, frozen in time like a painting or a snapshot" (Kimber 2015, 10)—reminiscent of a lyrical trope, most notably the dramatic monologue.[3]

Given Mansfield's desire to write a poetic prose, as well as her reading of Browning around the time "Poison" was written, it is not surprising that she would turn to the dramatic monologue as a means of creating both a lyrical and dramatic effect in her work. Just a few weeks after she composed "Poison", Mansfield completed "The Lady's Maid", a story that demonstrates not only a purposeful but a more adept use of the genre with its apparent but silent auditor, which

---

[3] Interestingly, in describing Browning, Oscar Wilde (1914) noted that "he will be remembered as a writer of fiction, as the most supreme writer of fiction, it may be, that we have ever had. His sense of dramatic situation was unrivaled [...]. He used poetry as a medium for writing in prose" (n.p). Mansfield, conversely, could be described as using prose to write the lyrical.

suggests that Mansfield was at least experimenting with the dramatic monologue around the time she wrote the earlier story. Further, aesthetic trends in modernism were also shifting toward experiments with the form.

Glennis Byron (2003) traces modern manifestations of the dramatic monologue to Oscar Wilde's writings on the mask, suggesting that for modernists the genre offered the opportunity to express and transcend personality. She uses T. S. Eliot's "Love Song of J. Alfred Prufrock" with its abstracted auditor as an example (112, 115). However, noting a shift in modern poetry back to the more authoritative speaker of the Romantic lyric—which Byron argues the Victorians rejected in turning to the more subjective speaker of the dramatic monologue (45)—she posits that

> The Modernists [...] appropriate the dramatic monologue primarily for the purposes of experimenting with poetic voice. And as the conventions associated with the dramatic monologue begin to lose their functional value and the undermining of any naturalistic sense of character leads to the fragmentation of the speaking 'I', a new kind of poem begins to evolve. (116)

As a poetic form, then, the use of the dramatic monologue sees a sharp decline for modern poets. In discussing the evolution of the dramatic monologue during the latter half of the 19th century, however, Byron notes that practitioners of the form began to adopt a more narrative structure, which she attributes to the rise in the popularity of the novel. As such, the narratives "become more distinct and separate from the moment of speaker-auditor exchange. The moment of telling usually becomes relatively static, and change, movement, is located within the narrative as narrative becomes an increasingly important element of the monologue" (92).

The dramatic monologue's trend toward the narrative at the end of the 19th century, when coupled with Mansfield's own tendency toward the lyrical, suggests a natural extension from the dramatic monologue to her use of it in prose. Thus, while modern poets turn towards the more authoritative, lyrical voice, Mansfield saw the value of the dramatic monologue as providing a means for appropriating another persona and exploring the views of her protagonist within a particular situation. Such utilization would certainly align with shifts towards the more psychological, interior nature of modern fiction, which is the focus of Meghan Hammond's (2014) book, *Empathy and the Psychology of Literary Modernism*. According to Hammond, inward-turning modernists sought "to promote cognitive alignment between reader and character" which, she argues, is evident in "empathetic forms that strive to provide an immediate sense of another's thoughts and feelings [... which] include interior monologues, stream-of-consciousness narration, narrative marked by anachrony and fragmentation, and rapidly shifting character focalisation" (3–4). The dramatic monologue offers a similar alignment between reader and character. According to Byron:

> [T]he function of the auditor are [sic] linked to the role of the reader. The dramatic monologue, with its absence of any clear guiding authorial voice, seems particularly designed to provide reader response, and almost from the start the reader has been considered to have a significant role to play. (2003, 21)

In this way, the dramatic monologue draws the reader in, giving her a sense of participation, which may be the reason that Mansfield turned to this technique. While the form may not fully invite empathy with the character in precisely the way Hammond discusses, it provides a means of exploring the subjectivity of the character allowing the reader at least to see through the speaker's perspective. Because the dramatic monologue emphasizes the character's internal nature as revealed dramatically, as a method it would have appealed to the modernist short fiction writer, especially one like Mansfield who often appropriated masks and was adept at developing dramatic tension as a tool for exploring character.

Although "Poison" does not clearly follow the taxonomy of the dramatic monologue, at one point in the story it becomes evident that the narrator is reflecting on events that happened in the past, implying that he is recounting the story to an auditor. However, like Eliot's auditor in "Prufrock" Mansfield's is indistinct:

> In fact, to put it shortly, I was twentyfour [sic] at the time. And when she lay on her back, with the pearls slipped under her chin and sighed "I'm thirsty, dearest. *Donne-moi un orange*," I would gladly, willingly, have dived for an orange into the jaws of a crocodile—if crocodiles ate oranges. (*CW*2, 257)

While the narrator has professed his passion for Beatrice in similar gestures earlier, such as his willingness to hold the groceries for years rather than to shock her sense of order, these other instances merely suggest that the narrator is speaking as in any first person narration, but it is in the passage above that he seems to truly break through the dramatic fourth wall. This is not to say that her attempt at the dramatic monologue in "Poison" is particularly successful, but at least it nods to her use of the genre. Certainly, she accomplishes the effect much more successfully in "The Lady's Maid" where we are truly immersed in the monologue of the narrator; in "'Poison" Mansfield relies more heavily on exposition.

The persona of the dramatic monologue further allows Mansfield to utilize the dramatic immediacy of the first person narrator while fully removing herself from the text, because the character's usurpation of the narration "signals that the speaker is not the [author. . .]; the use of the first person mode, however, pushes toward the lyric 'I' and suggests a real-life existence for the speaker" (Byron 2003, 14). This distance perhaps appealed to Mansfield who likely recognized that she was too close to the first person narrator of her *Pension* stories,[4] stories from which she later disassociated herself.

---

[4] For more detail on Katherine Mansfield's first person narrator in *In a German Pension*, see Martin (2013).

For this reason, Mansfield tended toward narrators who were more remote, a narrative strategy perfected in her more mature stories which are nonetheless able to get into the mind of her characters through her masterful use of free indirect discourse. Gerri Kimber (2015) notes in *Katherine Mansfield and the Art of the Short Story* that even when Mansfield presents us with an omniscient narrator, the narrator is unobtrusive and very often merges, via the use of free indirect discourse, with the character on the page, thus blurring the line between the reader and the characters' feelings and thoughts. The result, Kimber argues, is an "intimate method of storytelling" in which, for certain moments, "we become the character on the page" (16), much as Hammond's view of empathy suggests. Noting Mansfield's rejection of the conventional plot structure and dramatic action and her move toward a more character-driven story, Kimber stresses Mansfield's interest in the inner life of her characters and how they respond to their circumstances. By revealing the working of her characters' minds, Mansfield allows the reader to identify with the character through shared experience.

Yet, just as with the stories in *In a German Pension*, Mansfield had a strong personal and emotional tie to the events on which "Poison" appears to be based, as noted previously. In order to avoid any clear identification between herself and her narrator, however, Mansfield—despite her use of the first person narrator—is able to distance herself from the speaker by creating a more specific persona as well as by gendering the narrator male. While Mansfield frequently utilized male protagonists, cross-gendering was a device commonly used in the dramatic monologue, especially by its women practitioners (Byron 2003, 13). Doing so allows Mansfield, when questioning Murry's fidelity back in London, to dissociate herself from her own jealousy (which is manifest in the male speaker). But by making the male speaker the jealous one and making him the focus of the story, she can also emphasize how the masculine figure objectifies Beatrice, allowing the reader to see how he attempts to possess her in a way similar to how Browning's Duke desires to possess his duchess. Mansfield, though, turns that around by having Beatrice refuse to be possessed.

The Artist at Work

In her essay on the dramaturgical voice in Mansfield, Bowen, and Woolf, Anne Besnault-Levita (2008) makes specific note of the lyrical potential of the short story, especially as it was being practiced during the modern period, and notably how "the primacy of subjective experience seized at one 'spiritual moment' through a poetics of the apprehended aesthetic whole has indeed been exploited by those authors" (n.p.). While she does not discuss "Poison" directly, her comments on how Mansfield divorces her characters from any narratorial stance, and thus complicates the use of satire and irony more than if she just used free indirect speech, address one reason why Byron posits the dramatic monologue as an ideal political tool taken up in the 19th century, especially by women. The result is that readers must have a "higher awareness of the protagonists' inner conflicts and of the aesthetic or cultural contrast built up by the texts" (Besnault-Levita 2008, n.p.), a view that seems to align with Damrosch's notion of "refraction" and Hiddleston's of "worldliness". The result is that, as both Besnault-Levita and Byron contend in their separate studies, one must pay particular attention to grammatical features and linguistic codes employed by the persona. This makes genetic criticism and its emphasis on even the smallest authorial adjustments made in the generative process a valuable tool, especially for revealing character.

There are no overt allusions to Robert Browning in "Poison", or at least none manifest through direct quotation, and I don't want to overstate the influence of the poet. However, especially for this story, such allusions would fit the thematic emphasis. There *are*, though, direct allusions to Coleridge, Tennyson, and Pope, as Kimber and O'Sullivan reveal in their notes on the text. And in some instances, these references appear to be either misremembered or taken out of context. According to Pierre-Mark De Biasi (1996), in his essay "What is a Literary Draft? Toward a Functional Typology of Genetic Documentation", through the process of drafting, authors often co-opt source materials—what De Biasi calls exogenetic materials—and adjust them to fit the purpose of their stories. De Biasi explains that the will to referential veracity remains secondary to the organic primacy of the work: [...] the exogenetic detail is forced into the original context of the rough draft; but as the endogenetic [or compositional] logic develops, the writer can be seen abandoning, one after the other, over the course of the composition, all the realist characteristics that had been the initial reason for choosing such a demonstrative detail. As it meshes better and better with its context, the detail sometimes ends up becoming utterly unrealistic, if it doesn't simply run aground. (46)

In other words, the borrowed materials, in this case Mansfield's references to Browning, are adapted to the meaning of the text, which would explain why Mansfield either ignores or is not interested in the context of any of the allusions. First and foremost, according to De Biasi, the materials serve the purpose of the literary work the author is composing.

But for De Biasi, part of the process of appropriating the exogenetic materials, can include the full absorption of the borrowed text:

After undergoing its multiple transformations, the initial exogenetic element (for example, a topographical comment, a detail or a situation borrowed from a literary work) may have become perfectly untraceable: it has metamorphosed into an organic part of the text, which, for the reader, points only to the writer's imaginary and to the internal logic of the fiction, just like any other element of the work. (46)

Such, I would suggest, is the case with Mansfield's use of Browning. While there are no direct references to "My Last Duchess" in "Poison", certain traces remain, particularly in Mansfield's evocation of the significance of Beatrice's smile, which is reminiscent of the smile that spurs the Duke's jealousy of the unnamed duchess. The first reference to Beatrice's "sweet, teasing smile" is rather innocuous; however, the narrator later imagines Beatrice "smiling that secret smile, that languid, brilliant smile that was just for me" (*CW2*, 255, 256). The narrator echoes the Duke's comment, "But to myself they turned" (Browning 1842, line 9), referring to the duchess's gaze in the painting of her that he now keeps behind a curtain. Beatrice's secret smile, then, coalesces with the duchess's "spot of joy" and her "earnest glance", but most poignantly with the smile the Duke describes at the moment of crisis:

> Oh, sir, she smiled, no doubt,
> Whene'er I passed her; but who passed without
> Much the same smile? This grew; I gave commands;
> Then all smiles stopped together.
> (Browning 1842, lines 43–46)

It appears that Mansfield purposefully chose to emphasize Beatrice's smile and the narrator's feelings of possession to establish a reference to Browning's Duke. That she opted for the smile rather than the more referential "spot of joy" likely stems from its proximity to the Duke's commands to have the duchess killed.

Although Browning himself is recorded as having been ambiguous as to whether the "commands" specified the duchess's execution or her being sent to a convent (Friedland 1936, 676), the historical circumstances at least allude to her being killed by poison. Louis S. Friedland, the first critic to trace Browning's Duke to Alfonse II, the fifth duke of Ferrara, and the duchess to his young wife, Lucrezia de Medici, points out that while recent historians question whether Lucrezia was poisoned, rumors at the time suggested she was, and "the great genealogist of the Italian families, Count Litta, repeats the suspicion 'that her husband, through motives of jealousy, had poisoned her'" (672). If one interprets the Duke as having his wife killed, then poisoning seems the most logical means, for anything more overt or violent would certainly have aroused suspicion, and it corresponds with historical circumstances. This sets up an interesting correlation with Mansfield's title, perhaps another allusion to Browning's poem. For evidence of the male narrator's possessiveness, though, one need only recall his reasoning for wanting to marry Beatrice: "Not because

I cared for such horrible shows, but because I felt it might possibly perhaps lessen this ghastly feeling of absolute freedom, *her* absolute freedom, of course" (*CW*2, 256). A study of Mansfield's manuscript and typescript of the story, held at the Newberry Library in Chicago, reveals that Mansfield was very purposeful in creating the narrator's possessive nature. For example, just after noting the "secret smile" that "was just for me", the narrator asks: "'Who are you?' Who was she? She was – Woman'" (*CW*2, 256). The use of the capital "W" for woman reveals the speaker's objectification of Beatrice, making her the embodiment of womanhood. Seeing the evolution of the passage from the manuscript to the typescript reveals that this was a conscious choice for Mansfield:[5]

Manuscript (leaf 3)	**Typescript (leaf 3)**
"Who are you?" Who was she? She was—woman.	"Who are you?" Who was she? She was wWoman.

While it is difficult to say for sure whether the "w" of "Woman" in the manuscript is intended to be capitalized, the typescript shows that the "w" was originally lower-case, but Mansfield handwrote a capital "W" over what was evidently an error. Having the narrator essentialize Beatrice in this manner, Mansfield reveals how he strips Beatrice of her individual identity in order to more fully possess her, to possess the idea of what he wants her to be. This objectification later turns to worship. After Annette, their maid, announces

---

5 The following key is used to show revisions between the Manuscript and Typescript:
   [word] = KM's change of word or phrase or punctuation, etc., from previous version
   /word\ = KM's omission of word or phrase, etc., from previous version
   |word| = KM's addition of word or phrase, etc., from previous version
   ^word^ = KM's handwritten addition of word or phrase, etc., on current version
   word = KM's handwritten omission of word or phrase, etc., on current version
   *** = my omission, to distinguish from KM's own use of ellipses.

that there are no letters, the narrator celebrates: "I was wild with joy. I threw the paper up into the air and sang out: 'No letters, darling!' as I came over to where the beloved woman was lying in the long chair" (*CW*2, 258).

Manuscript (leaf 5)	**Typescript (leaf 5)**
I was wild with joy. I threw the paper up into the air and sang out: 'No letters, darling!' as I came over to where Beatrice was lying in the long chair.	I was wild with joy. I threw the paper up into the air and sang out: 'No letters, darling!' as I came over to where [the beloved woman] was lying in the long chair.

The manuscript merely has him come over to where Beatrice was lying. The change to "the beloved woman", then, shows a purposeful accentuation of his infatuation with her while simultaneously—by stripping her of her name—reduces her to an idea rather than acknowledging her as an individual.

Although the male narrator of Mansfield's story is overly possessive, like the Duke of Browning's poem, he is also as naïve as the Duke is suspicious. Thus, while he makes note of Beatrice's willingness to share her "radiance" with others, unlike the Duke he does not recognize that it probably suggests her promiscuity. With a note of dramatic irony, Mansfield has him exclaim that Beatrice would never poison anyone:

> "You—you do just the opposite. What is the name for one like you who, instead of poisoning people, fills them—everybody, the postman, the man who drives us, our boatman, the flower-seller, me—with new life, with something of her own radiance, her beauty, her—" (*CW*2, 259)

This is, of course, reminiscent of the Duke's more accusatory comments about the duchess, who is, contrasted with Mansfield's Beatrice, most likely innocent:

> She had
> A heart—how shall I say?—too soon made glad,
> Too easily impressed; she liked whate'er
> She looked on, and her looks went everywhere.
> Sir, 'twas all one! My favour at her breast,
> The dropping of the daylight in the West,
> The bough of cherries some officious fool
> Broke in the orchard for her, the white mule
> She rode with round the terrace—all and each
> Would draw from her alike the approving speech,
> Or blush, at least.
> (Browning 1842, ll. 21–31)

Antithetical to the Duke's cynicism, Mansfield's revisions of her own passage suggest that she is emphasizing her male speaker's gullibility. Not only does the narrator seem oblivious to Beatrice's wandering eye, but Mansfield's revisions show that she has him subordinate himself in the list of those with whom she shares herself.

Manuscript (leaf 8)	**Typescript (leaf 7)**
"And you," I said, taking the glass, "you've never poisoned anybody." That gave me an idea; I tried to explain. "You—you do just the opposite. What would be the name for one who like you . . . instead of poisoning people, filled them—not only me—but everybody—the postman, the man who drives us, our boatman, the flower-seller—with new life, with something of your own radiance, your beauty, your—"	"And you," I said, taking the glass, "you've never poisoned anybody." That gave me an idea; I tried to explain. "You—you do just the opposite. [What is the name for one like you who instead] of poisoning people, fill[s] them—/not only me – but\ everybody, the postman, the man who drives us, our boatman, the flower-seller, [me,]—with new life, with something of [her] own radiance, [her] beauty, [her]—"

In the manuscript, Mansfield writes that Beatrice "filled them —not only me—but everybody" with her radiance; the narrator takes the place of prominence. However, by the time the typescript is created, Beatrice "fill[s] them—everybody" and the narrator takes his place at the end of the list, seeming to defer the dominant place to others. The Duke, of course, refuses to share his duchess's glance with anyone. He wants full control. Interestingly, Mansfield also shifts the tense from the manuscript's "filled" to the typescript's "fills". Perhaps this is simply grammatical, but nevertheless such a change places the perspective in the present tense, situating the narrator's desire to prove (to himself as much as to Beatrice) that Beatrice is not one who would poison him in the more immediate present. But Mansfield's shift from "your" to the third person "her" at the end of the passage creates a greater distance from the actual character of Beatrice, making the claim seem more generic, rather than directly tied to Beatrice.

In the biographical context, though, one cannot help but see a portrayal of Mansfield herself in the betrayed narrator. Despite her efforts to remain untouched by Murry's infidelity, she nonetheless must have tasted the bitterness of betrayal, especially in his lack of sensitivity to her illness. She recognized the change in their relationship, the kind of change implied in the figurative dose of poison the man ingests at the end of the story. In a letter to Murry in which she discusses the story shortly after she wrote it, she notes: "The story is told by (evidently) a worldly, rather cynical (not wholly cynical) man *against* himself (but not altogether) when he was so absurdly young" (*Letters* 4, 119, emphasis in original). The same seems to be true of the Mansfield who, having grown more cynical of love after Murry's infidelity, both shores herself up stoically against her abused love but also laments the loss of a more idealized love she appears to have longed for.

Mansfield, though, reverses the circumstances of "My Last Duchess" by empowering Beatrice and thereby exacting her revenge on Murry. Beatrice maintains the upper hand, in essence avenging herself for being objectified, in much the same light that Mansfield steeled herself against Murry's hurtful acts. Beatrice (and Mansfield through her story) makes the first move by—whether literally or figuratively—supplying the male narrator with the first dose of poison. So, while it is easy to vilify Beatrice as a manipulative mistress, we cannot fully blame her for sowing the seeds of discontent in the relationship. The narrator's objectification of her reveals why she would want to escape. But Mansfield seems to want to accentuate Beatrice's callousness by editing out any but the most clearly feigned indications of her feelings for the narrator. Consider the changes Mansfield makes between the manuscript and the typescript at the moment Beatrice sees the postman—the "blue beetle"—approaching the villa:

Manuscript (leaf 4)	**Typescript (leafs 3–4)**
"Dearest!" breathed Beatrice.	"Dearest^,^" breathed Beatrice.
***	***
***	***
"What is it?"	"What is it?"
"I don't know," she laughed softly. "A wave of—a wave of affection."	"I don't know," she laughed softly. "A wave of—a wave of affection[,] |I suppose|."

Mansfield changes the exclamation point of the manuscript to a mere comma, emphasizing Beatrice's breathing and hinting at arousal, the effect of anticipation of the letter from her lover. But it also has the effect of deferring her passion from the narrator as the direct address to him is minimized. More importantly, the addition of "I suppose" deemphasizes her feeling of a "wave of affection". One can presume that she *does* feel this affection, but by qualifying it in this way, she not only deflects suspicion from herself and her anticipation of the letter, but also minimizes the extent to which he might interpret the affection as being evoked by himself. Of course, she allows him to think that he is the cause of the emotional outburst in order to appease him.

In relation to Browning's "My Last Duchess", however, perhaps the most significant changes that Mansfield made in the transition toward a final draft are found in the discussion of the fatal dose of poison.

Manuscript (leaf 6)	**Typescript (leaf 6)**
"It's the exception to find married people who don't poison each other—married people and lovers. Oh," she cried, "the number of cups of tea, glasses of wine, cups of coffee that are just tainted. The number I've had myself, and drunk, either knowing or not knowing—and risked it! The only reason why so many couples"—she laughed—"survive, is because the one is frightened of giving the other the fatal dose. That dose takes nerve … But it's bound to come sooner or later. There's no going back once the first little dose has been given. It's the beginning of the end, really. Don't you agree? Don't you see what I mean?"	"It's the exception to find married people who don't poison each other—married people and lovers. Oh," she cried, "the number of cups of tea, glasses of wine, cups of coffee that are just tainted. The number I've had myself, and drunk, either knowing or not knowing—and risked it[.] The only reason why so many couples"—she laughed—"^survive^,[6] is because the one is frightened of giving the other the fatal dose. That dose takes nerve[!] But it's bound to come sooner or later. There's no going back once the first little dose has been given. It's the beginning of the end, really[—d]on't you agree? Don't you see what I mean?"

One interesting shift is that Mansfield changes the exclamation point after "and risked it". The original punctuation emphasizes the risk that Beatrice has taken in relationships, but in changing this to a period, it appears to reduce the desperation of risking a relationship. A few sentences later, though, she changes the ellipses after "that dose takes nerve" in the manuscript to an exclamation point in the

---

[6] Mansfield underlines "survive" by hand, to ensure the emphasis noted in the manuscript.

typescript. Perhaps Mansfield simply wants to minimize the use of exclamation points and opts to emphasize the fact that administering the fatal dose takes nerve over the fact that she risked relationships. But the weight placed on the phrase the "fatal dose" suggests Mansfield wanted to accentuate Beatrice's own nerve in serving the initial dose to the narrator, that is, what she indicates is "the beginning of the end". And, of course, the Duke of Browning's poem had plenty of nerve to order the final dose. Rather than letting the male take ownership of her, Beatrice strikes first, establishing her independence, and beginning the process of distancing herself from him so that he cannot possess her. Complementing this, Mansfield makes a point of emphasizing "survive" in the transcript, having underscored it by hand—something that is not part of the manuscript. Unlike the duchess, she plans to survive, even if she must make a preemptive strike.

The final change in the passage is the substitution of a period for a dash leading to the question of "don't you agree". This change could be inconsequential, merely creating a more fluid rhythm. What is significant, though, is what precedes it. Beatrice notes that after the first dose is given, there is no turning back; the first dose is the "beginning of the end". The original period followed by the more formal question seems to suggest that the question is less rhetorical and more sincere. However, the creation of an elision implies that she assumes that he would obviously agree. It implies an affirmative response, accentuating the fact that the first dose is, in fact, the beginning of the end. Beatrice has initiated the end of the relationship.

Conclusion

The lack of any drafts of "Poison" beyond the one hand-written manuscript and the typescript found at the Newberry Library means that drawing any conclusions about Mansfield's possible allusions to Browning's "My Last Duchess" in the story must be tentative.[7]

---

[7]   After consulting *Katherine Mansfield: Manuscripts in the Alexander Turnbull Library* (1988) in conjunction with my research at the Newberry Library, I believe these are the only surviving versions of "Poison".

I do think, though, that the text retains enough of the original poem to make a compelling case, and the revisions that Mansfield makes between the extant versions at the very least reveal the shared theme of jealousy enhanced by the generic similarities between the works. In this way, "My Last Duchess" provides a dialogical context from which Mansfield builds her story, what De Biasi calls the "real role" of exogenetics, which can be "seen less as informing the act of writing than as offering it dialogic elements, which give a motivational and heuristic kick-start to the endogenetic process" (46).

An exploration of such dialogical elements provides insights into the writer at work, revealing Mansfield's artistic choices as she attempts to locate herself within the larger modernist enterprise. As I've tried to demonstrate, Mansfield's decision to incorporate elements of the dramatic monologue, of which Browning is one of the foremost practitioners, may have stemmed from her own desire to create a more poetic prose. Further, it suggests her attempt to manoeuvre within the broader modernist context, both in modernists' appropriation of the dramatic monologue and the modern turn toward more empathic readings. Likewise, her allusions to Browning's "My Last Duchess" provide a broader literary context from which to understand her narrator and his lover. To the extent that Mansfield intends to evoke the poem, she makes an artistic choice that, as Damrosch suggests in his notion of refraction, capitalizes on the connections in order to establish a dialogue between the two texts, one that not only adds meaning to her own story, but which also places her within the framework of world literature.

Postcolonial readings of Mansfield which take into account her place as a colonial outsider have revealed much of value both about her life and her work, but the emphasis placed on the aesthetic context of a work promoted by proponents of world literature provides not a replacement, but an alternative method for approaching an author, one that complicates rather than oversimplifies Mansfield's place in the literary economy.

Acknowledgement

Research for this project was completed through the funding of the Lester J. Cappon Fellowship for Documentary Editing, awarded by the Newberry Library, and through release time provided by Huntington University as part of the endowed Edwina Patton Chair. I would like to thank both organizations for their support.

Bibliography

Besnault-Levita, Anne. 2008. "The Dramaturgy of Voice in Five Modernist Short Fictions: Katherine Mansfield's 'The Canary', 'The Lady's Maid' and 'Late at Night', Elizabeth Bowen's 'Oh! Madam...' and Virginia Woolf's 'The Evening Party'." *Journal of the Short Story in English* 51: n.p. http://jsse.revues.org/909.

Browning, Robert. 1842. "My Last Duchess." Poetry Foundation. Accessed February 26, 2017. https://www.poetryfoundation.org/poems-andpoets/poems/detail/43768.

Byron, Glennis. 2003. *Dramatic Monologue*. London and New York: Routledge.

Casanova, Pascale. 2004. *The World Republic of Letters*. Cambridge and London: Harvard University Press.

Damrosch, David. 2009. *How to Read World Literature*. Chichester, West Sussex: Wiley-Blackwell.

De Biasi, Pierre-Marc. 1996. "What is a Literary Draft? Toward a Functional Typology of Genetic Documentation." Translated by Ingrid Wassenaar. *Yale French Studies* 89: 26–58.

Friedland, Louis S. 1936. "Ferrara and 'My Last Duchess'." *Studies in Philology* 33 (4): 656–84.

Hammond, Meghan Marie. 2014. *Empathy and the Psychology of Literary Modernism*. Edinburgh: Edinburgh University Press.

Hankin, Cherry A., ed. 1991. *Letters between Katherine Mansfield and John Middleton Murry*. New York: New Amsterdam Books.

Hiddleston, Jane. 2016. "Writing World Literature: Approaches from the Maghreb." *PMLA* 131 (5): 1386–95.

Kaplan, Sydney Janet. 1991. *Katherine Mansfield and the Origins of Modernist Fiction*. Ithaca, NY and London: Cornell University Press.

Katherine Mansfield: Manuscripts in the Alexander Turnbull Library. 1988. Wellington: Alexander Turnbull Library.

Kimber, Gerri. 2015. *Katherine Mansfield and the Art of the Short Story*. Basingstoke: Palgrave Macmillan.

Mansfield, Katherine. 1920a. "Poison [Manuscript]." Katherine Mansfield Papers (Box 1, folder 8), The Newberry Library: 8 leaves.

---. 1920b. "Poison [Typescript]." Katherine Mansfield Papers (Box 1, folder 9), The Newberry Library: 8 leaves.

Martin, Todd. 2013. "'Unmasking' the First-Person Narrator of *In a German Pension*." In *Katherine Mansfield and the (Post)colonial*, edited by Janet Wilson, Gerri Kimber and Delia da Sousa Correa, 76–86. Edinburgh: Edinburgh University Press.

Meyers, Jeffrey. [1978] 2002. *Katherine Mansfield: A Darker View*. New York: Cooper Square Press.

Sankar, S. 2016. "Literatures of the World: An Inquiry." *PMLA* 131 (5): 1405–13.

Wilde, Oscar. [1914] 2005. *Selected Prose of Oscar Wilde*, edited by Robert Ross. Urbana, IL: Project Gutenberg. Accessed May 2, 2017. http://www.gutenberg.org/files/1338/1338-h/1338-h.htm.

Young, Robert J. C. 2013. "World Literature and Postcolonialism." In *The Routledge Companion to World Literature*, edited by Theo D'haen, David Damrosch and Djelal Kadir, 213–23. Abingdon and New York: Routledge.

Katherine Mansfield: Homeostasis, Equanimity, and Fiction

Erika Baldt

Introduction: Mansfield and Mysticism

The first page of the August 1912 issue of *Rhythm*, following the table of contents, consists of an advertisement for Heal and Son of London featuring an illustration by Henri Gaudier-Brzeska (Binkes 2010, 154) with the words, "'A splendid bed, well covered around with a tent and adorned with a canopy'—THE MAHAVAMSA" (1). The text in question is known as *The Great Chronicle of Ceylon* and was published in London for the Pali Text Society in the same year the issue appeared. The *Chronicle* is 37 chapters long and describes the origins of Sri Lanka, beginning with the premise that "our Conqueror resolved to become a Buddha, that he might release the world from evil" (Geiger 1912, 1), a requirement of which is the renunciation of all desires. The very first words of the text, however, deal not with the content of the book, but with its form, stating:

> I will recite the Mahāvaṃsa, of varied content and lacking nothing. That (Mahāvaṃsa) which was compiled by the ancient (sages) was here too long drawn out and there too closely knit; and contained many repetitions. Attend ye now to this (Mahāvaṃsa) that is free from such faults, easy to understand and remember, arousing serene joy and emotion and handed down (to us) by tradition (attend ye to it) while that ye call up serene joy and emotion (in you) at passages that awaken serene joy and emotion. (1)

The speaker claims to have perfected the work of the sages by creating a text that is easily accessible to its audience on both a rational and an emotional level. Each chapter ends with the same claim that it was "compiled for the serene joy and emotion of the pious"

(Geiger 1912, 9). The *Chronicle* thus combines two perhaps conflicting ideas: the pleasure of earthly pursuits such as reading or listening to poetry and that of the renunciation of such pleasures in the pursuit of enlightenment.

Katherine Mansfield was of course the assistant editor of *Rhythm* at the time of the advertisement, which actually featured in two subsequent issues of the magazine. She and John Middleton Murry were also, according to Antony Alpers (1982), on intimate terms with Gaudier-Brzeska in 1912, so she would no doubt have been familiar with the advertisement, if not the text quoted in it (148–50). Yet unlike some of her peers, or even her husband, Mansfield never expressed interest in ancient texts such as these, later preferring instead the Russian path of Gurdjieff. However, many of the ideas expressed in *The Mahāvaṃsa* were already becoming part of popular culture during the years of *Rhythm*'s publication. As Julie Kane (1995) notes, "Eastern religious ideas continued to filter into Western consciousness throughout the early decades of the twentieth century" (331), and people like Pound, Eliot, and Woolf were toying with what was called "mysticism" (330). While Mansfield and Murry had many conversations on the subject, the meaning of the word itself remained unclear. In a letter written on the last day of 1922, only days before Mansfield's death, Murry (1983) attempted to articulate the ideas he had received from J.D. Beresford, telling Mansfield:

> He gave me a definition of the difference between mysticism & occultism: mysticism is an effort to get beyond the self and to come to union with a higher, outer reality: occultism is an attempt to penetrate into the self, inwardly, and involves a withdrawal & isolation from human life. (368)

Murry then stated, "Well, that didn't convince me at all", but he did go on to provide his own interpretation, suggesting that "a true penetration of the self, a true realisation is quite essential to mysticism" (368). Mansfield was never able to respond to Murry's comments. While hard and fast definitions such as these were never easy for Mansfield to support, the idea of "get[ting] beyond the self" was one she fully embraced, especially towards the end of her life. However, the path to such equanimity was fraught, as, I will argue, her stories show.

In order to understand Mansfield's relationship to "mysticism", we must first understand the ideas that were swirling about London at the time. Not all of them were given that title but all involved the concept that Murry describes of a "true realization" of the self. In 1894 Bertrand Russell (1999) wrote, "Our duty will consist in self-realization, but self-realization may of course be best attained by what is commonly called self-sacrifice" (56), and in 1896 Swami Vivekananda, one of those whom Kane identifies as bringing "Eastern religious ideas" (1995, 331) to the West, gave a lecture in London entitled "Practical Vedanta" in which he spoke of the "ideal", "the first step towards which is to give up selfishness, to give up self-enjoyment" (Vivekananda 2011, 238). Both are describing what the *Bhagavad Gita* refers to as an equanimity "with neither craving nor aversion", resulting in the attainment of "serenity at last" (2000, 58). One of the main tenets of Vedanta, a philosophy that encompasses ancient Hindu scriptures and other texts like the *Bhagavad Gita*, is that

> the purpose of life is to discover this Self within ourselves and realize its identity with Brahman, the transcendent Godhead. That is to say, the only logical goal in life is the discovery of our true nature, the knowledge of *who we really are*. (Johnson 2011, 22)

Such discoveries were not easily made, however, and Vivekananda identifies "two tendencies in human nature: one to reconcile the ideal with life and the other to elevate life to the ideal" (2011, 238). The first path is easier; the second requires more conscious effort.

Bergson ([1889] 2001), too, writes of these two tendencies in *Time and Free Will*. He claims that our consciousness has "an insatiable desire to separate", because such a state is more convenient: "as the self thus refracted, and thereby broken to pieces, is much better adapted to the requirements of social life in general and language in particular, consciousness prefers it, and gradually loses sight of the fundamental self" (128). Here again is the notion that there is one "true" or "fundamental" self that can and should be accessed, but, as Bergson goes on to say, it requires "a vigorous effort of analysis" (129). While it is unclear whether the Vedanta was known to Mansfield, Angela Smith (2003) notes that Bergson's ideas were "particularly significant for the *Rhythm* group" (106), so Mansfield would have been familiar with these concepts of the self.

The main issue for Mansfield, though, was the tension between the "two tendencies" that Vivekananda identifies. Referring to Polonius's "most sly, ambiguous, difficult piece of advice" in *Hamlet*, "to thine own self be true" (Mansfield 2002, 203), Mansfield exclaims with exasperation, "True to oneself! Which self? Which of my many— well, really, that's what it looks like coming to—hundreds of selves" (204). The quote is now one of Mansfield's most famous. What is mentioned less often, however, is the conclusion of that journal entry in which Mansfield juxtaposes the image of the frantic hotel clerk handing "the keys to the wilful guests" with an image that could be straight out of Bergson or even the *Bhagavad Gita* of a "free, disentangled, single" self:

> a self which is continuous and permanent, which, untouched by all we acquire and all we shed, pushes a green spear through the leaves and through the mould, thrusts a sealed bud through years of darkness until, one day, the light discovers it and shakes the flower free and—we are alive—we are flowering for our moment upon the earth. This is the moment which, after all, we live for, the moment of direct feeling when we are most ourselves and least personal. (*Notebooks* 2, 204)

According to Vedanta, "the highest center of spiritual consciousness" is represented by "the thousand-petaled lotus", and the goal of yoga and meditation is to reach this center in order for the individual to "[realize] his unity with Brahman", or the highest self (Johnson 2011, 49). While it is unlikely that Mansfield was consciously referencing those beliefs, the parallels remain, and, in fact, the image is not unlike the words of Mansfield's epitaph inscribed on the headstone of her grave—Hotspur's claim in *Henry IV, Part I* that "out of this nettle, danger, we pluck this flower, safety" (Alpers 1982, 385).

It is here, though, that one must make the distinction between Mansfield's inner world and her physical body, for no discussion of equanimity would be complete without reference to the physical conditions that required the selection of said epitaph for a woman of only 34 years of age. Though "mysticism" suggested that the pains of the body can be overcome by conscious effort, scientific developments at the turn of the 20th century were beginning to provide evidence to the contrary. While the word "equanimity" was derived from a Latin compound meaning equal mind,[1] another term was just coming into existence at around the time of Mansfield's illness that describes a similar, though unconscious, balancing in the body: homeostasis. Coined by Walter B. Cannon in 1926 (Brown and Fee 2002, 1595), the term was intended to describe

> that characteristic of an organism, notably a human or other animal body, according to which the organism maintains its own integrity and restores its own normal pattern of functioning, by means of internal readjustments, whenever it suffers a disturbance that is not fatal. For instance, homeostasis labels the process, and also the results of the process, by which the body-temperature is brought back to normal after over-heating or chill. (Joos 1962, 18)

With these processes, the body is able to adjust and readjust itself automatically. Cannon explained the rationale behind the etymology:

---

[1] See the definition of "equanimity" in *Oxford Living Dictionaries*: "from Latin aequanimitas, from aequus equal + animus mind".

Objection might be offered to the use of the term *stasis*, as implying something set and immobile, a stagnation. Stasis means, however, not only that, but also a condition; it is in this sense that the term is employed. *Homeo*, the abbreviated form of *homoio*, is prefixed instead of *homo*, because the former indicates "like" or "similar" and admits some variation, whereas the latter, meaning the "same," indicates a fixed and rigid constancy. (1929, 400–01)

While equanimity is an abstract notion referring literally to the mind but metaphorically to the inner self or spirit, homeostasis, is, as Cannon notes, a "condition" maintained without intervention by the intellect. It is, however, a condition of an optimally functioning body. Mansfield's tuberculosis, as well as her other conditions like arthritis and pleurisy, noted by Angela Smith (2000) as complications arising from a 1910 operation (51), meant that Mansfield would have most likely suffered from chronic pain, the effect of which makes both equanimity and homeostasis nearly impossible: "chronic pain, given its multidimensional nature, simultaneously affects multiple physiological systems, diminishes reserves, and decreases the ability to maintain homeostasis" (Shega et al. 2012, 115). Thus another strand is added to the "two tendencies" already identified. Along with controlling the mind in order to penetrate the self, Mansfield also needed to control or overcome the body, and her stories reflect an ambivalent engagement with the ideas of both equanimity and what would come to be known as homeostasis. For though she herself knew that what she wanted was that moment of being "least personal" and eventually that single "real" life she described, her fiction demonstrates the difficulty of divorcing the body from the mind, the mind from "all we acquire and all we shed" (*Notebooks* 2, 204).

Homeostasis: Mansfield's Irregular Regulation

Again, though the term "homeostasis" did not exist during Mansfield's lifetime, the ideas behind it did. In 1878, Claude Bernard (1885) described the processes by which birds such as condors maintain adequate oxygen levels in their blood despite flying at extremely high altitudes. He claimed that "all of life's mechanisms, however varied they may be, have always only one goal, that of maintaining the internal conditions necessary for life" (121–22).[2] Charles Richet (1900) then stated in the *Dictionnaire de Physiologie* that "life is a perpetual auto-regulation, an adaptation to changing exterior conditions" (721).[3] With her frequent consultation of doctors all over Europe, it is not only possible but likely that Mansfield was familiar with these concepts, especially considering that so much research was being done on lung function, of particular interest to a patient with tuberculosis. Regardless of whether she could claim any scientific knowledge, however, Mansfield's later fiction demonstrates concern for the body's [in]ability to regulate itself when threatened from without, made manifest through a preoccupation with poison.

The references to poison, either literal or metaphorical, are numerous in Mansfield's later work, and they speak to these contemporary concerns with physical balance. "A Married Man's Story", unfinished at the time of Mansfield's death, explores an unnamed narrator's relationship with his wife, the souring of which he suggests is related to his father's alleged poisoning of his mother. Indeed, the narrator's development is marked by the moment he believes his mother revealed to him the cause of her death:

> Did that visit happen? Was it a dream? Why did she come to tell me? Or why, if she came, did she go away so quickly? And her expression—so joyous under the frightened look—was that real? I believed it fully the afternoon of the funeral, when I saw my father dressed up for his part, hat and all. That tall hat so gleaming black and round was like a cork covered with black sealing-wax, and the rest of my father

---

[2] My translation. See the original text: "tous les mécanismes vitaux, quelque variés qu'ils soient, n'ont toujours qu'un but, celui de maintenir l'unité des conditions de la vie dans le milieu intérieur".

[3] My translation. See the original text: "La vie est une auto-régulation perpétuelle, une adaptation aux conditions extérieures changeantes".

was awfully like a bottle, with his face for the label—*Deadly Poison*. It flashed into my mind as I stood opposite him in the hall. And Deadly Poison, or old D.P., was my private name for him from that day. (*CW*2, 388)

The nonchalance with which the narrator comes to identify his own father for ever after with "deadly poison", as well as his perception of his mother's "joyous" expression upon exposing her husband's crime, suggests an abject fascination with the body's failure to "maintain its own integrity", in Joos's words (1962, 18). When the narrator finally, explicitly connects the event with his own life, it is in terms of giving in to this failure, of allowing himself to be overrun by stimuli:

"Who am I?" I thought? "What is all this?" And I looked at my room, at the broken bust of the man called Hahnemann on top of the cupboard, at my little bed with the pillow like an envelope. I saw it all, but not as I had seen before.... Everything lived, but everything. But that was not all. I was equally alive and—it's the only way I can express it—the barriers were down between us—I had come into my own world! (*CW*2, 390)

The broken bust of Hahnemann gives a clue as to how the narrator feels himself immune to the "auto-regulation" Richet identified. An 18th-century doctor considered the founder of homeopathy, Hahnemann, like the narrator's father, "was also an expert in chemistry", and

he was familiar with many of the symptoms caused by toxic agents and aware of the fact that a number of naturally occurring diseases closely resemble symptoms owing to intoxication: e.g. the intoxication induced by Belladonna resembles scarlet fever; that induced by quinine resembles malaria; and that induced by arsenic resembles cholera. It did not take him long to combine the idea of the replacement of similar diseases with that of the replacement induced by "artificial" intoxication: for example, he tried to use low doses of Belladonna to treat patients with scarlet fever and of arsenic to treat cholera. He intuitively understood that it was possible to discover specific remedies for a number of diseases, and therefore sought other potentially advantageous drugs and tested their "pathogenetic" power in healthy volunteers. (Bellavite et al. 2005, 445)

While Hahnemann's method relied on the belief that the body could regulate, if not cure, itself with the introduction of small amounts of poison, the narrator's distorted perception interprets the introduction of toxic elements as a way to remove boundaries, to destroy balance. His claim that "the barriers were down" suggests his sudden vitality and feeling of control over his life is actually a result of surrendering to the imbalance: "I love, I love this strange feeling of drifting—whither?" (*CW2*, 389).

The young nameless narrator of 1920's "Poison" faces a similar fate at the hands of his older lover, Beatrice, who claims that she herself has been poisoned by her previous two husbands, to that of the mother in "A Married Man's Story". As in "A Married Man's Story", "Poison" is full of references to poison and death from the lily of the valley, a toxic plant (Foster and Duke 2014, 18–19) that Beatrice wears and later actually bites (Mansfield 1920b, 259), to the figure of the postman as a beetle (257), which, in traditional superstition is a harbinger of death. Yet according to the narrator, Beatrice herself is a panacea:

> You—you do just the opposite. What is the name for one like you who, instead of poisoning people, fills them—everybody, the postman, the man who drives us, our boatman, the flower-seller, me—with new life, with something of her own radiance, her beauty, her—. (*CW2*, 259)

Though his words would suggest the narrator is being overwhelmed—that like the narrator of "A Married Man's Story", "the barriers were down between [them]" (*CW2*, 390)—they actually mimic a homeostatic process. Cannon identified one of the ways by which homeostasis is maintained as "storage by inundation", explaining "the analogy implied in this phrase is that of a bog or swamp into which water soaks when the supply is bountiful and from which the water seeps back into the distributing system when the supply is meager" (1929, 403). It is as if Beatrice's "radiance" is building up the narrator's reserves. However, as C. K. Stead (2015) notes of the story, "the account is essentially ironic" (245), and it becomes clear that those reserves have been metaphorically tainted. Discussing a "poison trial" featured in the newspaper Beatrice declares:

> "Haven't you ever thought"—she was pale with excitement—"of the amount of poisoning that goes on: It's the exception to find married people who don't poison each other—married people and lovers. Oh," she cried, "the number of cups of tea, glasses of wine, cups of coffee that are just tainted. The number I've had myself, and drunk, either knowing or not knowing—and risked it. The only reason why so many couples"—she laughed—"*survive*, is because the one is frightened of giving the other the fatal dose." (*CW2*, 258–59)

Her suggestion is that no one is safe from the threat of literal poisoning, but that the ubiquity of the toxins almost allows the victim to build up an immunity until the "fatal dose" is delivered and tips the balance. It is clear, however, that the young narrator has not yet developed such an immunity and has only just been exposed to "the first little dose" of Beatrice's poison. Unlike the narrator of "A Married Man's Story", who knowingly subjects himself to toxic elements, the narrator of "Poison" remains unaware of the disturbances from without that threaten to compromise his inner balance.

One of the more ambiguous symbols in the story that supports the narrator's misperception of events is the cigarette he smokes. While today it would be classified as another type of poison, in the story it becomes a sort of prop:

> There are times when a cigarette is just the very one thing that will carry you over the moment. It is more than a confederate, even; it is a secret, perfect little friend who knows all about it and understands absolutely. While you smoke you look down at it—smile or frown, as the occasion demands; you inhale deeply and expel the smoke in a slow fan. This was one of those moments. (*CW*2, 258)

The narrator sees the act of smoking as cathartic, which only adds to the irony of the story, for while he can "expel" the smoke from his lungs, he cannot rid himself of Beatrice's influence. A similar image appears in "At the Bay" as an indication of the metaphorical poisoning of Beryl Fairfield. One of the main strands of that story is Beryl's association with the Kembers. While she is infatuated with the handsome husband, she develops a more complicated relationship with Mrs. Harry Kember, whose notable attribute is her smoking:

> She was the only woman at the Bay who smoked, and she smoked incessantly, keeping the cigarette between her lips while she talked, and only taking it out when the ash was so long you could not understand why it did not fall. When she was not playing bridge—she played bridge every day of her life—she spent her time lying in the full glare of the sun. She could stand any amount of it; she never had enough. All the same, it did not seem to warm her. Parched, withered, cold, she lay stretched on the stones like a piece of tossed-up driftwood. (*CW*2, 351–52)

Mansfield here could be describing a case study in the failure of autoregulation. As noted above, one of the simplest examples of homeostasis in the human body is the regulation of temperature. Mrs. Harry Kember is not only unable to maintain her temperature despite excessive exposure to the sun, she is unable to retain moisture regardless of daily bathing in the sea. Yet it is not Mrs. Kember who suffers from this inability to maintain balance in either her life or her physical body, it is Beryl:

> suddenly [Mrs. Kember] turned turtle, disappeared, and swam away quickly, quickly, like a rat. Then she flicked round and began swimming back. She was going to say something else. Beryl felt that she was being poisoned by this cold woman, but she longed to hear. (*CW*2, 353)

As in "Poison" and "A Married Man's Story", the young, healthy person is threatened by those who have no control over their own bodies and therefore have nothing to lose; not only that, but just like the narrator of "Poison", or the mother of the narrator of "A Married Man's Story", Beryl is powerless to resist. The body's automatic response fails in spite of the demands of the rational mind, a situation with which Mansfield herself was all too familiar.

Yet while the stories themselves deal with the characters' lack of control, the form of all three belies the content. C.K. Stead praises the precision of "Poison", claiming it is a "beautifully written" story (2015, 245), and he also argues that "A Married Man's Story" is "a gripping and impressive fictional exercise" (1981, 45). Both stories, as well, see the characters attempting to restore order by putting their experiences into writing. "A Married Man's Story" is ostensibly the journal or diary of the narrator: "To live like this. . . . I write those words, very carefully, very beautifully. [. . .] isn't it staggering to think what may be contained in one innocent-looking little phrase? It tempts me—it tempts me terribly" (*CW*2, 382). It is as if the words provide the barriers lacking in the narrator's life, allowing all of his problematic temptations to be "contained". Meanwhile, "Poison" features not the narrator's but Beatrice's attempts to put the scene into words: "The Luncheon Table. Short story by—by—" (*CW*2, 256). Less successful or artful than the narrator of "A Married Man's Story", Beatrice and her imagined composition—specifically a short story—nevertheless are a reflection of what the narrator refers to as her "exquisite sense of order" (*CW*2, 255) that distracts him from her poisonous ways. "At the Bay", however, is the most interesting in that it mimics the lack of balance felt by its characters. Unlike its predecessors "Prelude" (1917) or "The Daughters of the Late Colonel" (1920), both of which comprise 12 sections of roughly similar length, "At the Bay" is divided into 13 parts, with the last consisting of only four sentences:

> A cloud, small, serene, floated across the moon. In that moment of darkness the sea sounded deep, troubled. Then the cloud sailed away, and the sound of the sea was a vague murmur, as though it waked out of a dark dream. All was still. (*CW*2, 371)

Beryl's "poisoning" by the Kembers is reflected in the environment as well as in the form of the story: Mansfield made the conscious decision to separate this part of the text from the rest for the American edition of *The Garden Party and Other Stories* (*CW*2, 372 n. 5), and the change suggests that she purposely distorted the symmetry of the earlier version.

Having this kind of control over a fictional world acted (almost) as an antidote for Mansfield's own pain and illness, just as it did for her characters, although she herself noted that the absence of physical stability as her condition worsened became both the impetus for and the result of periods of successful writing. In a letter to Dorothy Brett from Switzerland in August 1921, she describes her condition:

> The Furies have had me until today. Something quite new for a change—high fever, deadly sickness and weakness. I haven't been able to lift my head from the pillow. I think it has been a breakdown from too much work. I have felt exhausted with all those stories lately & yet—couldn't stop. (*Letters* 4, 269)

The stories to which she refers are "At the Bay" and "A Married Man's Story", and while the writing decimated her reserves, Mansfield nonetheless ends the paragraph with "but Heavens Brett— Life is so marvellous" (269). For Mansfield, like the speaker of *The Mahāvaṃsa*, if the form can give pleasure, then "serene joy and emotion" may follow, for both the reader and the writer. With a short story, there is more room for other voices, other selves, which was an important outlet for Mansfield, who, even until the end of her life, was unable to articulate a definitive answer to the question "*Who am I?*" (*Letters* 5, 340, original italics). As she noted in a letter to Murry of 26 December 1922:

> until that is discovered I don't see how one can really direct anything in ones self. "*Is there a Me.*" One must be certain of that before one has a real unshakeable leg to stand on. And I don't believe for one moment these questions can be settled by the head alone. It is this life of the *head*, this formative intellectual life at the expense of all the rest of us which has got us into this state. (*Letters* 5, 340–41, original italics)

Here Mansfield is moving not only from questions of homeostasis and the maintenance of physical balance, but to those of equanimity, the answers to which cannot be determined by either the physical being or the "intellectual life". The self or, as she argued, the *selves* must be accessed in a different way.

Towards Equanimity

The ability to slough off one of her selves and take on another was key to both the content and form of Mansfield's writing. In "A Cup of Tea", for example, the first introduction to the protagonist Rosemary Fell is an attempt to describe her, which can only be done, it seems, "if you took her to pieces" (*CW2*, 461). The rest of the story is about Rosemary attempting to unify those pieces through the single unselfish act of offering assistance to a Miss Smith, a "little battered creature" (463). Her motives are questionable—the "thrilling" (463) idea of taking the girl home is the result of disappointment at not being able to buy a small, expensive box that leaves her feeling that "there are moments, horrible moments in life, when one emerges from shelter and looks out, and it's awful. One oughtn't to give way to them. One ought to go home and have an extra-special tea" (462). Importantly, Rosemary does not feel hunger—her desire for "an extra-special tea" is not rooted in a biological urge to maintain homeostasis[4]—in serving the girl she is serving herself. It does, however, give her a purpose she had not previously had in her aimless, pampered existence, a purpose which disintegrates almost as quickly as it is formed when her husband sees the poor Miss Smith. His compliments break Rosemary to pieces again: "Pretty! Absolutely lovely! Bowled over! Her heart beat like a heavy bell. Pretty! Lovely!" (466). Her husband's words become part of her consciousness as she repeats over and over inside her own head the phrases he used to describe the other woman. At the end, of course, she reverts to her original state, playing up her "dazzled exotic gaze" (467) and asking for the box that had originally inspired the endeavor. The story illustrates Bergson's notion of "the self refracted" and the difficulty, if not impossibility, of balancing the mind.

A similar effect occurs in "The Stranger", but, this time from the husband's perspective. Hammond has been without his wife for nearly a year, and her arrival is further delayed even while he stands on the wharf to collect her. Once she arrives, his mind is settled: "She was here to look after things. It was all right. Everything was" (*CW2*, 245). After the strain of the wait, the sight of his wife restores Hammond's equanimity, but the feeling is short lived:

> Hammond never knew—never knew for dead certain that she was as glad as he was. How could he know? Would he ever know? Would he always have this craving—this pang

---

[4] According to Cannon (1929), "Hunger is characterized by highly disagreeable pangs which result from strong contractions of the empty stomach" (417), a state which may apply to Miss Smith but not to Rosemary herself.

like hunger, somehow, to make Janey so much part of him that there wasn't any of her to escape? He wanted to blot out everybody, everything. (247)

As with Rosemary, the feeling of imbalance is described *"like hunger"*, but one no "extra-special tea" could sate. The word "craving" is also used in the *Bhagavad Gita* to refer to that which must be eliminated for the achievement of serenity. The other essential is lack of aversion, which Hammond too finds impossible. Upon learning that his wife's delay was caused by another passenger dying in her arms, "he had to hide his face" as he comes to the realization that the dead man will always be haunting their time together, and "they would never be alone together again" (*CW2*, 249). Hammond's sense of self is so dependent on his wife that an event he has no part in, a man he has never and will never meet, can destroy whatever equanimity he may have had.

For Mansfield's own part, however, Hammond's loss is her gain. In describing—becoming—the character and his loss, she restored balance within herself. Writing about the composition of the story to Murry on November 3 1920, seemingly immediately upon its completion, she claims,

> Here it is under my hand—finished [. . .] My depression has gone, Boge, so it was just this. And now its here—thank God. [. . .] What a QUEER business writing is. I don't know. I dont [sic] believe other people are ever as foolishly excited as I am while Im working. [. . .] Ive *been* this man *been* this woman. Ive stood for hours on the Auckland Wharf. Ive been out in the stream waiting to be berthed. Ive been a seagull hovering at the stern and a hotel porter whistling through his teeth. It isn't as though one sits and watches the spectacle. That would be thrilling enough, God knows. But one IS the spectacle for the time. If one remained oneself all the time like some writers can it would be a bit less exhausting. It's a

lightning change affair, tho. But what does it matter.
(*Letters* 4, 97, original italics)

It is almost as if in separating herself—not only by occupying the minds of Hammond and his wife but those of inanimate objects as well—Mansfield is able to exorcise whatever demons were plaguing her. She acknowledges that it is not what others do, and, indeed, her process seems to be the exact opposite of renunciation of craving or aversion; but, as she says, "what does it matter"? Here it seems that Mansfield has found a way to be "least personal" (*Notebooks* 2, 204), and it comes not from controlling her bodily health or reaching the thousand-petaled lotus, but through writing. According to Angela Smith (2000), "If such a moment occurs, the *personal*, obsessive self-analysis and self-consciousness, will be irrelevant as a harmony of mind and spirit will be achieved" (142, italics in original). Inward balance or "harmony" can only be achieved by allowing the self to simply *be*, without external influences or internal scrutiny. Though the work describes the seeming impossibility of achieving such enlightenment while one's self is subject to the opinions and actions of others, as are Rosemary's and Hammond's, the stories themselves "awaken serene joy and emotion" that, for Mansfield at least, was a way of accessing that fundamental unity.

While writing provided Mansfield with a way to balance the two sides of the mind, the attachment and aversion, a physical balance continued to remain elusive. Whether considered spiritually or scientifically, Mansfield's ability to achieve what she always sought—what the *Bhagavad Gita* calls "serenity at last"—was severely limited by pain and illness. Yet Mansfield was the first to articulate these limitations in a letter to Murry in October 1920:

> And then suffering—bodily suffering such as Ive known [...]. It has changed forever everything—even the *appearance* of the world is not the same—there is something added. *Everything has its shadow.* Is it right to resist such suffering? Do

you know I feel it has been an immense privilege. Yes, in spite of it all. (*Letters* 4, 75)

Even as the suffering itself seems to put her further from a place of physical balance, it allows her the "privilege" of seeing in a new way, of writing in a new way. Just as *The Mahāvaṃsa* describes those "who have overcome darkness with the light of insight" (Geiger 1912, 18), Mansfield was able to turn the "shadow" into her own kind of "self-realization".

Bibliography

Alpers, Antony. [1980] 1982. *The Life of Katherine Mansfield*. Oxford: Oxford University Press.

Bellavite P., A. Conforti, V. Piasere, & R. Ortolan. 2005. "Immunology and Homeopathy. 1. Historical Background." *Evidence-Based Complementary and Alternative Medicine* 2 (4): 441–52. http://doi.org/10.1093/ecam/neh141.

Bergson, Henri. [1889] 2001. *Time and Free Will*. Translated by F.L. Pogson. Mineola, NY: Dover.

Bernard, Claude. [1878] 1885. *Leçons sur les phénomènes de la vie, communs aux animaux et aux végétaux*. Paris: J.-B. Baillière et fils. http://gallica.bnf.fr/ark:/12148/bpt6k62986637/.

Bhagavad Gita. 2000. Translated by Stephen Mitchell. New York: Three Rivers Press.

Binkes, Faith. 2010. *Modernism, Magazines, and the British Avant-Garde: Reading Rhythm 1910–1914*. Oxford: Oxford University Press.

Brown, Theodore M. and Elizabeth Fee. 2002. "Walter Bradford Cannon: Pioneer Physiologist of Human Emotions." *American Journal of Public Health* 92 (10): 1594–595. https://www.ncbi.nlm.nih.gov/pmc/articles/PMC1447286/pdf/0921594.pdf.

Cannon, Walter B. 1929. "Organization for Physiological Homeostasis." *Physiological Reviews* 9 (3): 399–431.

Foster, Steven and James A. Duke. 2014. "Lily-of-the-Valley." In *Peterson Field Guide to Medicinal Plants and Herbs of Eastern and Central North America*, 18–19. Boston: Houghton Mifflin Harcourt.

Gaudier-Brzeska, Henri. 1912. Advertisement for Heal & Son. *Rhythm* 2 (7–9): 1.

Hankin, C.A., ed. 1983. *The Letters of John Middleton Murry to Katherine Mansfield*. New York: Franklin Watts.

Johnson, Cliff, ed. [1971] 2011. "What is Vedanta?" *Vedanta: An Anthology of Hindu Scripture, Commentary, and Poetry*, 17–24. Studio City, CA: InnerQuest Publishing.

Joos, Martin. 1962. "Homeostasis in English Usage." *College Composition and Communication* 13 (3): 18–22.

Kane, Julie. 1995. "Varieties of Mystical Experience in the Writings of Virginia Woolf." *Twentieth Century Literature* 41 (4): 328–49.

Oxford Living Dictionaries. 2017. "Equanimity." Oxford University Press. https://en.oxforddictionaries.com/definition/equanimity

Richet, Charles. 1900. "Défense (Fonctions de)." In *Dictionnaire de Physiologie* 4: 699–721. Paris: Félix Alcan. https://archive.org/stream/dictionnairedeph04rich#page/720/mode/2up.

Russell, Bertrand. 1999. "Ethical Axioms." In *Russell on Ethics: Selections from the Writings of Bertrand Russell*, edited by Charles R. Pigden, 53–56. New York: Routledge.

Shega, Joseph W., et al. 2012. "Persistent Pain and Frailty: A Case for Homeostenosis." *Journal of the American Geriatrics Society* 60 (1): 113–17.

Smith, Angela. 2000. *Katherine Mansfield: A Literary Life*. Basingstoke: Palgrave.

———. 2003. "Katherine Mansfield and *Rhythm*." *Journal of New Zealand Literature* 21: 102–21.

Stead, C.K. [1977] 1981. "Katherine Mansfield: The Art of the 'Fiction." In *In the Glass Case: Essays on New Zealand Literature*, 29–46. Auckland: Auckland University Press.

———. 2015. "Katherine Mansfield and the Fictions of Continental Europe." In *Katherine Mansfield and Continental Europe*, edited by

Janka Kaščáková and Gerri Kimber, 236–51. Basingstoke: Palgrave Macmillan.

The Mahāvaṃsa, or The Great Chronicle of Ceylon. 1912. Translated by Wilhelm Geiger, assisted by Mabel Haynes Bode. Oxford: Oxford University Press.

Vivekananda, Swami. 2011. "Excerpt from 'Practical Vedanta: I'." In *Vedanta: An Anthology of Hindu Scripture, Commentary, and Poetry*, edited by Cliff Johnson, 238–42. Studio City, CA: InnerQuest Publishing.

Fairy Stories and War

Katherine Mansfield, Fairy Tales and Fir Trees: "the story is past too: past! past!—that's the way with all stories"

Gerri Kimber

As a child, Katherine Mansfield was an avid reader of fairy tales. Her childhood friend Marion Ruddick (1928) recorded:

> We read and re-read Grimms and Hans Andersen's fairy tales, The Princess and the Goblins, Alice in Wonderland of course, and a book we liked very much called Christmas Tree Land. It was a German fairy tale about two children who, when visiting their grandmother in her German castle went daily accompanied by their nurse to a fir wood on a nearby hill; there while the nurse was overcome by sleep, the children entered a door in one of the trees and day after day had the most wonderful adventures. (24)

Mrs Molesworth's *Christmas-Tree Land* (1884)

Mrs Molesworth's (1981) enormously popular children's book, *Christmas-Tree Land*, beautifully illustrated by Walter Crane, was first published in 1884. Didactic in tone, its fantasy element nevertheless thrilled young readers—as it clearly did Mansfield and Marion—who revelled in the fairy-tale adventures of its brother and sister protagonists, Rollo and Maia. Following the death of their mother, Rollo and Maia are sent away to live in the castle of their relative, Lady Venelda, since their father, who spends long periods away from home, is unable to take care of them. The pine forest in which the castle is situated is the most dominant feature of the book: "And far as the eye could reach stretched away into the distance, miles and miles and miles, here rising, there again sweeping downwards, the everlasting Christmas-trees!" (189). Maia and Rollo spend many happy hours exploring the forest, where they meet Silva and Waldo, fairy forest children who live in an isolated cottage, and Godmother, a divinely beautiful wise woman, who seems both old and young, and who leads them on various adventures, tells them stories, and finally allows them a visionary glimpse of Santa Claus's garden of Christmas trees. In discussing this vision, Anita Moss (1988) notes, "Of particular interest is the powerful extent to which [Mrs Molesworth] enlists the dream vision to subvert the constraints of the moral tale so prevalent in Victorian children's literature" (106). Mansfield seemingly never forgot this book; though none of her extant writings mentions it specifically (as was the case with almost everything she read as a child), nevertheless, its influence can be perceived in a number of her stories. Seared into her memory was Mrs Molesworth's many descriptions of those pine trees, whose antipodean counterparts, of course, are prevalent in the New Zealand landscape. In *Christmas-Tree Land*, "the feeling of mystery caused by the dark shade of the lofty trees, standing there in countless rows as they had stood for centuries, the silence only broken by the occasional dropping of a twig or the flutter of a leaf" (Molesworth 1981, 32), is the defining feature of the book, where the forest could almost be considered a character in its own right.

Further on in her memoir, Ruddick told of how, as children, on a picnic to Days Bay near Wellington, Mansfield regaled everyone with her own rendering of "Hansel and Gretel", holding her audience completely spellbound:

> We loved the part about the guardian angels protecting the children as they slept, and were thrilled when Gretel pushed the old witch into the oven and especially liked the part where they found the row of children stiff with honeycrust which fell off when Gretel touched them with a wand of juniper.
>
> We always listened to Katie's stories with interest. She not only could tell them but she could write them. When she

told stories she drew on her store of fairy tales and legends. (Ruddick 1928, 49–50)

From 1903–06, Mansfield and her two older sisters were sent to London to be educated at the liberal girls' educational institution, Queen's College, in Harley Street. Mansfield's story "The Pine-Tree, the Sparrow and You and I", published in the Queen's College school magazine in December 1903, resembles a tale that Mrs Molesworth herself might have written, so closely does it replicate that fantasy forest of pines where magical things happen and trees are anthropomorphised into living beings:

> He was a tall, stately pine-tree. So tall, so very tall, that when you stood underneath and looked right up through the branches you could not see the top. How very fond you were of that pine-tree. We used to go and see it every day. He sang the most beautiful songs and told the most lovely stories; but he always seemed a little sad, somehow. (*CW*1, 10)

It was the first of Mansfield's 'baby' stories—with little children as protagonists, and meant for a specific audience; it is also, however, the first story by Mansfield where the narrator is male—in this case the father of the little girl:

> "No–o–o–o" you said, crying much harder. "It's about zem poor 'icle spawows." I sat right down on the bed and felt like Mummy feels when the cook says she's going to leave, "dinner-party or no dinner-party."
> We went to see them the first thing next morning. Alas! As soon as I saw our old friend, I knew something must be the matter. He was crying and moaning—and then—and—then, you found three little dead sparrows. Poor, poor little darlings. You held them in your pinafore, and I quite forgot Mummy would be cross. (*CW*1, 12)

The emotional state of the father at that precise moment, trying to comfort his emotionally overwrought little daughter, is cleverly portrayed, presaging Mansfield's adult use of free indirect discourse to convey the interior thoughts of her characters. There is humour here too, in the reported speech of the cook and the presumed reactions of the mother.

The influence of Walter Rippmann

Another story by Mansfield, "She", written in 1904, though never published, is of much greater interest than "The Pine Tree". It is a hallucinatory story, steeped in her school-girl reading of Oscar Wilde and the Decadents, thanks, in large part, to Walter Rippmann (1869–1947), the brilliant young German Professor at Queen's College, born in London of a German father and an English mother (and who changed his German name to the more anglicised Ripman during World War One), who, of all the teachers at the school, had the greatest influence on Mansfield. He became Professor of German at Queen's in 1896, aged just 27, and stayed for nearly 20 years.

Evelyn Payne, Mansfield's older cousin, who left Queen's College in the summer of 1903 to study at the all-female Oxford college, Lady Margaret Hall, was less impressed with Rippmann, claiming he was "rather fat and flabby, with very well-oiled hair, and his voice had a thick lisp" (Alpers 1980, 31). Nevertheless, he was a brilliant scholar, having taken the Tripos Examinations at Cambridge in Classics, Medieval and Modern Languages, and Indian Languages:

> [He] was an admirer of Oscar Wilde, of Walter Pater, and of art nouveau. In contrast to most of the other professors, he was "young and ardent", and a man of great social charm. With his more able original students, he was ready to spend time in stimulating conversation, introducing them to new ideas and encouraging them to discover their own potentialities. A select group was invited to visit his house in Lad-

broke Grove, where he would talk to them of his literary heroes, show them his collection of Japanese prints, and introduce them to an exciting new world. (Kaye 1972, 127)

Mansfield would become one of Rippmann's favoured students, invited to his bohemian home at 72 Ladbroke Grove, which he shared with a journalist and an artist, and which was decorated in an art nouveau style, as well as with Japanese prints, which were then hugely popular. There he would give "rose teas", with rose petals scattered in the hearth, under the soft rose glow of his art nouveau lamps. Mansfield would never have seen anything quite like it. It is probably not an exaggeration to state that in introducing the impressionable Mansfield to the works of Wilde, Pater and other writers of the fin-de-siècle and Decadent movements (especially Arthur Symons, Ernest Dowson, Paul Verlaine and Nietzsche), Rippmann would alter the course of her reading—and writing life. At this point in time, Mansfield was an open vessel, absorbing every influence that came her way.

As a result of these decadent influences, in "She", the godmother from *Christmas-Tree Land* is now transformed from a childhood fantasy figure to a fin-de-siècle goddess of Death:

> One day, he walked by the river. The sun was hidden behind the clouds. The wind moaned as though in pain. The tall trees shook their branches in despair. Winter was at hand. But the river flowed on, calm and restful. And his heart was desolate. It moaned with the wind—Ah, for one sight of Her!!! Then a thought flashed across his brain. Why not go to the river and bury himself in its depths, and see her again, for always and for ever. And he gave one hoarse cry, and then ah, he saw her again. She stretched out her arms, with her lips parted, with her eyes luminous, and clasped him to her heart. She held [him] in her arms as she would a little child, but as her arms touched him, he felt all his sorrows, his tears and his bitterness fade away into the past, become buried with the past. Then he looked up at her. "Take me with you" he moaned,

"take me with you." And she looked at him and smiled at him, and clasped him still more tightly in her arms and took him.

Death. Death. And her name was—ah! how well we know her you and I. She who came with our Forefathers, and will stay while this little universe will remain. Too often do we bar our doors against her, and watch her entrance with blinding tears. Her name was Death. (*CW*1, 14–15)

The image of a mystical river is a popular one in decadent literature—a liminal space acting, like a window, both as a boundary and a threshold. Another influence for this story is the prose poem "The Visit", by Ernest Dowson, another writer introduced to the impressionable Mansfield by Rippmann, via her reading of Arthur Symons's *Studies in Prose in Verse* (1904), which had recently been published and which contained a whole chapter on Dowson as well as a fascinating chapter on Wilde. Mansfield's notebooks, as late as 1909, contain numerous quotes from Symons's book, a particular favourite. In Dowson's "The Visit", the dreaming protagonist is also taken by Death:

As though I were still struggling through the meshes of some riotous dream, I heard his knock upon the door. As in a dream, I bade him enter, but with his entry, I awoke. Yet when he entered it seemed to me that I was dreaming, for there was nothing strange in that supreme and sorrowful smile which shone through the mask which I knew. And just as though I had not always been afraid of him I said: "Welcome."

And he said very simply, "I am here."

Dreaming I had thought myself, but the reproachful sorrow of his smile showed me that I was awake. Then dared I open my eyes and I saw my old body on the bed, and the room in which I had grown so tired, and in the middle of the room the pan of charcoal which still smouldered. And dimly I remembered my great weariness and the lost whiteness of

Lalage and last year's snows; and these things had been agonies.

Darkly, as in a dream, I wondered why they gave me no more hurt, as I looked at my old body on the bed; why, they were like old maids' fancies (as I looked at my grey body on the bed of my agonies)—like silly toys of children that fond mothers lay up in lavender (as I looked at the twisted limbs of my old body), for these things had been agonies.

But all my wonder was gone when I looked again into the eyes of my guest, and I said:

"I have wanted you all my life."

Then said Death (and what reproachful tenderness was shadowed in his obscure smile):

"You had only to call." (Thornton 2003, 212)

Close to the draft of "She" in her notebook, Mansfield copied out, in the original German, Heinrich Heine's lyrical poem "Der Tod", ("Death"), on the themes of death, love and dreaming:

Our death is in the cool of night,
Our life is in the pool of day.
The darkness glows, I'm drowning,
Day's tired me with light.

Over my head in leaves grown deep,
Sings the young nightingale.
It only sings of love there,
I hear it in my sleep. (*CW*4, 11)

Heine's *Book of Songs*, in which the poem appears, mixes autobiographical references, folklore, vivid evocations of nature, and narrative. In 1904, then, Mansfield was steeping herself in fin-de-siècle literature and poetry as well as earlier, German Romantic poetry, and, more importantly, reflecting this influence in her own literary endeavours. It was also in 1904 that one of Mansfield's close friends, Vere Bartrick-Baker, lent her the original Lippincott's magazine serialisation of Oscar Wilde's *The Picture of Dorian Gray*. Mansfield was soon hooked and obtained a copy of the book itself, which became almost a sacred tome for her during the next few years. She filled her notebooks with quotations from it and tried to imitate the wit in aphorisms of her own. For some time thereafter, Mansfield would refer to herself as the "White Gardenia" in her notebooks, referencing one of the preferred flowers of Oscar Wilde.

Another story of Mansfield's printed in the *Queen's College Magazine*—and the most outstanding—was "Die Einsame" ("The Lonely One"), published in March 1904. Its German language title was taken straight from her cousin Elizabeth von Arnim's latest bestseller, *The Adventures of Elizabeth in Rügen*, which had been published just a few weeks before, and where "Die Einsame" was the name of a resort on the beautiful Rügen Island in Germany, famous for its sandy beaches, chalk cliffs, and lagoons. More importantly, the German title of Mansfield's own story also hints at her continuing obsession with Walter Rippmann and her desire to be liked by him, whilst the contents, replete with decadent, symbolist and fin-de-siècle motifs, reveal just how much she had absorbed from Rippmann's suggested extra-curricular reading, as well as her memories (perhaps subconscious) yet again, of the pine-forest, flower-laden landscape in Mrs Molesworth's *Christmas-Tree Land*:

> All alone she was. All alone with her soul. She lived on the top of a solitary hill. Her house was small and bare, and alone, too.
> All day long she spent in the forest, with the trees and the flowers and the birds. She seemed like a creature of the forest herself, sometimes.
> [...]
> In the forest, in the forest, silence had cast a spell over all things. She plucked a great bouquet of daffodils and snowdrops, and tenderly held them to her, and tenderly kissed their fresh spring faces. (*CW1*, 20–21)

The repetitive phrases add to the hauntingly poetic, lyrical, almost mythical quality of the prose. The magical silence of the forest and the bouquets of sweet-smelling flowers are influenced by Mrs Molesworth's fantasy book, *Christmas-Tree Land*. And who better to write about isolation and loneliness than Mansfield, that moody, difficult adolescent, whose frequent preference for her own company, together with her notorious "moods", marked her out as different from the other students at Queen's College. Alienation and loneliness were to become themes that Mansfield would pick up time and again in her mature stories. And there is another theme here—death—prevalent in Mansfield's adolescent and early adult stories, as we have seen. Here, the anonymous protagonist, part wood nymph, part sea nymph, in the end almost seems to have her wishes fulfilled in going to her death:

> Now the water was creeping, higher to her waist, and now it was at her throat. She could barely stand. "Take me," she cried piteously, and looking up she saw—the boat and the figure had gone.
> [...]
> Then a great wave came, and there was silence. (*CW*1, 21)

Back in Wellington by December 1906, following her three years of schooling in London, Mansfield's haven during the long 18 months in New Zealand she spent waiting for permission from her father to return to London, was the Parliamentary Library, where she spent many hours reading an eclectic range of books. In March 1908—the start of autumn in New Zealand—Mansfield was to be found nestled in the library, writing a strange diary entry, where the proliferation of pine trees echoes yet again that favourite book from childhood, Mrs Molesworth's *Christmas-Tree Land*, but now woven into a more heady, fin-de-siècle prose style:

> A wet afternoon in the Library—in March. I have read most strange books here—one on the Path to Rome, one of Maori Art - - - Through the long avenue of pine trees, where the

shadow of Night crept from tree to tree. The Autumn afternoon it really would be better to call it so. This is what I want—the little asphalt path like a mauve ribbon, the great fragrant warm sweetness of the pine needles massed & heaped together, ruddy with perfume. Then the trees—hundreds there seem in the dull light, a vast procession of gloomy forms. Now here, now there, the shades of night are trooping softly, the air is heavy with a faint uneasy sound, a restless beating to & fro, a long unceasing sigh, & far away in the distance there is a dreary waste of grey sea—a desert of heaving water.

Grey, grey—there is no light in it at all, & the autumn air is cold with the coldness of drowned men. And Night is rising out of the sea—a ghastly broken form, & the autumn world sinks into that broken embrace, pillows its tired head upon that pulseless heart.

There is a little asphalt path like a mauve ribbon, and it is fringed with a vast procession of pine trees. In this dull light there seem to be hundreds of them. They are huddled together and muffled in their gloomy shadows.

On the earth a fragrant sweetness & pine needles, massed & heaped up, ruddy with perfume. And through the black lace-like tracery of trees a pale sky full of hurrying clouds. Far away in the distance a dreary waste of grey sea, a desert of heaving water.

Grey, grey... there is no light at all, and the autumn air is cold with the coldness of traceless spaces. Out of the grey sea creeps the ghastly, drowned body of Night. Her long dark hair swam among the branches of the pine trees, her dead body walks along the little mauve ribbon of an asphalt path. She stretches out her arms and the autumn world sinks into that frozen embrace, pillows its tired head upon that pulseless heart.

And the long procession of pine trees, huddled together, are ghostly fearful snowmen at the wedding with Death. (*CW*4, 90)

The predominant words here are grey, pine, trees, cold; ghostly, lifeless forms are everywhere. The only colour present is to be found in the little mauve asphalt path that winds like a ribbon through the narrative, a motif for Mansfield's diminishing hopes of leaving grey and dull Wellington for the decadent, mauve-coloured delights of London. While her New Zealand roots were imprinted in her brain, to resurface time and again in her fiction, Mansfield's three years in London had effectively cut the ties between herself and her parents' stuffy, middle-class, colonial world. She wanted none of it. If there was a choice to be made between art nouveau interior décor and purple sofas in Ladbroke Grove, or a grand house in Wellington, with its incumbent dull round of parties and the same old faces, the decision was an overwhelmingly easy one.

Hans Christian Andersen's Fairy Tales

Another childhood literary influence on Mansfield was Hans Christian Andersen, whose tales, as noted above, had fascinated her as a child. Mrs Molesworth, in an article she herself wrote on Andersen in 1888, the year Mansfield was born, said:

> The very sound of his familiar name brings with it a rush of the sweetest associations: of Christmas trees and Christmas chimes; of midsummer fancies in the scented pine-woods; of the very happiest hours of happy childhood, past and yet living in memory forever. (1888, 665)

Even as a world-weary, cynical 18-year-old in Wellington, Mansfield found herself returning to Andersen's strange, magical tales. On June 12, 1908, she wrote to her sister Vera:

Have you lately read Hans Andersen's Fairy Tales? If you have a copy in the house do look up the Fir Tree. The last sentence is so astonishingly Chopin I read it over & over— and the simple unearthly words flood your soul like the dying phrase of a Majorca nocturne. (*Letters* 1, 48)

As Mansfield read her copy of Andersen's tales she must have been struck by the similarity between her own position (desperately wanting to be somewhere else, with no power to make that happen), and that of the anthropomorphised protagonist. In the fairy tale, a fir tree is so anxious to grow up and experience greater things that he simply cannot appreciate living in the moment:

"Perhaps I may be destined to tread this glorious path one day!" cried the Fir Tree rejoicingly. "That is even better than traveling across the sea. How painfully I long for it! If it were only Christmas now! Now I am great and grown up, like the rest who were led away last year. Oh, if I were only on the carriage! If I were only in the warm room, among all the pomp and splendor! And then? Yes, then something even better will come, something far more charming, or else why should they adorn me so? There must be something grander, something greater still to come; but what? Oh! I'm suffering, I'm longing! I don't know myself what is the matter with me!" (Andersen 1893, 210)[1]

This passage echoes so many diary entries of Mansfield's at this time, hating Wellington and its colonial inhabitants, hating her parents and her family even more, and holding out for a glittering future in that city of delights, the heart of Empire, London. Eventually cut down, taken into a house, and decorated on Christmas Eve, topped with a beautiful gold star, the fir tree expects to be admired over the

---

[1] Special thanks go to Fiona Oliver, curator at the Alexander Turnbull Library, Wellington, New Zealand, for locating this copy in the library's collections, which is, I believe, the version Mansfield is referring to.

whole of Christmas. Instead, after one day of glory, when his beautifully decorated branches are plundered for their toys and treats, he is placed in the attic and left to rot. In the spring, now brown and withered, he is taken outside, a little boy removes the gold star—the only decoration remaining—and he is chopped into bits and burnt.

Psychologically of course, Mansfield could relate to the fir tree's anxious and futile longing for an idealised future which would never come, and she was now wise enough to recognise it. Jackie Wullschlager (2002) suggests the tale portrays a certain psychological type—an individual who cannot be happy in the moment because they always expect something even greater to happen to them in the future; continually disappointed, their life becomes one of constant regret. Thus, the fir tree is "a fantasist, vain, fearful, restless, afflicted with the trembling sensitivity of the neurotic, manically swinging from hope to misery" (248).

Andersen's tale, originally published in 1844 together with "The Snow Queen", was written very much with the adult reader in mind. Its bourgeois, non-threatening setting enabled its fatalistic tone to be more readily accepted, and allowed the reader to identify with the tragic fir tree's demise. Andersen had written tales with unhappy endings before (see "The Little Mermaid" and "The Steadfast Tin Soldier"), but "The Fir Tree's" note of "deeply ingrained pessimism, suggesting not only the mercilessness of fate but the pointlessness of life itself, that only the moment is worthwhile" (Wullschlager 2002, 249), was an innovative departure for the author. The final lines of the story, which Mansfield likened to a "dying phrase of a [Chopin] Majorca nocturne", are as follows:

> The boys played in the garden, and the youngest had on his breast a golden star, which the Tree had worn on its happiest evening. Now that was past, and the Tree's life was past, and the story is past too: past! past!—that's the way with all stories. (Andersen 1893, 214)

"The Fir Tree" is also a tragi-comic self-portrait by Andersen, as Wullschlager notes, and "harshly perceptive. Andersen, like his tree was a fantasist, vain, restless, a trembling oversensitive neurotic who swung madly from hope to despair" (Wullschlager 2005, 430). The tale would also, of course, have brought back memories of Mrs Molesworth's *Christmas-Tree Land*. Fir trees and pine trees, seemed to litter Mansfield's adolescent consciousness in a quite remarkable way.

Indeed, one of Mansfield's earliest stories, "A Happy Christmas Eve", published in the Wellington *High School Reporter* in 1899 when she was just eleven, seems to have been written with Andersen's "The Fir Tree" in mind:

> "As you break up today, I am going to take you with me to town, to get the presents for our tree." For the Courteneys were going to have a tree for the poor children that year. [...]
>
> Such a funny crowd it was that came that night, ragged and dirty, but having a look of curiosity on their faces. When they had all come, the study door was thrown open and the Christmas tree was seen in all its splendour. I wish I could have let you see the delight on the faces of the children. Really it was a sight to behold. The tree was loaded with sweets, fruits and presents and there was a present for everyone besides the sweets. Then there were games, supper at which the children ate very heartily, more games, and then they went home. (*CW*1, 6)

The story concerns the plight of the poor from the point of view of a little rich girl, revealing how the young Mansfield was mindful of such disparities in society; the largesse of the rich family towards the poor tantalisingly presages elements of one of her most celebrated stories, "The Garden Party".

There are numerous other connections between Mansfield and Andersen. Both writers were innovative. Mansfield's short stories broke new ground. She rejected traditional story-telling concepts, developing experimental techniques of her own; her stories evolve over the course of time into "slices of life"—glimpses into the lives of individuals, families, captured at a certain moment, frozen in time like a painting or a snapshot. On the whole, a single, "main" event is revealed and developed, no case is presented for or against their actions or their life; they simply "are". Like Mansfield, Andersen's gifts were those of a miniaturist, whose skills were somehow lost in the broad canvas of a novel (though he wrote several), and were far better contained in the short story medium. Wullschlager notes the reasons that made Andersen a revolutionary writer: as well as the fact that he merged the fairy tale with images of the everyday world around him,

> he was the first person to take the fairy tale as a literary form and to invent new ones of his own. [...] Andersen was a breath of fresh air, an authentic story-telling voice which carried conviction and truth in language that was simple without being banal, and that everyone could understand. (2002, 146)

Eventually he would become known as the artist who idealized the world of middle-class childhood. Andersen once wrote: "I don't know how other writers feel! *I* suffer with my characters, I share their moods, whether good or bad, and I can be nice or nasty according to the scene on which I happen to be working" (quoted in Wullschlager 2005, 425, original italics). And Mansfield too, wrote:

> Ive *been* this man, *been* this woman. Ive stood for hours on the Auckland Wharf. Ive been out in the stream waiting to be berthed—Ive been a seagull hovering at the stern and a hotel porter whistling through his teeth. It isn't as though one sits and watches the spectacle. That would be thrilling enough, God knows. But one IS the spectacle for the time. (*Letters* 4, 97)

For both writers it seems that the act of creating characters seems to be almost an act of *possession*.

On his deathbed, after an illness of several months, what caused Andersen most regret was the absence of music in his life. Even as a young child he had always had an interest in music, with an excellent singing voice, though not good enough to become a singer at the Royal Theatre in Copenhagen, his first choice of profession. As an adult he delighted in attending concerts and operas, and never lost his passion for music. The apogee of art was, to his mind, the realm of *tone*. For communicating his musical impressions to others he employed a language replete with imagery, rich in metaphor, vibrant with passion and emotion, as can be seen in those final lines from "The Fir Tree". Mansfield, of course, was an accomplished cellist and singer, and so music, with its seemingly endless referential modalities, is used in her own stories in a significant way. An obvious example is of course, "The Singing Lesson". In the story, a singing teacher, Miss Meadows, has received a letter from her fiancé, breaking off their engagement. Her heartbreak is reflected in almost every syllable of the story:

> Good Heavens, what could be more tragic than that lament! Every note was a sigh, a sob, a groan of awful mournfulness. Miss Meadows lifted her arms in the wide gown and began conducting with both hands. "... I feel more and more strongly that our marriage would be a mistake...." she beat. And the voices cried: *Fleetly! Ah, Fleetly*. What could have possessed him to write such a letter! (*CW2*, 236–37)

Only a writer with a feel for music and its effects, could have written such a story, and understood how music has the ability to reflect our deepest moods and desires.

Other elements which define both writers' geniuses include an individual colloquial manner, together with a lightly ironic social satire. Like Andersen, Mansfield considers the nature of urban life—and how people survive it—with its access to modern comforts on one hand, and extreme poverty on the other. Andersen's tale "The Old House" is a musing on mortality and transience, a story of a little boy's friendship with a wealthy old man, but where the man's house is the true protagonist:

> Down yonder, in the street, stood an old, old house. It was almost three hundred years old, for one could read as much on the beam, on which was carved the date of its erection, surrounded by tulips and trailing hops. There one could read entire verses in the characters of olden times, and over each window a face had been carved in the beam, and these faces made all kinds of grimaces. One story projected a long way above the other, and close under the roof was a leaden gutter with a dragon's head. The rain water was to run out of the dragon's mouth, but it ran out of the creature's body instead, for there was a hole in the pipe. (Andersen 1893, 98)

The old man dies, his house is eventually pulled down, and a new, modern house is erected in its place, though sticking out of the earth, in a little part of the garden, the spirit of the old house still dwells, in the form of a little tin soldier, once gifted to the old man by the little boy, and the remains of the beautifully gilded leather wallpaper, now reduced to a little rag of pig-skin. *Sic transit Gloria mundi*, Andersen tells us: death is as inevitable as life, but the spirit of the house lingers on and does not quite die.

A similar theme is taken up by Mansfield in her early story, "The House", dating from 1912 (and not republished after its appearance in *Hearth and Home* on November 28, 1912 until the Edinburgh edition of her *Complete Works* in 2012, a century later). The story begins with prose that takes us back to Mansfield's schoolgirl infatuation with the Decadents, in water-logged tones of grey and amethyst:

> Another day ended! Darkness was pouring into the world like grey fluid into a greyer cup—no amethyst twilight this, no dropping of a chiffon scarf—no trailing of a starbroidered mantle … a sense of smudging over—that was all. Fallen leaves spattered the pavement. Still over wall and housefront the Virginia creeper draggled her tousled tresses. And

the cold wind was full of the shuddering breath of winter. (*CW*1, 304)

A young and impoverished office worker shelters from the evening rain in the porch of an empty house. She falls asleep and dreams of a life of wealth and happiness in the house, with roaring fires, beautiful interiors, rich food and an adoring husband and children—the opposite, in fact, of her quotidian life. The next morning, however, the girl is found dead, still in the porch of the empty old house. The passers-by speculate on the girl's death and its implications for the house itself:

> It'll be called 'aunted now.
> […]
> 'It'll always be empty now.'
> 'Yes, always empty now … (*CW*1, 311)

As with Andersen's story "The Old House", people may die, but the spirit of the house lingers on.

Mansfield's "A Fairy Story" from 1910, published in the little magazine *Open Window* under the pseudonym Katherina Mansfield, a modernist fairy-tale about a woodcutter's daughter who moves to the great metropolis thus betraying the love of her life, is in fact, a homage to Andersen himself, who is mentioned by name, as are a dozen or so of his fairy tales. He even appears as a shadowy ghost-figure in the tragic denouement:

> And there crept into the room a worn-out, bent old ghost, who lifted up the Boy's frail body, and laid him on a bed. An old ghost, who moaned and muttered about the 'Little Sea Maid' and 'The Snow Queen,' as he smoothed the Boy's hair. (*CW*1, 203)

The story is also full of allusions to Rippmann and all he taught her. Indeed, the central character, "The Wanderer", is based on Rippmann himself:

"Well?" he said sharply, as the Girl stood by the door.

"I want to look at your books," said she. He glanced at her curiously. Her wonderful face gleamed strangely at him, from billow and billow of white pinafore.

"I'm—I'm quite exceptional," she said, hastily, "I'm very advanced."

"Oh, are you?" said the Wanderer.

"Don't think of what I *look* like; as Mr. Shaw says, 'You Never can Tell.'"

"Hang thee, sweet wench," said the Wanderer, "come along here—you know the 'Open Sesame' and I'll show you the books."

And two hours later, they were both sitting on the floor—And he was reading her Omar Kháyyám, and she was looking into Arthur Symons.

[...]

And he told her of London, of Spain, of Paris, of Brussels, and again London.

And he taught her his ethics of life, and that unselfishness signifies lack of Progress—and that she must avoid the Seven Deadly Virtues. And she printed a little text, and hung it above her washstand—"*The strongest man is he who stands most alone.*"

[...]

And the Wanderer did not forget her. He sent her a postcard of Maxim Gorki, and a little book "The Virgins of the Rocks"; she did not understand it, but it gave her beautiful dreams. (*CW*1, 201–02)

As well as a heady mix of the fairy stories of the Grimm brothers and Hans Andersen, the fantasy delights of *Christmas-Tree Land* by Mrs Molesworth, the story is replete with the Decadent literature introduced to the impressionable 14-year-old Mansfield by her German teacher Walter Rippmann, remembered seven years on and fictionalised.

For de Mylius (2006), Andersen, a proto-modernist in both his personal life and his art, "managed to show us that everyday phenomena might reveal the essence of poetry, the true fairy tale of life" (176). The marvellous itself, as Mansfield knew instinctively, is inherent in modernity, since modernity consists of an interplay between enchantment and disenchantment, the exact two themes explored in the above story, one which deserves far more critical attention than it has received to date. Mimicking the fairy tale, imitating the gestures of children's literature, the stories discussed in this chapter, behind this surface, reach far beyond both these genres.

Bibliography

Alpers, Antony. 1980. *The Life of Katherine Mansfield*. London: Viking.
Andersen, Hans Christian. 1893. *Stories for the Household*. New York: McLoughlin Brothers.
Kimber, Gerri. 2016. *Katherine Mansfield: The Early Years*. Edinburgh: Edinburgh University Press.
Molesworth, Mrs. [1884] 1981. *Christmas-Tree Land*. London: Macmillan.
---. 1888. "Hans Christian Andersen." *Time* June (18): 665–72.
Moss, Anita. 1988. "Mrs Molesworth: Victorian Visionary." *The Lion and the Unicorn* 12 (1): 105–10.
De Mylius, Johan. 2006. "'Our time is the time of the fairy tale': Hans Christian Andersen between Traditional Craft and Literary Modernism." *Marvels & Tales: Journal of Fairy-Tale Studies* 20 (2): 166–178.
Ruddick, Marion. 1928. "Incidents in the Childhood of Katherine Mansfield." Unpublished typescript, MS-Papers-1339. Alexander Turnbull Library, Wellington, New Zealand.
Symons, Arthur. 1904. *Studies in Prose in Verse*. London: J. M. Dent.
Thornton, R. K. R., ed. 2003. *Ernest Dowson: Collected Poems*. London: Bloomsbury.
Wullschlager, Jackie. 2002. *Hans Christian Andersen: The Life of a Storyteller*. Chicago: University of Chicago Press.
---, ed. 2005. *Hans Christian Andersen: Fairy Tales*. London: Penguin.

Consuming Identifications: Food Politics in Mansfield's "A Suburban Fairy Tale"

Elsa Högberg

> When I pass the apple stalls I cannot help stopping and staring until I feel that I, myself, am changing into an apple, too—and that at any moment I may produce an apple, miraculously, out of my own being like the conjuror produces the egg [...]. When I write about ducks I swear that I am a white duck with a round eye [...]. There follows the moment when you are *more* duck, *more* apple or *more* Natasha than any of these objects could ever possibly be, and so you *create* them anew. (Mansfield, *Letters* 1, 330; emphasis in original)

It is tempting to read Katherine Mansfield's mature work via Henri Bergson's idea of the artist's "sympathetic identification" with objects.[1] However, the mode of identification described in the epigraph above, in which the boundary that habitually separates subject and object breaks down, also produces a distinctly modernist effect of the uncanny in her short fiction (see Hanson 2011, 122). The process by which the subject becomes another (person, animal or thing) is performed in Mansfield's stories through animism and telepathy as aesthetic devices, both of which, according to Freud, belong to the realm of the uncanny. In her animistic fictional universe, things and animals express a startling and often disturbing interiority, as in "Prelude" (1918), where the objects in Linda Burnell's bedroom assume a sinister mental life, or when a fox necklet in its box makes a crying noise at the end of "Miss Brill" (1920), as if it were buried alive. Mansfield's aesthetic achievement also includes an original exploration of telepathy: "the spontaneous transmission of mental processes"

---

[1] On Mansfield and Bergson, see Eiko Nakano (2002, 2011) and Angela Smith (2000, 10–14, 69–71, 79–81, 128–30).

beyond ordinary communication, in which a person may share another's thoughts and emotions (Freud 2003, 141–42).[2]

If we follow Mansfield's reflection on ducks and apples, then it appears that identification and affective transmission enable the shaping of the modernist short story as a formally rigorous project; the artist's imperative to become *"more* duck, *more* apple" in order to *"create* them anew" asserts the formalist notion that art creates rather than imitates life. In Freudian terminology, these lines depict the writer's projection of their interiority onto the world. For Freud (1987a), artists hold a primitive, neurotic and childlike belief in "the omnipotence of thought": the animistic idea that "they can alter the external world by mere thinking"—or, we could add, writing (87). While Freud describes the omnipotence of thought inspiring art in transhistorical terms, the artist's ambition to recreate the material world by unsettling perceptual habits and subject-object boundaries is a central principle of literary modernism in particular. In this chapter, I propose that Mansfield's farsighted engagement with animism and telepathy goes beyond Freud's theorisation of these processes as regressive and narcissistic. More contemporary scholarship on affect and animism, such as that of Teresa Brennan (2004), Graham Harvey (2006) and Jane Bennett (2010), might offer illuminating perspectives on the communication of affect between writer, text and reader at work in Mansfield's fiction. I will nonetheless linger on Freud's writings on occult, uncanny phenomena as a particularly compelling framework for reading Mansfield and, more specifically, the effective ways in which she creates animistic and telepathic relations to address social and political injustice. To this end, I focus on her depiction of hunger and food in the posthumously published story "A Suburban Fairy Tale", Mansfield's indignant response to the prolongation of the Allied blockade of Germany after the armistice, which exacerbated an already severe food crisis in the country.[3] Written in 1919, the year in

---

[2] For accounts of animism and telepathy in Mansfield's fiction, see Clare Hanson (2011) and Janet Wilson (2013, 2016).

[3] Antony Alpers (1984) notes of "A Suburban Fairy Tale": "evidently a comment on the famine suffered in Germany after the First World War, and

which Freud's "The Uncanny" was published, this story demonstrates Mansfield's exceptionally innovative use of defamiliarising, animistic literary techniques.

When Freud speaks of animism and the omnipotence of thought, his observations read like a critique of a romantic-modernist literary tradition. It is within literature's power, he claims, to bring about the reader's return to a primitive animistic worldview, and to cultivate "the narcissistic overrating of one's own mental processes" (Freud 2003, 147; 1978a, 85–90). Seen from this perspective, literature builds a defence against the socio-political, material world in its function as a discharge of the writer's wishes and desires. Such artistic autonomy does not amount to the subject's mastery of an object world, however; on the contrary, it emerges in "a regression to times when the ego had not yet clearly set itself off against the world outside and from others" (Freud 2003, 143). In "The Uncanny", Freud discusses telepathy and animism as phenomena that occur when this line of separation is no longer clearly drawn. He opens his essay by positioning the uncanny in the realm of aesthetics, which he defines as "relating to the qualities of our feeling" (2003, 123).[4] Elsewhere, he reflects on the affinity of art with magic and the occult: the "magic of art", he writes, lies in its ability to "produc[e] emotional effects—thanks to artistic illusion—just as though it were something real" (Freud 1978a, 90). For Freud, it is in the regime of magic and the omnipotence of thought that art becomes "a conventionally accepted reality in which [...] symbols and substitutes are able to provoke real emotions" (1978b, 188).

The Freudian association of art's occult dimensions with the artist's capacity to manipulate and provoke emotions has many affinities with Mansfield's notion of artistic metamorphosis. When she

---

apart from *Stay-laces* (1915), the only known instance of K. M.'s writing a story to make such a point. The manuscript [...] is dated '15 iii 1919'" (562).

[4] As a psychoanalyst not usually concerned with aesthetics, Freud takes an interest in the uncanny as an affect because it brings about the return of unconscious and repressed material (2003, 123).

describes the successful artist as a conjuror who magically becomes the objects of her art, Mansfield also makes this transfiguration a question of aesthetic form and design: "but that is why I believe in technique", she writes, "because I don't see how art is going to make that divine *spring* into the bounding outlines of things if it hasn't passed through the process of trying to *become* these things before recreating them" (*Letters* 1, 330; emphasis in original). Her romantic-modernist conviction that art should transmit deep emotion also converges with Freud's view of aesthetics and the psychological ground of art.[5] The lyricism and romantic impulse of Mansfield's mature work puts into practice her notion that "without emotion writing is dead; it becomes a record instead of a revelation, for the sense of revelation comes from that emotional reaction which the artist felt and was impelled to communicate" (*CW*3, 643–44). Given these resonances, it is perhaps not surprising that so much scholarship on Mansfield's work has assumed a biographical approach (see Burgan 1994; Moran 1996; Smith 1999, 2000). However, I would like to align myself with a recent, aesthetic turn in Mansfield criticism, where the focus is on the historical resonances and socio-political effects of her stylistic strategies. Such an approach, which differs significantly from Freud's framing of art as fundamentally narcissistic, might reveal how Mansfield reinvents the short story genre by making it central to modernist expressions of aesthetic virtuosity. In her hands, the medium of the short story unsettles any sense of a safe distance between writer, text and reader, and the politically charged transmission of affect is achieved through the artist-magician's astonishing technical skill.

Mansfield's "*spring* into the bounding outlines of things" suggests Bergsonian identification as explained by T.E. Hulme; both his and Mansfield's work appeared in *The New Age* in 1910–11. In his notes on "Bergson's Theory of Art", Hulme (1922b) stresses the de-familiarising capacity of art, where the "veil" habitually distinguishing

---

[5] Freud saw the writer's reworking of biographical source material as a particularly interesting object of literary study; see, for example, "The Interest of Psycho-Analysis from the Point of View of the Science of Aesthetics" (Freud 1978b, 187).

the mind from the material world is made "transparent" by the artist's intuition. For Hulme, the creative process brings about a sympathetic identification with objects that assigns them individuality and interiority, thereby unsettling the "distinct outlines" separating them from the subject (301–02; see also Hulme 1922a, 287–88). This blurring of the subject-object boundary recalls the occult dimension of aesthetics as theorised by Freud, with one important difference: for Freud, the animistic world of art is by no means sympathetic but deeply unsettling, since it brings about the shock of the unfamiliar. Bergson's idea of identification continues to offer a productive lens for Mansfield critics, particularly in the light of recent, political and ecocritical work on animism and material vitality, much of which demonstrates that it is not backwards or regressive to attribute interiority and complex communication to non-human forms of life. On the contrary, animistic and vitalist worldviews have been proved to resonate with contemporary science as well as environmentalist and egalitarian projects.[6] Mansfield's work deserves further study in this contemporary light, as the scholarship of Janet Wilson (2016), Aimee Gasston (2014) and Melinda Harvey (2011) attests. Even so, I see the Freudian uncanny as the realm where the social consciousness of Mansfield's work emerges most forcefully.[7]

In Mansfield's fiction, animism is often associated with social exclusion. As Roger Robinson (1994) puts it, "Mansfield wrote almost compulsively of outcasts [...] and fringe dwellers" (4), and in two remarkable stories, "Miss Brill" (1920) and the unfinished "A Married Man's Story" (1921), she conjures animistic encounters to convey a keen awareness of the protagonists' marginalisation. As the despised Miss Brill returns home to her claustrophobic "room like a cupboard",

---

[6] See, for instance, Jane Bennett (2010, Chapter 5 in particular) and Graham Harvey (2006); see also Harvey's 2013 collection, especially the essays by Max Velmans, Matthew Hall and Val Plumwood.

[7] On this point, I concur with field-defining critics—notably Smith (1999), Hanson (2011) and Gasston (2014)—all of whom recognise a grappling with pervasive social changes, and particularly those caused by World War I, in Mansfield's creation of uncanny effects.

she puts her fox necklet back into its box: "but when she put the lid on she thought she heard something crying" (*CW*2, 254). In "A Married Man's Story", the narrator, who was bullied at school, describes himself as having been "an outcast" until the moment of revelation where he sees the things in his familiar room in a way he has never seen them before: "everything lived, but everything. But that was not all. I was equally alive and [. . .] the barriers were down between us" (390). This phrasing—"the barriers were down"—captures a notion implied in much of Mansfield's work: that an animistic universe fosters inclusive and egalitarian relations. I have written elsewhere on Mansfield's use of lyrical vocality, and the cry in particular, as a means of foregrounding the reality of social inequality (Högberg, 2018). In "Life of Ma Parker" (1921), for instance, an uncanny fusion of voices, where Ma Parker's dead grandson speaks through her, gives us an acute sense of her hardship, and of the direct way in which her poverty sustains the comfortable life of the "literary gentleman" for whom she works.

Similar devices can be traced in "A Suburban Fairy Tale", where a birdlike little boy hears the sparrows in the garden speak, communicating their hunger to the well-fed family. He eventually becomes one in a flock of grotesque hybrid creatures that change rapidly from sparrows into boys, then back into sparrows again. When his parents finally attune their ears to the sparrow-boys' cry, they turn into birds and fly away, "out of sight—out of call" (*CW*2, 173). The social pathos of this story works through affective transmission and identification with marginalised figures, but it is also distinctively political in its critique of the politics of food and hunger during the Allied blockade of Germany. Written in March 1919, the story could well be read as an allegorical response to the prolongation of the blockade from the armistice until July 1919, when it was lifted following the signing of the Versailles Treaty. This prolongation was a political strategy aimed at preventing a Bolshevik revolution and the revitalisation of military power in Germany (Howard 1993, 161, 170, 185). A few days after the armistice, on November 17, 1918, Mansfield (*Letters* 2, 291) commented in a letter to Ottoline Morrell on "the loathsome press about Germany's cry for food"—a reference to the extensive British reporting about imminent famine in the country. Just as the hungry sparrows are shut out from Mr and Mrs B.'s homely dining room, these reports about starvation reached a Britain where wartime food administration was largely successful (see Barnett 1985). In sharp contrast to the desperate situation on the continent, public health and nutrition levels in Britain even improved during the war (Winter 1977, 489, 499–503).[8] This contrast is accentuated by the setting of the story close to the end of rationing, with Mr and Mrs B. indulging in gluttonous dreams about food now available: Scotch hares, dates, "a glut of cheese" (*CW*2, 171–72). As in her pre-war story "Germans at Meat" (1910), Mansfield links gluttony to political dominance and aggression, but here the tables are turned: while her earlier caricature of food-obsessed Germans functioned as a trope for the country's threatening military power in the years leading up to the war, "A Suburban Fairy Tale", uses the figure of the hungry sparrow to highlight the Allied nations' exacerbation of the humanitarian crisis caused by food shortages in Germany during the blockade.[9]

The title already announces the in-between position of this text with regard to Freud's schema in "The Uncanny": the story begins with a realist "ground of common reality" (Freud 2003, 156)—the reality of food prices and rationing in a London suburb—then fairy tale elements are introduced to create an uncanny effect. As Sarah Shieff (2014) observes, it is in moments "when something ruffles the surface of the everyday world—that dark, fey quality" that Mansfield's "debt

---

[8] As Gasston (2013) observes, however, food in wartime Britain did become "a sparse commodity, reduced to its use value while provoking a richly imaginative fantasy life" (165).
[9] In his "Introductory Note" to *In a German Pension* (1911) for the 1948 Constable edition of Mansfield's collected stories, John Middleton Murry (1948) recalls a decisive reason for Mansfield's reluctance to have this satiric volume republished, despite generous offers during and after the war: her conviction that it would be unfair to take advantage of the anti-German sentiments prevailing in Britain at the time (695–96).

to the world of the fairy story is clearest" (73–74).[10] While the traditional fairy tale "openly commits itself to the acceptance of animistic beliefs", the writer of fiction based on realistic premises can intensify the impact of the uncanny: "we react to his fictions as if they had been our own experiences" (Freud 2003, 156–57). This is exactly what Mansfield is doing in "A Suburban Fairy Tale". The setting of the story, a rich English breakfast in the B. family's "cosy red dining-room" (*CW2*, 170), is *heimlich* in a sense foregrounded by Freud: "intimate, cosily homely; arousing a pleasant feeling of [...] secure protection, like the enclosed, comfortable house" (2003, 127). From the first page, we are drawn into this intimate sphere through free indirect discourse, where the narrator's voice blurs with those of Mr and Mrs B. This world has its windows symbolically shut onto the garden, which is cold, threatening and full of shrieking sparrows. *Heimlich* also refers to animals in the sense of "tame, associating familiarly with humans" (Freud 2003, 126), but this is not the case with Mansfield's birds: "the sparrows' little voices were like ringing of little knives being sharpened" (*CW2*, 172). Diane McGee notes that Mansfield tends to disrupt the common association of food with a secure and intimate home setting (2001, 81, 87), and such disturbance is achieved by the uncanny voices in this story.

It is the voice of the birdlike son, Little B., that brings about the intrusion of the sparrows' foreign, piercing cry into his parents' sheltered reality:

> "O-oh!" cried Little B. so suddenly and sharply that it gave them quite a start—"Look at the whole lot of sparrows flown onto our lawn"—[...]. And while he spoke, even though the windows were closed, they heard a loud shrill cheeping and chirping from the garden. (*CW2*, 171)

---

[10] Shieff (2014, 75) suggests that Oscar Wilde's fairy tale "The Happy Prince", with its birds and social commentary, may have been a source of inspiration for Mansfield's story.

Walking over to the window, Little B. pleads with his parents that they feed the hungry sparrows, but they do not hear. As he watches the birds, they turn eerily into little boys flapping their arms and squeaking "want something to eat, want something to eat!" (*CW*2, 172). The next moment, Mr and Mrs B. see their son through the window as one of the sparrow-boys. Telepathy, which is "taken for granted" in magical and animistic thinking (Freud 1978a, 81, 85), is a key strategy in the social critique delivered by this text. Little B.'s communication with the birds is telepathic in Freud's sense: the "spontaneous transmission of mental processes" where "one becomes co-owner of the other's knowledge, emotions and experience. Moreover, a person may identify himself with another and so become unsure of his true self; or he may substitute the other's self for his own" (Freud 2003, 141–42). Hearing a call for food in what appears as nonsensical noise to his parents, Little B. identifies with the sparrows so completely that he becomes one of them. His uncanny metamorphosis en acts Mansfield's notion of the artist's "*spring* into the bounding outlines of things"—an expression, as I have suggested, of what Freud calls the omnipotence of thought. The omnipotence of thought amounts to affective transmission as a strategic principle of literature: "by the moods [the writer] induces and the expectations he arouses he can direct our feelings" (Freud 2003, 158).[11] Moreover, the aesthetic effect of the uncanny can only emerge when we identify with a character (ibid.), just as we are made to identify with Little B. and the sparrow he becomes.[12]

---

11 See also Nicholas Royle's compelling notion of a "telepathy effect" specific to narrative fiction, where telepathy and clairvoyance emerged as essentially literary processes with the advent of psychoanalysis (2003, 256–76).
12 In "The Daughters of the Late Colonel" (1920), a sparrow's cry is used similarly as a device for creating identification: "some little sparrows [. . .] chirped on the window-ledge. 'Yeep—eyeep—yeep.' But Josephine felt they were not sparrows, not on the window-ledge. It was inside her, that queer little crying noise. [. . .] Ah, what was it crying, so weak and forlorn?" (*CW*2, 281).

Aimee Gasston (2013) traces an analogy across Mansfield's fiction between reading and eating, and argues compellingly that the trope of insatiable hunger has been employed persistently to figure the very form of the modern short story. In "A Suburban Fairy Tale", Mansfield's formal use of fairy tale elements elicits a strong desire for food; the sparrows' ravenous cry—"*cheek-a-cheep-cheep-cheek!*"—is repeated three times, interspersing three mirage-like apparitions of abundant dishes floating magically in the air (*CW*2, 171–72). This strategy transmits an acute, physical sense of the birds' predicament, and unsettles the initial safe distance between living room and garden—a distance that even the shut windows fail to uphold. When Little B. makes his appearance as a sparrow-boy, he seems to have entered the garden through the glass, and when his parents, recognising their son among the hybrid creatures, eventually open the window to feed the flock, it is too late. The boy-sparrow transformation is uncanny because it shakes Mr and Mrs B.'s prosaic world, and the realist framing of the story. Hearing, finally, an intelligible request: "want something to eat, want something to eat" (*CW*2, 172), they—and we— are compelled to adopt a child's animistic worldview, and forced thereby to face the uncomfortable reality of our neighbours' poverty and hunger.

At the end of World War One, as Angela Smith (1999) points out, Mansfield and Freud both redefined foreignness as an inextricable part of the self, a redefinition prompted as much by the dislocation of boundaries caused by the war (Smith cites Wilfred Owen's poem "Strange Meeting", where a dead German soldier appears to the poet in a dream: "I am the enemy you killed, my friend") as by the emergence of Freudian psychoanalysis (2–3).[13] Such a reappraisal is at work in "A Suburban Fairy Tale", where our unwilled identification with the abject sparrows is an effect of the Bergsonian "aesthetic emotion" skilfully created by Mansfield: the "direct communication" of affect beyond the habitual, "stock type" emotions we commonly

---

13   Clare Hanson (2011), too, sees the uncanniness of Mansfield's fiction as a distinctly modern form of the uncanny associated in particular with World War I (128).

experience (Hulme 1922c, 310–12). In the case of British responses to the German food crisis, such a stock type emotion would be Mr B.'s rage: "all this talk about famine [...] all a Fake, all a Blind" (*CW*2, 172). The food blockade was particularly severe until the end of March 1919, when Mansfield's story was written, and most British reports from Germany that spring agreed that the country was "on the verge of starvation" (Howard 1993, 162, 183). However, there was an intense "historical and propaganda dispute" regarding the extent, even truth, of these reports, and whether the blockade did indeed lead to famine—a debate that pervaded the first historical accounts of the period (161, 168–69) and continues among scholars today (see Howard 1993; Vincent 1985; Marks 2013, 650–51). It is nonetheless widely recognised that the blockade had an undeniable impact on the German people's health; it aggravated the widespread starvation and malnutrition that drastically increased mortality during the war, particularly among children and the elderly (Howard 1993, 161–62; Vincent 1985, 137–39, 145). "A Suburban Fairy Tale" should be considered in this light. When Mansfield casts Mr B.'s speculation and deafness to the sparrows' cry as cold cynicism, she plants in us a sharp sense that the political calculation underlying the extension of the blockade as well as the consequent propaganda dispute occurred at the inestimable cost of civilian suffering. This is the repressed reality that emerges in the story through the disclosing function of the uncanny, which is, after all, "everything that was intended to remain secret, hidden away, and has come into the open" (Freud 2003, 132).

      How, then, can we read Little B. in this context—a weak, sparrow-like child who eventually becomes a sparrow? Even before his transformation, the boy appears as a strange bird next to his stout parents: "he was undersized for his age, with legs like macaroni, tiny claws, soft, soft hair that felt like mouse fur and big wide-open eyes. [...] And Mrs B. loved him as only weak children are loved" (*CW*2, 170–71). Showing potential symptoms of malnutrition at his parents' generous breakfast table, Little B.'s body takes the uncanny shape of an undernourished German child. C. Paul Vincent (1985) points to clear differences in terms of health between English and German children from 1916, when famine had become widespread in Germany. While the English child (although "never blessed with a surplus of food") "was fortunate to have maintained a level of nutrition necessary for more than mere subsistence", at the time of the armistice "the state of health of Germany's children was truly appalling", with soaring death rates from various diseases as a consequence (136–39). Tuberculosis, "the most widespread and deadly of Germany's wartime illnesses", affected children aged one to five in the final years of the war; tubercular mortality among this group had increased by 100 per cent in 1919 compared to 1914 (137–38). Given Mansfield's own suffering from tuberculosis, she was perhaps particularly sensitive to this distressing development, and would no doubt have concurred with Vincent: "many of these children died, and one is therefore forced to consider how many may have survived had the Allies abrogated the blockade at the initial signing of the armistice" (139). This is one of the reflections that Mansfield compels her reader to make through her portrayal of Little B.'s birdlike features and uncanny metamorphosis.

The social pathos of "A Suburban Fairy Tale" emerges with particular force in Mansfield's startling depiction of Little B.'s voice: a boy's piercing cry ("O-oh!") fusing with that of a sparrow ("*cheek-a-cheep-cheep-cheek!*") to vocalise the urgent, legitimate demand of a hungry, foreign child ("want something to eat, want something to eat"; *CW*2, 171–72). The replacement of the initial exclamation mark with a full stop in the last two iterations of this demand reinforces its emphatic legitimacy. As in several other stories by Mansfield, such as "Life of Ma Parker", "A Married Man's Story", "A Man and His Dog" (1922), and "The Canary" (1922), the voice and the lyrical cry function here as channels for affective transmission—the process by which an emotion strongly felt by the artist is conveyed to the reader. That Mansfield herself thought of the vocal potential of writing in such terms becomes evident notably in a striking image of the artist as a caged songbird, which recurs throughout her work. In a letter to her husband John Middleton Murry from October 20, 1919, she writes: "oh, it is agony to meet corruption when one thinks all is fair—the big snail under the leaf—the spot in the childs [sic] lung [...]. Hanging in our little cages on the awful wall over the gulf of eternity we must sing—sing" (*Letters* 3, 37). "Corruption" had two particular connotations for Mansfield towards the end of the war: tuberculosis—illness corrupting the body—and the moral and political corruption she associated with the war. Her figuration of corruption as affectively charged material for lyric expression recalls a frequently cited passage from another letter to Murry written on February 3, 1918:

> Ive [sic] two "kick offs" in the writing game. *One* is joy—real joy [...] and that sort of writing I could only do in just that state of being in some perfectly blissful way *at peace*. Then something delicate and lovely seems to open before my eyes, like a flower without thought of a frost or a cold breath—knowing that all about it is warm and tender and "steady." And *that* I try, ever so humbly to express.
>
> The other "kick off" is my old original one, and (had I not known love) it would have been my all. Not hate or destruction [...] but an *extremely* deep sense of hopelessness—of everything doomed to disaster. [...] There! as I took out a cigarette paper I got it exactly—*a cry against corruption* that is *absolutely* the nail on the head. Not a protest—a *cry*, and I mean corruption in the widest sense of the word, of course. (*Letters* 2, 54)

The image of the opening flower, another recurring motif in Mansfield's writing from this period, both exemplifies and describes the lyric impulse characterising much of her mature work, while the cry against corruption suggests a lyric voice no longer at peace to communicate emotions "recollected in tranquillity".

Considered alongside two resonant, contemporaneous reflections, her notion of lyrical writing as outlined in this passage is not merely post-romantic: it is also decidedly modernist. A diary entry from April 1920 contains a vivid, poetic depiction of the self flowering in "the moment of direct feeling when we are most ourselves and least personal" (*Notebooks* 2, 204). The modernist doctrine of impersonality pervades Mansfield's lyricism, as does the psychoanalytic privileging of experience that exceeds the conscious and rational; in a remark from October the same year about the impact of psychoanalysis on contemporary fiction, she suggests that a "subconscious ... wisdom" can emerge as "a sort of divine flower" in the work of a "*possessed*" and "*inspired*" artist (*Letters* 4, 69; emphasis in original). These words retain the occult implications that also appear in the epigraph to this chapter: an artist inspired by an initial emotion or impulse may become possessed (animistically, or telepathically) by the objects of her art to the point of becoming them. If the "direct feeling" inspiring "A Suburban Fairy Tale" was indignation against the corruption—the "perversion or destruction of integrity in the discharge of public duties" (*OED* 2017)—widely associated with the Allied blockade in the months following the armistice, Mansfield creates a process of consuming identification (the artist becoming a sparrow; Little B. becoming a starving child) that forcefully transmits that indignation to the reader. It is against this background that we should understand her outcry when reading "the loathsome press about Germany's cry for food", in a letter written on November 17, 1918:

> why don't they fly at each other kiss & cry & share everything—One feels that about nations—but alas! about individuals, too. *Why* do people hide & withdraw & suspect—as they do? [...]. I think it is *lack of heart*: a sort of blight on them which will not let them ever come to full flower. (*Letters* 2, 291)

Read as a social comment, this reflection would be idle and naïve with its quick shift of attention from the German food crisis to reserved individuals; it illustrates what Con Coroneos (1997) calls an "over-writing of love" in Mansfield's letters during the war years (201). However, if we relate it to her representation elsewhere of the war in terms of corruption and flowering, we can appreciate it as a way of voicing her conviction that post-war art must be driven by intense emotion. Privately calling Virginia Woolf's 1919 novel *Night and Day* "a lie in the soul" ("the war has never been, that is what its message is"), she wrote to Murry that artists must engage with the devastating consequences of the war by finding "new expressions new moulds for our new thoughts & feelings" (*Letters* 3, 82). Such writing should not take the shape of explicit socio-political commentary ("I dont want G. forbid mobilisation and the violation of Belgium" [ibid.]), but a remodelling of habitual, cognitive and affective "moulds".[14] Mansfield's own *"cry against corruption"* in "A Suburban Fairy Tale"—"Not a protest—a *cry*"—achieves such manipulation through its vocal and uncanny qualities. The cry that can only be heard, at first, as the threatening and unintelligible noise of abject birds eventually morphs into the voice of a single, loved son. Mansfield thereby attunes our ears to the acute needs of the starving children on the continent, as well as to the widespread suffering exacerbated by the food blockade and the cynical mindset endorsing it.

There is also another, immediately political side to Mansfield's engagement with wartime food and health policies. In Britain during the war, there was a massive public investment in the health of children up to five years, so that child welfare improved considerably. This support of infant and child welfare spanned the social spectrum and included a systematic organisation of antenatal and postnatal care (Winter 1977, 496–503). J. M. Winter (1977) draws attention to "the mixture of philanthropy and patriotism" that enabled these wide-ranging measures in mobilising popular approval and substantial funding: the movement for child welfare was "bolstered by the support of all those who wanted to maximize the future military potential of the country" (498–99, 502). Widespread concern about the high infant mortality and poor nutrition levels of the pre-war years engendered, for many, a determination to build the manpower needed for a

---

14 T. E. Hulme (1922b) uses the term "mould" in his account of Bergson's theory of art: habitual perception, he writes, "runs in certain moulds"—perceptual structures that produce "a practical simplification of reality" (302).

strong military.[15] "A Suburban Fairy Tale" no doubt expresses Mansfield's outrage at this aspect of the public efforts to improve children's health, and the ways in which they worked to breed future soldiers. Later in 1919, she wrote to Ottoline Morrell about the Versailles peace celebrations: "I have a food complex [...] when I think of all these toothless old jaws guzzling for the day—and then of all that beautiful youth feeding the fields of France" (*Letters* 2, 339).

Viewed in the light of the British "cult of the child" (Winter 1977, 498), "A Suburban Fairy Tale" assumes political as well as ethical dimensions, particularly through Mansfield's symbolic use of the sparrow figure. As Shieff (2014) observes, the process by which Mansfield projects her interiority onto the objects of her art, thereby animating them, has an important consequence: each such object comes to signify as "*more* than itself—that is, as a symbol" (78). This is true of the sparrows in "A Suburban Fairy Tale". The well-known biblical paradox about sparrows applies to Little B.: "are not five sparrows sold for two farthings, and not one of them is forgotten before God?" (Luke 12: 6).[16] Each single sparrow is loved and cared for, but also a commodity to be sold and eaten,[17] and Mr and Mrs B.'s loving attempt to feed their son to make him into a strong and healthy boy is similarly equivocal. In the context of British wartime investments in a new

---

[15] Vincent observes that "concern for the health of future soldiers was deepened by the recognition that large numbers of men were deemed by the army to be unfit for combat duty on grounds of poor health": in 1917–18, this figure was over 40 per cent (1985, 499). We can only speculate about whether health problems might have played a part in Mr B.'s failed attempts to "chuck his job and join the Army" during the war (*CW*2, 170).

[16] All biblical references are to www.kingjamesbibleonline.org.

[17] Cf. Gene Stratton-Porter (2017) on "the common custom in the East of catching small birds, and selling them to be skinned, roasted and sold as tid-bits"; sparrows were "an article of commerce in the days of Jesus, just as they are now in the Far East" (online). Melinda Harvey (2011) notes that the animals populating Mansfield's fiction tend to be "diminutive, unostentatious": "innocuous enough to remain uncaged, or unsavoury enough to avoid being eaten" (207). She gives the sparrow as an example of such animals, but in "A Suburban Fairy Tale", the sparrow's biblical function as a food item is significant.

generation of recruits, young boys effectively became sparrows. The human-animal distinction upheld in the biblical value judgement breaks down as Little B. turns into a bird: "are not two sparrows sold for a farthing? and one of them shall not fall on the ground without your Father. But the very hairs of your head are all numbered. Fear ye not therefore, ye are of more value than many sparrows" (Matthew 10: 29–31).[18] While the more cynical advocates of the children's welfare movement might claim to care for Little B. as God is said to care for each unique human being, the boy's transformation suggests that he is ultimately *not* "of more value than many sparrows", but food for the war machine.

To conclude, the pathos and uncanny dimensions of "A Suburban Fairy Tale" give us a sharp sense of the unequal distribution of food in Europe at this historical moment, and of the wartime uses of food and starvation as weapons for political ends. After the war in particular, as Sydney Janet Kaplan (1991) notes, Mansfield's writing expresses "outrage against a society in which privilege is so marked by indifference to the misery of others" (192). These words capture the socio-political force of "A Suburban Fairy Tale" and several other works among her post-war fiction. If Mansfield believed in the artist-magician's capacity to change the terms of the external world through the process of writing, her masterly use of animism, telepathy and uncanny metamorphosis reaches far beyond the narcissism that Freud associated with art as a form of magic. In this, her work demonstrates the vital, social and political role of affective transmission in the modernist short story—an area that has only begun to be explored.

Bibliography

Alpers, Antony, ed. 1984. *The Stories of Katherine Mansfield*. Auckland: Oxford University Press.

Barnett, L. Margaret. 1985. *British Food Policy during the First World War*. Boston: George Allen & Unwin.

---

[18] See also Luke 12: 7: "But even the very hairs of your head are all numbered. Fear not therefore: ye are of more value than many sparrows".

Bennett, Jane. 2010. *Vibrant Matter: A Political Ecology of Things.* Durham, NC: Duke University Press.

Brennan, Teresa. 2004. *The Transmission of Affect.* Ithaca, NY: Cornell University Press.

Burgan, Mary. 1994. *Illness, Gender, and Writing: The Case of Katherine Mansfield.* Baltimore, MD: Johns Hopkins University Press.

Coroneos, Con. 1997. "Flies and Violets in Katherine Mansfield." In *Women's Fiction and the Great War*, edited by Suzanne Raitt and Trudi Tate, 197–218. Oxford: Clarendon Press.

Freud, Sigmund. [1953] 1978a. "Totem and Taboo: Some Points of Agreement between the Mental Lives of Savages and Neurotics." In *Totem and Taboo and Other Works.* Vol. 13 of *The Standard Edition of the Complete Psychological Works of Sigmund Freud.* Translated by James Strachey (in collaboration with Anna Freud, assisted by Alix Strachey and Alan Tyson), vii–162. London: Hogarth Press and the Institute of Psycho-Analysis.

———. [1953] 1978b. "The Claims of Psycho-Analysis to Scientific Interest." In *Totem and Taboo and Other Works.* Vol. 13 of *The Standard Edition of the Complete Psychological Works of Sigmund Freud.* Translated by James Strachey (in collaboration with Anna Freud, assisted by Alix Strachey and Alan Tyson), 163–90. London: Hogarth Press and the Institute of Psycho-Analysis.

———. [1919] 2003. "The Uncanny." In *The Uncanny*, translated by David McLintock with an Introduction by Hugh Haughton, 123–62. London: Penguin.

Gasston, Aimee. 2013. "Consuming Art: Katherine Mansfield's Literary Snack." *Journal of New Zealand Literature* 31 (2): 163–82.

———. 2014. "Phenomenology of Beings at Home: The Presence of Things in the Short Fiction of Katherine Mansfield and Virginia Woolf." *Journal of New Zealand Literature* 32(2): 31–51. Special issue, "Katherine Mansfield: Masked and Unmasked," edited by Harry Ricketts and Anna Jackson.

Hanson, Clare. 2011. "Katherine Mansfield's Uncanniness." In *Celebrating Katherine Mansfield: A Centenary Volume of Essays*, edited by Gerri Kimber and Janet Wilson, 115–30. Basingstoke: Palgrave Macmillan.

Harvey, Graham. 2006. *Animism: Respecting the Living World*. New York: Columbia University Press.
———. ed. 2013. *The Handbook of Contemporary Animism*. Durham: Acumen.
Harvey, Melinda. 2011. "Katherine Mansfield's Menagerie." In *Katherine Mansfield and Literary Modernism*, edited by Janet Wilson, Gerri Kimber and Susan Reid, 202–10. London: Continuum.
Högberg, Elsa. Forthcoming. "Katherine Mansfield's Lyricism and Jacques Rancière's Politics of Aesthetics." *Modernism/modernity*.
Howard, N.P. 1993. "The Social and Political Consequences of the Allied Food Blockade of Germany, 1918–19." *German History* 11 (2): 161–88.
Hulme, T.E. 1922a. "The Note-Books of T.E. Hulme." *The New Age* 30 (22): 287–88.
———. 1922b. "The Note-Books of T.E. Hulme." *The New Age* 30 (23): 301–302.
———. 1922c. "The Note-Books of T.E. Hulme." *The New Age* 30 (24): 310–12.
Kaplan, Sydney Janet. 1991. *Katherine Mansfield and the Origins of Modernist Fiction*. Ithaca, NY: Cornell University Press.
Marks, Sally. 2013. "Mistakes and Myths: The Allies, Germany, and the Versailles Treaty, 1918–1921." *The Journal of Modern History* 85: 632–59.
McGee, Diane. 2001. *Writing the Meal: Dinner in the Fiction of Early Twentieth-Century Women Writers*. Toronto: University of Toronto Press.
Moran, Patricia. 1996. *Word of Mouth: Body Language in Katherine Mansfield and Virginia Woolf*. Charlottesville, VA: University Press of Virginia.
Murry, John Middleton. [1945] 1948. "Introductory Note" to "In a German Pension." In *Collected Stories of Katherine Mansfield*, 695–96. London: Constable.
Nakano, Eiko. 2002. "Intuition and Intellect: Henri Bergson's Influence on Katherine Mansfield's Representation of Places." *Journal of Postcolonial Writing* 40 (1): 86–100.

Nakano, Eiko. 2011. "Katherine Mansfield, *Rhythm* and Henri Bergson." In *Katherine Mansfield and Literary Modernism*, edited by Janet Wilson, Gerri Kimber and Susan Reid, 30–41. London: Continuum.

Oxford English Dictionary Online. 2017. "corruption, n." Oxford University Press. Accessed January 20, 2017. http://www.oed.com/view/Entry/42045?redirectedFrom=corruption.

Robinson, Roger. 1994. "Introduction: In from the Margin". In *Katherine Mansfield: In from the Margin*, edited by Roger Robinson, 1-8. Baton Rouge, LA: Louisiana State University Press.

Royle, Nicholas. 2003. *The Uncanny*. Manchester: Manchester University Press.

Shieff, Sarah. 2014. "Katherine Mansfield's Fairytale Food." *Journal of New Zealand Literature* 32 (2): 68–84. Special issue on "Katherine Mansfield: Masked and Unmasked", edited by Harry Ricketts and Anna Jackson.

Smith, Angela. 1999. *Katherine Mansfield and Virginia Woolf: A Public of Two*. Oxford: Clarendon Press.

---. 2000. *Katherine Mansfield: A Literary Life*. Basingstoke: Palgrave.

Stratton-Porter, Gene. 2017. "Sparrow." *International Standard Bible Encyclopaedia Online*. Accessed January 20, 2017. http://www.internationalstandardbible.com/S/sparrow.html.

Vincent, C. Paul. 1985. *The Politics of Hunger: The Allied Blockade of Germany, 1915–1919*. Athens, OH: Ohio University Press.

Wilson, Janet. 2013. "Mansfield as (Post)colonial-Modernist: Rewriting the Contract with Death." In *Katherine Mansfield and the (Post)colonial*, edited by Janet Wilson, Gerri Kimber and Delia da Sousa Correa, 29–44. Edinburgh: Edinburgh University Press.

---. 2016. "Katherine Mansfield and *Anima Mundi*: France and the Tradition of Nature Personified." In *Katherine Mansfield's French Lives*, edited by Claire Davison-Pégon and Gerri Kimber, 125–42. Leiden/Boston: Brill/Rodopi.

Winter, J. M. 1977. "The Impact of the First World War on Civilian Health in Britain." *The Economic History Review* 30 (3): 487–507.

Treasure and Rot: Preservation and Bequest in Mansfield's Short Fiction

Aimee Gasston

The ideas I want to explore in this chapter are not new, in terms of either Mansfield scholarship or literary history: the polarities of permanence and impermanence; preservation and decay; truth and corruption; and art and mortality are well-traversed territory. These very Keatsian themes—what Ali Smith (2007) refers to as Mansfield's "twinned impetus", the inexorably "linked expression of joy and grief" (xxi)—run through all of her work in a way that is so deeply rooted that it might seem to barely warrant commentary at all. Lorna Sage (2002) perhaps put it best when she wrote with characteristic salience: "Mansfield's work speaks about what's irretrievably lost, material, mortal, *unless it is turned to artifice*" (81). Beyond that, one might think, what more is there to say on the subject?

Nonetheless, I would here like to examine these antitheses as materially manifested in the themes of treasure and rot in my favourite of all Mansfield's stories, the exquisitely wrought, panoramic, subtle, shimmering "At the Bay". I would like to think about what a story is, what it does and what Mansfield's stories continue to do in her absence—in short, what a story contains and what it passes on. To quote Lorna Sage on Mansfield again: "In her stories she could (and regularly did, between 1917 and 1921) pull off the illusionist feat of storing infinite riches in a little room" (2002, 79–80). By examining these riches, I will begin to develop a theory of preservation and bequest, by which we can view Mansfield's stories as treasure houses which store and pass on both riches and obligations to writers and readers. As Mansfield wrote to Ida Baker in 1920: "thats [sic] what writing means to me—to enrich—to give" (*Letters* 4, 57). In 1922, she wrote to the South African writer Sara Millin: "I think the only way to live as a writer is to draw upon one's real *familiar* life—to find the treasure in that as Olive Shreiner did" (*Letters* 5, 80, original italics).[1] Mansfield was not the first to conceptualise literature as a type of treasure. The symbolist poet Stéphane Mallarmé viewed poetry as "the jewellery of mankind" (qtd in Cain and Furbank 2004, 27), while Walter Pater (1998), whom the young Mansfield revered so much, saw the aim of life as "to burn always with this hard, gemlike flame" (236); life which should be transposed into art. Later, in his 1936 essay "The Storyteller", Walter Benjamin (1999) would draw attention to the way in which Leskov depicts the gem-cutter as the "perfect artisan" (106) in his stories, drawing a comparison between storytellers and refiners and polishers of jewels.

Similarly, Susan Stewart (1993), in her incisive book *On Longing*, writes of miniature books and their popularity from the 15th century onward. Many of these were covered in jewels and worn like necklaces, the book's "gemlike properties [...] reflected in its adornment by real gems" (41). Sometimes books were even made with metal pages with Stewart quoting James Dougald Henderson's 1928 description of one: "silver gilt, three quarters of an inch high, with a narrow panel on the front cover [...] enameled in natural colours, a pansy with stems and leaves", with the front cover boasting "an engraved cobweb from which hangs a spider", its "body [...] a pearl and the head [...] a wee ruby" (41). One of the most bizarre and successful descriptions in Mansfield's "At the Bay" relates to the two little boys by the water's edge who "twinkled like spiders" (*CW2*, 350)—Ali Smith picks up on this phrase in her Introduction to the Penguin edition of Mansfield's stories to assert that the "whole notion of spider is re-seen because of the verb" (2007, xxi). The phrase ought not make sense at all, yet absolutely does—it makes sense before you think it through,

---

[1] Gillian Boddy (1994) also draws upon this quotation in her exploration of "the ways in which Mansfield 'found treasure' during the last months of her life" (174). Boddy's essay explores the biographical and postcolonial aspects of "At the Bay" to conclude that the "pains Mansfield was enduring also mixed inevitably with the treasure of the past" (187). This essay will continue Boddy's argument with an extended analysis of the textual ambivalence of the story.

with its oddity only apparent as you turn it over in your hands. It is an example of Mansfield's deftness in selecting from her word-hoard and juxtaposing her treasures, making words yield far more than their literalness and letting language coruscate. It signifies, makes meaning, but remains resistant to direct translation. Rather like a jewel it demonstrates what Roland Barthes (2006) would refer to as "the ultimate power of signification" (59), sparkling with a plurality of possible meanings.

The mesmeric opening paragraphs of "At the Bay" also twinkle like spiders yet, like the act of twinkling itself, the treasure they offer is fleeting and impermanent; blink and you will miss it. The resilient permanence of gold, silver and pearls ironically suffuses a thoroughly transient, mortal scenery which initially appears to be held in a state of suspension. We have "marigolds" and "pearls of dew" (*CW*2, 342); the shepherd's coat decorated with "a web of tiny drops"; "big spots of light gleam" in the mist while "silvery beams broaden" (*CW*2, 343). A goldfinch flies over the shepherd's head, turning to the sun; even the swamp which the sheep stray over is yellow with the gleam of gold (*CW*2, 344). The "glittering sea [is] so bright that it made one's eyes ache to look at it" (*CW*2, 343). Yet that word "ache" is just one of many counterpoints to the rich, sumptuous promise of these scenes, a stinging reminder of age and decay. The physical frames of the shepherd and his old sheep-dog are also reminders of frailty, the shepherd's mortality pointedly pronounced in Mansfield's description of him as "grave" (*CW*2, 344). The pearls of dew do not remain as such; we are reminded of another tireless natural force—gravity—by the "splashing of big drops on large leaves" and then there is "something else—what was it?—a faint stirring and shaking, the snapping of a twig and then such silence that it seemed someone was listening" (*CW*2, 343). This sensation of someone listening is especially uncanny and ominous; it captures the anticipatory state of waiting for disruption or decay which permeates Mansfield's most tranquil scenes as well as the experience of her readers. We approach and then leave Mansfield's stories expecting to be stirred, shaken or snapped like twigs. Relying on similar imagery, later in the story Linda Burnell compares herself to a leaf: "Along came Life like a wind and she was seized and shaken; she had to go" (*CW*2, 354). Elsewhere, with more of a sense of solid fatalism than precariousness, the Trout family dog lies on his back seemingly awaiting death:

> His blue eye was turned up, his legs stuck out stiffly, and he gave an occasional desperate sounding puff, as much as to say he had decided to make an end of it and was only waiting for some kind cart to come along. (*CW*2, 356–57).

If the opening paragraphs of the story conjure tranquillity, it is an assuredly uneasy one. While the "whole of Crescent Bay [i]s hidden under a white sea-mist" (*CW*2, 342), there is a sense that what is covered by the mist is unlikely to be as pure as its hue. The neighbouring Daylight Cove might allude to shadows as much as light—Mansfield wrote in a letter before she knew she had contracted tuberculosis of the urgent need to "make use of a short daylight" (*Letters* 1, 94). If the uncanny is, as Freud (1990) argued, what is "concealed and kept out of sight" (345) Mansfield's stories return to the notion of death as uncanny not only to probe the hypocrisy of those public rituals which seek to sanitise it but also to undo its mystery by continually sweeping it out from under the carpet of her fiction. In part six of "At the Bay", a manuka flower is described intricately for almost a paragraph's duration; it is depicted as a "deep bronze" "bell" (*CW*2, 354) with Mansfield appropriating metallic imagery once more while alluding to mortality, nudging us to wonder for whom these particular bells might toll. The paragraph ends with Linda Burnell's reflection: "Who takes the trouble or the joy—to make all these things that are wasted, wasted.... It was uncanny" (*CW*2, 354). This moment recalls a comment of Mansfield's to John Middleton Murry in a letter of November 1919:

> Its as though, even while we live again we face death. But *through Life*: that's the point. We see death in life as we see death in a flower that is fresh unfolded. Our hymn is to the

flower's beauty—we would make that beauty immortal because we *know*. (*Letters* 3, 96)

It is the knowledge of death, the imminent rotting of the flower that blazes for a day, which intensifies its flashing beauty. Not long after this moment, we find Jonathan Trout exclaiming in Linda's presence: "The shortness of life! The shortness of life! I've only one night or one day, and there's this vast dangerous garden, waiting out there, undiscovered, unexplored" (*CW*2, 366). Like Mansfield herself, Jonathan Trout knows the importance of getting "so much into a short time" (*Letters* 1, 94). His statement is easily aligned with Mansfield's view of the short fiction form, speaking to the richness of rendering required by its brevity and ever-looming ending. When Jonathan Trout begins to sing lines from an opera moments later, the lyrics chosen are "Would ye hear the story / How it unfolds itself ..." (*CW*2, 366), in a self-referential gesture.² Once the story begins to unfold, we are aware that we advance towards its ending, and it is the approaching ending which instigates awareness of our own demise or rot and makes us cling to any treasure offered up so tightly. When Stanley Burnell misreads Jonathan Trout, conceiving of his purportedly eccentric ideas as flawed, he complains of his conversation as always influenced by "some rot he'd been reading" (*CW*2, 345). Rot inflects Mansfield's stories and is what makes their treasure glow all the more brightly. She changed the way we read, inciting an increased intensity of absorption and appreciation as if reading were a model for living— her stories are illuminated because "we *know*" the resonant meaning of their endings. As Valerie Shaw (1998) observed, referring to the episodic nature of the 20th-century short story, the "brevity of the form [...] is directly imitative of the modern experience of being alive" (17).

Brevity is a rich seam in "At the Bay", one of Mansfield's longest stories. The story records the space of "just one day" to which Jonathan Trout refers—the sun tracing its arc from start to finish, yet

---

2   The lines Trout cites are from Pagliacci (or "Clowns"), an Italian opera by Ruggero Leoncavallo which meditates on the relationship between life and art, first performed in 1892.

another piece of gold that saturates the piece. Yet there is literal treasure too. Towards the middle of the story we are shown a notice in Mrs Stubbs's shop window, which announces:

> LOST! HANSOME GOLE BROOCH
> SOLID GOLD
> ON OR NEAR BEACH
> REWARD OFFERED (*CW*2, 349)

This echoes a comment of the narrator in Virginia Woolf's (2003) "The Mark on the Wall" (written earlier in 1917—a story which Katherine told Virginia she "liked tre-*men*dously"; *Letters* 2, 170) whose narrator declares: "how very little control of our possessions we have", imagining "opals and emeralds" to "lie about the roots of turnips" (78). Elsewhere in "At the Bay", Stanley Burnell bemoans that fact that he "can't keep a single possession to [himself]" (*CW*2, 347). The notice also links to the contemporaneous story "The Voyage" in terms of both its device and theme. In that story, Fenella looks up to see framed text above her bed, which reads:

> Lost! One Golden Hour
> Set with Sixty Diamond Minutes.
> No Reward Is Offered
> For It Is Gone For Ever! (*CW*2, 379)

In each example the comedic capitals offset the seriousness of the messages which ruminate on loss and perilousness, saving the tone from mawkishness. Their manufactured quaintness somehow works to evoke a nostalgia and yearning akin to loss, each notice joining cry with Jonathan Trout: "The shortness of life! The shortness of life!" (*CW*2, 366). They beg us to question what sort of treasure it is with which we should choose to endow the hour that is our life: the gold brooch mourned by the sign in the shop, or the "fat chuckle" which emanates from its proprietor who gladly knows "Freedom's best!" (*CW*2, 361)?

The word "gold" features 12 times throughout "At the Bay", yet only twice does it refer to the precious metal—in the example above and in the later beach scene where Beryl drops jewellery into her mother's lap before swimming—one item lost, one cast off. While gold is one of the most stable chemical elements, resistant to rust and corrosion, the remainder of Mansfield's references are decidedly ephemeral; things that cannot be easily grasped. We have patches of sunlight, the sky coloured a "pale gold" (*CW*2, 366), marigolds, nasturtiums, a goldfinch ruffling its breast feathers in the sun, the sand at the bottom of the sea: "when you kicked with your toes there rose a little puff of gold-dust" (*CW*2, 353). Gold is neither lost nor solid—it is all around, but decidedly not in a treasure chest, nor in a safe or a bank.[3]

While Beryl thinks alone in her room at night "Oh, what a joy it is to own things! Mine—my own!", the boldness of her statement is undercut by the childlike question that follows it: "My very own for ever?" (*CW*2, 368). This unanswered question, containing that foreboding, anomalous word so often applied by humans to situations it does not suit—"forever"—echoes Kezia's hopeless interrogation from earlier in the story: "Does everybody have to die?" (*CW*2, 358). These questions dance with Alice's rather beaten-up parasol, referred to grimly and appropriately as a *"perishall"* (*CW*2, 359; italics in original); they hover with the strong smell of seaweed on the beach which precedes its decay. They foreshadow Harry Kember's proclamation "Oh, rot!" which indicates not only his disbelief in Beryl but also a wider disenchantment with the world; an absence epitomised by his "bright, blind terrifying smile" (*CW*2, 370).

In a letter of February 7, 1922 which Mansfield wrote to Murry from Paris, she quotes from *Anthony and Cleopatra*: "Like to a vagabond flag upon the stream / Goes to and back, lackeying the varying tide / To rot itself with motion" (*Letters* 5, 51). This phrase is,

---

3   We might remember at this point the profession of Mansfield's father, the banker Harold Beauchamp, whom the young Mansfield transposed in "Juliet" (1906) as "a general merchant, director of several companies, chairman of several societies, thoroughly commonplace and commercial" (*CW*1, 38).

Mansfield writes, both "terrible" and revealing of a "terribly deep psychological truth" which she pins on the phrase "*rots* itself" (51). "I understand that phrase better than I care to", Mansfield explains, "I mean—alas!—I have proof of it in my own being" (51). Despite this confession, perhaps for Murry's sake, the phrase which Mansfield omits from her Shakespeare (1997) quotation, which precedes and explains the vagabond simile is: "This common body" (2638). The idea of the body rotting would likely have terrified Mansfield, yet what comes through in the quotation is not the threat of disease which befalls an unlucky few but instead the "common body" which "rots itself with motion", petitioning death through life.[4] We rot, not with stagnation but motion, as if it is life's propulsive effort which invites decay rather than counteracting it, like the story whose flow quickens its termination.

Some counterpoise to this inescapable decay can be found in what is described in "Bliss" as "all this blissful treasure" (*CW*2, 149) of which the world is made up. If Linda Burnell's life is a "ship that got wrecked everyday" (*CW*2, 355), it is perhaps one in need of appreciation for "what gets chucked up from wrecks" (*CW*2, 350). Her stifled existence bears sharp contrast with that lived out by the children of the story whose probing fingers find blissful hidden treasure made up of sea-smoothed glass in the sand: "The lovely green thing seemed to dance in Pip's fingers. Aunt Beryl had a nemeral in a ring, but it was a very small one. This one was as big as a star and far more beautiful" (*CW*2, 350). Perhaps treasure is less likely to be found in Beryl's jewellery box than in Mrs Fairfield's kitchen, where "the sun stream[s] on to the yellow varnished walls and bare floor" and "[e]verything on the table flashed and glittered" around the "old salad bowl filled with yellow and red nasturtiums" (*CW*2, 347), in ageing Jonathan's hair "speckled all over with silver, like the breast plumage of a black fowl" (*CW*2, 367) or the "fire (which) blazed in him" (*CW*2, 365). It might be

---

[4] Another writer with whom Mansfield shares rich affinities is Samuel Beckett (1965), whose Pozzo with similar devastation summarises in *Waiting for Godot*: "They give birth astride the grave, the light gleams an instant, then it's night once more" (89).

found in "the sunlight [that] seemed to spin like a silver coin dropped into each of the small rock pools" (*CW*2, 356); or in the sea which is "that marvellous transparent blue, flecked with silver" and "sand at the bottom [that] looked gold"; or the bush outlined against the sunset which "gleam[ed] dark and brilliant like metal" (*CW*2, 366).

Towards the end of the story, in a gesture of hope, Linda observes this same sunset to find "something infinitely joyful and tender in [the] silver beams" which extend out over the sky. There is a creeping sense of a capacity for grasping joy, beauty and freedom—of realising that a life made up increasingly of "glimpses, moments, breathing spaces of calm" (*CW*2, 355) might be all she needs to begin to rebalance the dormant life she has not quite chosen. Mansfield famously described in a letter of February 3, 1919 to Murry her "two 'kick offs' in the writing game" as "joy—real joy" and "an *extremely deep sense of hopelessness*". In expressing the latter, her writing takes the expression of "*a cry against corruption*" (*Letters* 2, 54, italics in original)—a counter-assertion to the rot of injustice, decay, dishonesty, cruelty. The moments of freedom and beauty she depicts in her stories are the fleeting pieces of treasure which work against a wider network of corruption, oppression, hopelessness and entropy.

Reflecting on a photograph of herself as a small child sent to her by her sister, Mansfield was dismayed that the picture did not match her self-image of "a sweet little laughing thing, rather French, with wistful eyes under a fringe, firmly gripping a spade, showing even then a longing to dig for treasure with her own hands" (Mantz and Murry 1933, 64). Mansfield's grandfather, Arthur Beauchamp, was an unsuccessful gold prospector (38) and it is possible Mansfield feared his genetic inheritance; she saw the photograph as depicting a "little solemn monster" who grasped her spade with "the greatest reluctance" (64). The photograph referred to is collected in Gerri Kimber's (2016) recent biography of Mansfield's early years and reveals Mansfield's reflection to be characteristically self-deprecating (28). Nevertheless, Mansfield's desire to dig for treasure is better borne out by her life's work than childhood photographs. In some ways, those stories function themselves as a type of family photograph album, though one with extended reach and resonance. As Kimber sets out in her biography, in "At the Bay" Mansfield captured her mother, Annie Beauchamp, as Linda Burnell (37), her Uncle Val Walters as Jonathan Trout (2016, 58), as well as the geography of Days Bay (75–77). Mansfield herself wrote of "At the Bay":

> It is so strange to bring the dead to life again. Theres my grandmother, back in her chair with her pink knitting, there my uncle stalks over the grass. I feel as I write "you are not dead, my darlings. All is remembered. I bow down to you. I efface myself so that you may live again through me in your richness and your beauty." And one feels *possessed*. (*Letters* 4, 278)

Not only possessed, through fiction Mansfield is also able to possess, and pass on possessions. Here, she conceives of the short story as a preserving mechanism which is not only capable of sustaining and exploring memory but also revivifying the deceased. Through her fiction she is able to perpetuate the riches her relatives have left to her, working to balance the rot and corruption of death while not denying its necessity, facing it through life.

On October 1, 1920, Mansfield wrote, again to Murry: "'One must tell everything—everything.' That is more and more real to me each day. It is, after all, the only treasure heirloom we have to leave—our own little grain of truth" (*Letters* 4, 57). Martin Heidegger (2000) similarly defined the essence of art as the "setting-into-work of truth", summarising the purpose of art as "the creative preserving of truth in the work" (196). This is what Mansfield left all of us—a treasure hoard composed of gleaming grains of truth. Furthermore, all her work practises a state of what Heidegger termed "being-towards-death", each story keenly aware of approaching endings; *memento mori* is the lingering message of each. In her strongest work, she revivifies those loved ones she has lost and gently, persistently reminds us that we will die too, so we might live to grope the treasure about our feet. She addresses her own fear that there will be "no time to explain what could be explained so simply", by setting forth the ineffable, alternately meaningful and meaningless complexity of life using only the most straightforward of words. "Grain" is an appropriate metaphor for the words Mansfield chose—it captures well the resolute, unpompous prose in which she set forth her creative preserving of truth.

It has been observed that, during Mansfield's life, "very few *possessions*—in the material sense—were precious to her" and those that were "she was likely to give away, impulsively, to any who seemed to be 'her people'" (Mantz and Murry 1933, 81; italics in original). Less than six months before she died, in a letter of August 7, 1922, Mansfield wrote to Murry about her will in a letter which was left for him at her bank in London to be read after her death. Written a week before her official will, it concluded: "I seem, after all, to have nothing to leave and nobody to leave it to" (*Letters* 5, 235).[5] Jean-Paul Sartre (1999) might have disagreed, keenly aware as he was of all the things that Mansfield left behind in her literature, as if in compensation for an absence of material endowments. During World War Two, he recorded his ambition to "write short stories of a similar kind to K. Mansfield" (145). By this, he meant writing stories which would

> present meaning still adhering to things [...] and—in order to exhibit it—to show rapidly some of the objects that secrete it, and to make their equivalence felt; in such a way that these solids would drive away and annul each other in the reader's mind, just as one event drives away the memory of another, and there would eventually remain on the horizon of this motley chaos only a discreet, tenacious meaning—very precise, but escaping from the words forever. (145)

---

[5] There were of course some possessions, including a gold watch and chain for Ida Baker (1985)—one golden hour set with sixty diamond minutes perhaps, which Mansfield would silently urge her to seize. Baker interpreted it differently, recalling in her memoir: "Her watch and chain on the mantelpiece I took at once. It was a symbol or pledge, which she had left me to assure me that she was still going forward and on" (229).

Here, Sartre presents Mansfield's work as radiating meaning which is not literal and perhaps more than literary—it is as if the nimbly complex structures of the stories which she creates might be better described as a series of material things, created by a sculptor rather than a writer. They contain illuminated objects—evidencing Mansfield's belief that the artist should "single out, [...] bring into the light, [...] put up higher" (*Notebooks* 2, 267)—to be experienced rather than explained, as if reading Mansfield were a type of aesthesis; a direct experience of the material world rather than comprehension through description. Sartre's comment reveals Mansfield's legacy as both profound and manifold—a refulgent literature containing a myriad of carefully chosen objects, to each of which a "discreet, tenacious meaning" attaches. It is a rich inheritance.

And so many have prospered from what Mansfield left behind—her literary endowment; that which Virginia Woolf (1980) referred to when she wrote of finding public libraries "full of sunk treasure" (126). I have mentioned Woolf already, but Woolf had a friend in later life whom Mansfield would not live long enough to meet—Elizabeth Bowen. Bowen did not read Mansfield until after she had published her first volume of stories in 1923, at which point her first thought was that people would say that she had copied Mansfield—and they did.[6] Over 30 years later, Bowen (1956) wrote an Introduction to an American edition of Mansfield's stories published by Vintage, in which she sets out a detailed, reverent and personal tribute. In it, she describes the New Zealand stories such as "Prelude", "At the Bay" and "The Doll's House" as being on "a quite other, supreme level", possessing a "living-and-breathing reality [that] at once astonishes and calms us" (xxii). The piece ends with these words:

---

[6] As Bowen (1961) set out in her introduction to her first story collection: "I read *Bliss* when I had completed that first set of my stories which were to make *Encounters*—then, admiration and envy were shot through with a profound dismay: I thought, 'If ever I am published, everybody will say I imitated her.' I was right: this happened" (10).

The stories are more than moments, instants, gleams: she has given them touches of eternity. The dauntless artist accomplished, if less than she hoped, more than she knew. Almost no writer's art has not its perishable fringes: light dust may settle on that margin. But against the core, the integrity, what can time do? Katherine Mansfield's deathless expectations set up a mark for us: no one has yet fulfilled them. Still at work, her genius rekindles faith; she is on our side in every further attempt. The effort she was involved in involves us—how can we feel her other than a contemporary? (xxiv)

So much is said in this short paragraph which reverberates with Mansfield's prose and her ambitions—the gleams we have seen in "At the Bay", immaculately, uncannily preserved like that mirror Kezia spies in the room she shares with her grandmother—"very strange [...] as though a little piece of forked lightning was imprisoned in it" (*CW2*, 357), at once fleeting and permanent. This is what another dazzling artist whose prose has also been touched by Mansfield, Ali Smith (2013), calls the ability of the short story, as perfected by Mansfield, to deal uncompromisingly in "the purely momentary nature of everything, both timeless *and* transient" (29). We have that word "perishable" beside an observation of Mansfield's driving, doughty integrity which was so closely linked to the meaning of that word; the integrity which gave her access to those "touches of eternity" in her work. Finally, we have her aesthetic challenge, the obligations she passed on to the writers that followed her, the success of which is conveyed in Bowen's description of them as "deathless expectations" which still call to be answered. These expectations were ones which Woolf and Bowen sought to meet; ones which Simone de Beauvoir (1993) also responded to in *The Second Sex*, where she described the way Mansfield captured those "luminous moments of happiness" which demonstrate the "free surge of liberty" usually "reserved for man" (653); ones now responded to bravely by Smith in her stories and novels. Mansfield is our indefatigable contemporary.

As Jacques Derrida (1982) wrote in "Signature Event Context", for writing to be writing, "it must continue to 'act' and to be legible even if what is called the author of the writing no longer answers for what he has written, for what he seems to have signed" (316). It is this act of iterability, the text's ability to remain still at work, still haunting, still giving, by which we can judge the generous riches of Mansfield's literary bequest.

Bibliography

Beckett, Samuel. 1965. *Waiting for Godot*. London: Faber.
Baker, Ida. 1985. *Katherine Mansfield: The Memories of L.M.* London: Virago.
Barthes, Roland. 2006. "From Gemstones to Jewellery." In *The Language of Fashion*, 54–59. London: Bloomsbury Academic.
Beauvoir, Simone de. 1993. *The Second Sex*. Edited by H. M. Parshley. London: Everyman's Library.
Boddy, Gillian. 1994. "'Finding the Treasure,' Coming Home—Katherine Mansfield in 1921-22." In *Katherine Mansfield: In from the Margin*, edited by Roger Robinson, 173–88. Baton Rouge, LA and London: Louisiana State University Press.
Bowen, Elizabeth. 1956. "Introduction." In *Stories* by Katherine Mansfield, v–xxiv. New York: Alfred A. Knopf and Random House.
———. 1961. *Encounters*. London: Ace Books.
Benjamin, Walter. 1999. "The Storyteller: Reflections on the Works of Nikolai Leskov." In *Illuminations*, edited by Hannah Arendt, 83–107. London: Pimlico.
Cain, A. M., and P. N. Furbank. 2004. *Mallarmé on Fashion: A Translation of the Fashion Magazine* La Dernière Mode *with Commentary*. New York and Oxford: Berg.
Derrida, Jacques. 1982. "Signature Event Context." In *Margins of Philosophy*. Translated by Alan Bass, 307–30. Chicago: Harvester Press.
Freud, Sigmund. 1990. "The 'Uncanny'." In *Art and Literature*, edited by James Strachey, 335–76. London: Penguin.

Heidegger, Martin. 2000. "The Origin of the Work of Art." In *Basic Writings*, edited by David Farrell Krell, 139–212. London: Routledge.

Kimber, Gerri. 2016. *Katherine Mansfield: The Early Years*. Edinburgh: Edinburgh University Press.

Mantz, Ruth Elvish, and John Middleton Murry. 1933. *The Life of Katherine Mansfield*. London: Constable.

Pater, Walter. 1998. *The Renaissance: Studies in Art and Poetry*. London: Senate.

Sage, Lorna. 2002. *Moments of Truth: Twelve Twentieth-Century Women Writers*. London: Fourth Estate.

Shakespeare, William. 1997. *The Norton Shakespeare*. Edited by Stephen Greenblatt, Walter Cohen, Jean E. Howard, and Katharine Eisaman Maus. London and New York: W. W. Norton & Company.

Sartre, Jean-Paul. 1999. *War Diaries: Notebooks From a Phoney War 1939–1940*. Translated by Quintin Hoare. London and New York: Verso.

Shaw, Valerie. 1998. *The Short Story: A Critical Introduction*. London and New York: Longman.

Smith, Ali, 2007. "Introduction." In *The Collected Stories* by Katherine Mansfield, v–xxx. London: Penguin.

---, 2013. *Artful*. London: Penguin.

Stewart, Susan. 1993. *On Longing: Narratives of the Miniature, the Gigantic, the Souvenir, the Collection*. Durham, NC and London: Duke University Press.

Woolf, Virginia. 1980. *The Diary of Virginia Woolf*. Vol. 2. *1920–1924*. Edited by Anne Olivier Bell with Andrew McNeillie. New York and London: Harvest / Harcourt Brace Jovanovich.

---, 2003. *A Haunted House: The Complete Shorter Fiction*. Edited by Susan Dick. London: Vintage.

Death by Ink: The Symbolism of Ink in Katherine Mansfield's "The Fly"

Janka Kascakova

> With a single drop of ink for a mirror,
> the Egyptian sorcerer undertakes to reveal
> to any chance comer far-reaching visions of the past.
> (Eliot [1859] 2008, 9)

In spite of its short length, especially compared to some of Mansfield's other famous stories, "The Fly" remains one of her most discussed texts. In fact, one could argue that "what we do not know about it is not for want of telling".[1] It has been, after all, at one point the subject of what John Hagopian (1964) fittingly refers to as "a critical guerrilla warfare" (385).[2] But the attention given to particular symbols or elements of the story is surprisingly uneven; while some have been dissected and assessed from multiple angles, the very killing weapon—ink—is, in most cases, strangely neglected. Out of the large number of interpretations of this story, many either do not mention ink at all or refer to it only in passing without any attempt at tackling its possible symbolic value (see Jacobs 1947; Bledsoe 1947; Wright 1955; Assad 1955; Bell 1960; Rea 1965; Bateson and Shakevitch 1962; Meyers [1978] 2002). Others offer quick and often unsatisfactory insights into their understanding of the place they assign the ink within the symbolic meaning of the story. Joe D. Thomas (1961a), for example, maintains that "by every literary tradition and every law of associative psychology, these darkly oozing patches must be identified with the boss's grief; they are the one perfectly obvious

---

[1] Words borrowed from Mansfield's review of *The Sleeping Partner* by M. P. Willcocks entitled "The 'Sex-Complex'" where, however, they apply to the topic of sex education (*CW*3, 501).
[2] Hagopian refers to the back and forth discussion about "The Fly" taking place mostly in *The Explicator* in the 1940s through to the 1960s.

symbol of the story" (261). Unfortunately, after Clinton W. Oleson's (1961) critical attack on his reading, Thomas was no longer willing to defend this position, calling it his "weakest [...] assumption" (Thomas 1961b, 586). However, both Robert Stallman (1945) and Ted Boyle (1965) respectively, also associate the ink with the grief the boss suffers; Stanley Greenfield (1958) indirectly supports this reading but includes the added symbolism of time. Time is also Hagopian's (1964, 386) response, but no further discussion ensues in any of their analyses, and the ink is thus assigned a supporting role rather than being treated as one of the central symbols of the story, which is the premise of this chapter.

More recent readings of the story continue aspects of the early critical reception; Vincent O'Sullivan (2011) comments on the ink only parenthetically, noting that "to be drowned in ink" is a "sardonic note [...] from a writer who thought writing, pure and simple, so diminished life" (22). Parenthetically again, but closer to the argument of this chapter, Clare Hanson (2011) hesitantly hypothesizes that the ink constitutes, "*perhaps*, a self-referential allusion to the process of writing" (126; my emphasis). The most detailed discussion of the ink as well as two other liquids, blood and milk, in both (what she called) "the life-writing" and "the art-writings" was offered recently by Diana Harris (2014, 52). She first construes it as a symbol of the afterlife, but later, however, adds another interpretation, claiming that in "The Fly" the ink "stands for blood" (54). She comments on "the way in which [Mansfield] interrogated the meaningless waste of young lives lost on the dual battlefields of war and disease with pen and ink" (52), and later reads the boss in "The Fly" as "the kind of anonymous English officer who has been so often blamed for the loss of countless lives through stupidity and blind obedience to orders", or as the "men who condemn young men to war and can barely remember why" (63). She concludes that the story is "a strong anti-war protest" (64), but at this point in her discussion does not consider the ink, and the possible implications of its use by the boss that would further support this line of argument.

The relatively frequent glossing over of the ink in the story is rather surprising for several reasons, the first and foremost being that it was, figuratively speaking, Mansfield's life-blood, the liquid that enabled her to express herself and spread her ideas through writing. That something so dear to her was used in such an unambiguously negative context should have alerted the critics to its significance from the outset. Secondly, although symbolic references to all kinds of insects, especially flies, pepper her writings, and they are more often than not drowning or drenched, the liquid is usually milk or cream;[3] it is only in this last story that it changes from the white stickiness of the beverage symbolizing her increasing health problems that were gradually slowing down her movements,[4] to the darkness of ink. This shift indicates that *her* dying is caused by a different agent than that of whoever is symbolized by the fly in her story and that the medium is thus very important. Thirdly, if ink was indeed insignificant and seen by Mansfield as just some kind of liquid necessary for the way she had decided her literary fly would die, then anything else would have done: water, tea, coffee, milk or the "little drop of whisky" (*CW*2, 477) which the boss offers to the frail Woodifield; all of these are arguably more appealing to a fly than ink. Lastly, all the associations of ink with literature, culture, education but also politics and propaganda, together with the extent to which World War I, more than any other war, was directly connected with literature and poetry (see Fussell [1975] 2000; Todman 2007; Winter [1995] 2010), point towards a much greater significance of this particular symbol than has previously been thought.

My reading of the story builds on the previous ones, especially those that see "The Fly" not only as a strong anti-war protest in general, but as a direct reaction to this particular conflict and the

---

[3] See Harris (2014) for an extensive discussion of these examples.
[4] Interestingly, Virginia Woolf's very vivid recollection of her last meeting with Mansfield also includes "a glass of milk and a medicine bottle" on her writing table, as the first observation about her surroundings (Woolf 1980, 226).

British war and post-war attitudes.[5] The particular emphasis on ink reinforces many arguments made earlier and further clarifies who Mansfield held responsible for the disaster. Unlike most other readings that focus on interpreting mainly who the victim and the perpetrator are, that is, who is symbolized by the boss and the fly, this reading advocates the need to assign equal attention both to how and by what means the tragedy occurred.

As Mansfield famously expressed in a letter to Murry, she was unable or unwilling to write explicit or openly critical works about the war like those of the World War I poets serving in the trenches; there was no "bang out" telling about "the deserts of vast eternity" for her (*Letters* 3, 97–98; November 16, 1919). Instead, and unlike her pre-war stories of *In a German Pension*, which are sometimes heavy-handed in their mockery of the Germans, by the end of her career, Mansfield was well able to deliver a quite radical upbraiding in a much more subtle way. Thus "The Fly", in all its seeming intimacy and covertness, should be put alongside Owen's or Sassoon's most critical war poems. Its inclusion of ink, not for its original purpose of writing, but as a makeshift murder or killing weapon (depending on the extent of its deliberate use for evil purposes), actually constitutes a bitter accusation of the abuse of ink in countless ways that caused, prolonged, or in any way influenced the war and made it into one of the deadliest events of human history.

The drops falling on the hapless insect read almost like part of a mythological or biblical tale. Their number, three, and its symbolism of fullness or completeness suggest that this amount is indeed symbolic, not actual, and that they represent something else rather than, to put it bluntly, the scientifically accurate amount of some sticky liquid required for the demise of an insect of a certain size. The number's value is also ambiguous and thus befitting the gradual build-up of tension in the crucial part of the story: according to common superstition, the number three can bring both good and bad luck, and there

---

[5] See also Joanna Scutts (2009) who, although not taking ink into consideration, also reads the story as a comment on the post-war political issues, notably the commemoration of the fallen.

is indeed a tension between these two. A first-time reader might well wait in suspense, together with the boss, wondering whether the fly will survive the third drop and escape; whether the "*plucky* little devil" (*CW2*, 479; my emphasis) will also be "lucky".

Finally, through different historical periods, cultures, or fields of study, the number three is commonly associated with objects, characters or phenomena that are on the one hand distinct or separate, and on the other inseparably joined by some common link or principle: a triangle has three edges that can even have different angles but when combined form a geometric shape; the Trinity consists of three distinct persons who together create one God; to some extent Cerberus's[6] three heads can each move separately but are attached to one body, to mention but a few of the many possible examples. It seems to be the case with the three drops too; they are made of the same substance, and before being dropped one by one on the fly, they belonged to the liquid in the inkpot. It therefore makes sense to search for three different, but somehow connected elements that the three drops of ink could possibly symbolize. With respect to the realities of the Great War, especially in the way it differed from any other previous conflict, they could be identified as politics, propaganda and education/knowledge (not necessarily in that order).

The first drop of ink is thus the documents issued and exchanged among politicians or diplomats—all that potentially deadly bureaucratic activity which, as a direct result, brought about a whole generation of young men lost on the battlefields. There are, of course, many examples to choose from but the best for illustration are the most notorious ones, the greatest bureaucratic milestones of the Great War: its outset, the stalemate at the Western front and the Versailles Treaty.

The outset is a fitting example of not only the abuse of power but definitely of ink too. The time between the assassination of Archduke Franz Ferdinand and the call to arms was marked by a shameful

---

[6] In Greek mythology, Cerberus is the three-headed dog that guards the gates of the Underworld.

tragicomic charade of exchanging diplomatic notes and ultimata that were not meant to solve anything and were expressly written so that their stipulations could not possibly have been met. In July 1914, the German Ambassador to Vienna, Count Heinrich von Tschirschky, assured the German Chancellor Bethmann-Hollweg (in writing) that the note including demands on Serbia for compensation for the assassination of the Archduke "is being composed so that the possibility of its acceptance is practically excluded" (MacMillan 2013, 531). Winston Churchill was clearly aware of this game and believed "the Austrian ultimatum to Serbia [to be] the most insolent document of its kind ever devised" (Soames 2001, 95).[7] As such, it was not a real attempt at peace negotiations, but a humbug designed to appease the demands of propriety or the long-standing rules of the game, while the main powerful players had already decided on, and were preparing for, a military conflict. Just as with the boss in the story, for politicians the war is an experiment, a sport they play on an imaginary giant European chessboard or rather, in both cases, on a piece of paper. Engulfed in documents, plans and rules, they are never close enough to the destruction and tragedies of war, and do not take into account human lives other than statistically.

In this context, it is worth taking a closer look at one element of the unavoidable and routinely assumed inspiration for the story, Gloucester's complaint from *King Lear*: "As flies to wanton boys are we to th' gods. / They kill us for their sport" (Shakespeare 2005, 4.1.36–37) and its counterpart in Mansfield's text. When reading critical studies of "The Fly", one occasionally comes across what appears to be simply a typo: the spelling of the boss as "the Boss". One in fact wonders why Mansfield did not use the upper case "B"; it would make sense especially if, as some claim, her boss represents God, whom she arguably resented for the death of her brother. Mansfield, however, uses the lower case "b" deliberately, and in spite of the insubstantial visual difference, her choice is highly significant for the interpretation of the symbolism of the boss, and materially problematizes the

---

[7] To Clementine Churchill, July 24, 1914.

reading of the boss as God. Shakespeare's Gloucester, after all, talks about "gods" in the plural and Mansfield's boss in the singular means that he is only one of many representations of gods or boys that play with their prey.

This reading is further reinforced when the whole universe and philosophy of *King Lear*, not just this familiar quote, is taken into consideration. Although apparently pre-Christian, *Lear* has a very inconsistent system of faith, and while gods are often mentioned and praised or blamed for all kinds of things, there is also a great deal of scepticism, and a belief that for some people they are just an excuse for their deeds. All in all, *Lear*, and by extension Mansfield's "The Fly", are not concerned with the divine, but instead primarily contemplate humanity. Thus, rather than God understood as a theological concept, the boss is one of the many "small" (hence lower case) gods, the people in positions of authority who rule over the lives of others, and have the power to make them miserable. Alternatively, if read ironically, he can equally represent those who view themselves as gods and act accordingly, without having the necessary skills or potential to fill the role. This reading is also supported by the change that Mansfield made to the name of her main character. Originally called "the manager", the alteration, as W. H. New (1996) argues, is not a casual semantic one; it "implies class categories in action, and potentially an undercutting of the social power ostensibly enjoyed by the story's erstwhile 'manager'" (58). What is more, as New further demonstrates, the term has metaphoric possibilities when its etymology is taken into account:

> As a medieval word deriving from the French *boce*, or "bump," the word "boss" (as in the modern "emboss") refers to a prominence or protuberance, one that is sometimes hollow. And the phonologically associated term "boss-eyed" (meaning "crooked" or "one-sided") derives from an English dialect usage meaning "make a mess of" or "bungle". (58)

As he concludes, with this and other single-term revisions, Mansfield "added an allusive complexity to this story, hinting at qualities of personality, motivations for behavior, and limitations of sympathy and vision" (58). In consequence, even such a minor change as substituting the lower case 'b' for an upper case 'B' in "the boss", as insignificant as it may seem, and as inadvertent as it most likely is, may affect the interpretation of the symbol and distort the reading of the whole story.

As the war progressed, much of it was again fought with ink on paper. Even if Mansfield was not aware of the sham "peace" negotiations before it started, she certainly knew more than enough about the way it was being conducted. The many personal losses among her family, friends and acquaintances, her own experience when passing through war-torn France and the daily news of the dead and missing would have destroyed any illusions she might have harboured and made her more than agree with Siegfried Sassoon's (1983) daring claim that the war (if it ever was) was no longer a question of necessity or of defence of some noble ideal, but a political game that was "being deliberately prolonged by those who have the power to end it" (173).

In this respect, it is worth noting that Sassoon does not blame the suffering of the soldiers on "the military conduct of the War" but on "the *political errors* and insincerities for which the fighting men are being sacrificed", that is, on the bureaucracy and uninformed decisions of the politicians (1983, 173–74; my emphasis). This affinity of Mansfield's and Sassoon's ideas does not seem to be entirely coincidental; she was knowledgeable about his struggle and attempts not to return to the front, as he wrote his declaration while convalescing at Lady Ottoline Morrell's house, being actively supported by her and Bertrand Russell, and Mansfield was at that time in London and in frequent contact with Ottoline. Sassoon's "Act of Wilful Defiance" was finished on June 15, 1917; and on June 16 Mansfield wrote to Morrell: "I want to talk to you about Sassoon (who seems to me at present, in the *Dostoievsky* sense, 'delirious')", which, as an editorial note explains, in this context means he was anguished, and "in the grip of an *idée fixe*" (*Letters* 1, 310–11, n2).

Finally, although not the only one, the Versailles treaty is arguably the ultimate example of an "ink-stained" piece of paper that, while professing to end killing and bring peace, was to some extent a form of political revenge on Germany, contributing to the fact that after a relatively brief respite, the war was rekindled and became even deadlier and more atrocious than before. Mansfield herself commented very negatively on the preparations for the celebrations of the Treaty, visualizing on the one hand those eager to celebrate as "toothless old jaws guzzling for the day" in the "workhouses throughout the land", whilst on the other hand noting the "beautiful youth feeding the fields of France". Such a contrast made her exclaim: "Life is almost too ignoble to be borne. [...] I keep seeing these horrors, bathing in them again & again" (*Letters* 2, 339).

The second of the drops might well be the war propaganda, the external representation of the first drop (politics), and at the same time the most directly obvious abuse of ink for war purposes. The echoes of its clichés appear in the boss's musings, as if his mind, facing the sad fact of his son's death in war, is no longer able to create personal responses and has to resort to stale war rhetoric and military idiom: "that was the right spirit", "never say die" (*CW*2, 479) or "look sharp" (*CW*2, 480); such phrases read like the slogans from recruitment posters or the empty ramblings of a senior officer to his decimated soldiers. What is more, one of the most notorious propaganda clichés of the Great War, the reference to Belgium as "plucky little Belgium", trampled by the German army on its way to war, is echoed in the boss's reference to the fly as "a plucky little devil". All these meaningless mantras are infused with the same heavy irony and bitterness as the World War I poems that mimic the falsely cheerful and highly inappropriate euphemisms concealing unspeakable horrors and destruction: "'Poor young chap,' I'd say—I used to know his father well; / Yes, we've lost heavily in this last scrap" (Sassoon 1918, n.p.). The boss sounds and acts like both the "kind" politician and the propaganda copywriter. He encourages, cheers the fly on, praises its persistence and fighting spirit, underplaying his own role in its suffering, and the fact that, without his actions, it would not need to show those commendable qualities and struggle for its life.

The last drop is the abuse of knowledge in all its forms and shapes, together with the use of human intelligence and skill for evil purposes. It is also a bitter accusation of misguided education which, instead of making people lead better lives, destroys them. It is a well-known fact that while the working class had the highest total number of casualties, when it came to a percentage share, the heaviest losses out of all the different social layers were sustained by the students and graduates of public schools, and the universities of Oxford and Cambridge. This was caused not only by the fact that they were immediately made junior officers and were therefore responsible for leading the charges, but that their classical education, full of heroes, battles and heroic deaths, was made the standard of behaviour and in many cases even meant they willingly enlisted for service. Many of these young men, just like Mansfield's brother, had unrealistic views of war gleaned from books; they yearned for adventure and could not imagine not returning to tell their heroic tales or even worse, that there would be no tales worth telling. The dark drop of ink on the fly here represents the dark side of education and its dangers, resonating with Wilfred Owen's (1920) accusation that "old lies" are being fed "to children ardent for some desperate glory" (n.p.).

But it is not only classical education that is taken to task. Engineers, architects and mechanics on both sides were incessantly using their skills and knowledge to create better, faster, deadlier ways of killing, maiming and getting rid of the largest possible number of enemy soldiers. The greatest irony is that this military experimentation, while deadly on the battlefield, contributed to the rapid progress of science used for peaceful purposes, and was in many ways instrumental in increasing the standard of life of late 20th-century Europeans.

Another aspect of this kind of abuse of ink, the one closest to Mansfield's heart, are the literary representations of or reactions to the war. Judging from her literary reviews, she had a real bone to pick with those authors who, instead of attempting to capture the truth, were only perpetuating the old myths and clichés, and supporting the established beliefs and practices. These, among her most openly critical texts, are often almost vicious in their sarcasm. There is, for example, her review of *Desire and Delight* by F.E. Penny, a novel about a woman named Rosemary who marries an officer and, while waiting for him to return from the war, works as a hospital nurse. When he does return, he is no longer happy and charming, but gloomy and sulking. "What can have happened to him? Could a year at Gallipoli spent among the dead and dying account for it?" (*CW*3, 512), asks Mansfield sarcastically. As she observes with a great deal of contempt,

> women like Rosemary, once they have secured their [husband], will send him off to the wars without a murmur, hear of his being wounded with a thrill of pride, and confide in their best friends "even if Maurice died I suppose I should just have to carry on". (*CW*3, 513)

She is even more derisory in her review of W. B. Maxwell's novel *A Man and his Lesson*, the story of a man who is saved from his disgrace and that of his family after he falls in love with a married woman, by the arrival of the war at the right moment. "Hurrah for August 1914! He is saved. Off he goes to be honourably killed. Off he goes to the greatest of all garden parties—and this time there is no doubt of his enjoying himself" (*CW*3, 511). Maxwell, although a First World War veteran himself, does depict the atrocities of the war, yet his response is stereotypically British, male and patriotic. The dark side of the war is as nothing compared to the lessons it teaches. And here follows another of Mansfield's sarcastic questions:

> Where else shall a man learn the value of brotherly love, the wisdom and friendliness of the generals at the Base, the beauty of Mr. Lloyd George's phrase "the War to end war", the solid worth and charm of a London restaurant, a London club, a London theatre? (*CW*3, 511)

But the most ferocious attack is reserved for the last of the war novels she reviewed, and the one that apparently touched her most deeply in a negative sense: Gilbert Frankau's *Peter Jackson*. To illustrate its alleged insincerity and bad taste, Mansfield, in her review, piles up all the lexical as well as conceptual clichés she could possibly find. The war is "the Great Hunting", London the "Heart of Empire", the pre-war period is referred to as "the stale old days before 1914", and Germans are the "Beasts in gray, [with] murder, rape and plunder in their swinish eyes" (*CW*3, 571–72). The upper-classes, according to Frankau, had the moral duty to go and defend the country "from which they draw their riches and their education" and whoever did not was "surely anathema marantha, the moral leper, the pariah among his kind" (572).

It is easy to see why Mansfield was so upset with this text, more than any other. Not only did it remind her of the mistaken ideals that brought her brother to an early grave, it also touched a sensitive spot when denouncing in no uncertain terms the ones who chose not to serve, such as her own husband Murry. To Mansfield the novel is "nothing but a roaring hymn in praise of killing, for killing is the Job of Jobs" (*CW*3, 572–73). Her emotional involvement is reflected in her overall assessment of this work which is rather unfair; for all its trite patriotism and formulaic writing, Frankau's novel does not really promote war and killing, but rather the proverbial English stiff upper lip that remains unshaken and loyal even when facing trenches, mud, death and subsequent shell-shock. The main character does not like war and hates to leave his comfortable existence, but sees it as his duty and would never contemplate thinking otherwise.

However, it would be a mistake to read "The Fly" as Mansfield's attack on others and a case of pointing fingers in all directions. She is, after all, one of those who "drop" ink on paper and therefore has to be wary of the potential consequences, not only in her published writing, but every single time her pen touches the inkpot. Just like any other writer, therefore, she must be included in the blame as well. In this respect, J. Lawrence Mitchell's (2014) article offers a further, chilling implication of the meaning of ink as a cause of death. He mentions Mansfield's 1914 patriotic letter to her mother's friend Laura Bright which was (without her knowledge) published in the Wellington *Evening Post* and considers the possibility that it influenced Mansfield's only brother Leslie's decision to enlist. It is thus conceivable that Mansfield's violent grief and apparent survivor's guilt was not only of a general kind, but due to feelings of responsibility for her brother's death, and that therefore, in "The Fly", she contemplates the perils of writing, even her own.[8]

Of course, although discussed and divided into three groups, all these instances of the abuse of ink cannot in reality be separated; they intermingle and are interdependent. This is not only implied in the symbolic meaning of their number, as discussed earlier, but also prompted by Mansfield's recorded admiration of Bergson's philosophy. Although the drops fall one by one, the reader does not seem to be invited to see them separately, but as "one in the other, each permeating the other and organizing themselves like the notes of a tune" (Bergson 1910, n.p.). Paraphrasing Bergson's example of the swing of the pendulum making one sleepy: it is not the third drop that kills the fly (not the last sound that makes one fall asleep), but "the rhythmic organization of the whole" (1910, n.p.), that is, the joint impact of the fly's original dip in the inkpot and the three drops from the boss. This has however one further implication. Mansfield is not saying that everything that happens to the soldiers or ordinary people is due to someone else's decision. They are not entirely, as Meyers has it, "helpless people" ([1978] 2002, 234). The fly has no business in the inkpot in the first place, and would probably have died there anyway. This can be linked to the passage from "At the Bay" where Jonathan Trout confesses his own voluntary imprisonment, comparing himself to a fly. Jonathan does not invent the cage, the room symbolizing patriarchal society, but he "flies" in voluntarily and chooses to stay, not strong or brave enough to break free. Similarly, the fly in the eponymous story flies into the inkpot of its own choice, possibly out of curiosity or lured by the smell, and

---

8   Both Hanson (2011, 125) and Mitchell (2004, 40 and 2011, 38) also argue that Mansfield had strong feelings of guilt following the death of her brother.

just like Jonathan Trout, but more literally, has got itself into a sticky mess from which it is very difficult to escape (and which is also reminiscent of the mud of the trenches). Mansfield thus acknowledges every individual's personal responsibility for their lives and shows that no matter how slight, one always has a chance to influence one's destiny against the small gods attempting to destroy it.

The last unimposing, but nevertheless indispensable, piece of the puzzle regarding the symbolic structure of "The Fly", and one that is even more neglected than the ink, is the blotting-paper, which at first serves as the stage for the ink-dropping scene, and later plays a role in the conclusion when, the fly dead and the grief forgotten, the boss sends the harried "old dog" Macey to fetch another "fresh" sheet. Its presence in both cases gives further weight to the significance of ink in the story, and complements the meaning of its symbolism argued for in this chapter. The fly, spread out on a piece of paper, evokes the political and military manoeuvres played out usually in offices far away from the actual battle, the newspaper statistics and debates, and the depiction of war in novels: even if well meaning, they are all theoretical, distant and detached from the actual conditions and suffering of the soldiers at the front. The fact that the paper is specified as blotting paper adds further options for interpretation. It is hard to write on properly as it is too absorbent and the writing would get blurry, an indication perhaps that the distance of the authorities from actual soldiers blurs their vision, and their ability to perceive individual human suffering. Moreover, the attribute "blotting" repeated twice in such a very short text, draws attention to the connotative meaning of the word, that of tarnishing, disgracing, dishonouring, as well as to the verb "to blot out" that evokes the attempts at covering, obscuring, or obliterating unpleasant or painful facts from memory, a power that the victors and the powerful ones have, creating official history using ink and paper to serve their purposes. The fly is thus killed on a piece of paper, thrown into the waste-paper basket of history, and the boss is provided with a "fresh" sheet, both the blank cheque to continue his actions and an indication that history will repeat itself.

As with most Mansfield stories, this one is written in a way that renders it universal and timeless, its symbolism enabling the readers to apply the text to different circumstances and their own experience, not necessarily similar to that of Mansfield; it is a symbolic story of loss, grief and memory, that can be read and interpreted in many ways. However, at the same time, by including several specific details, Mansfield made sure there would be no doubt that it is also a story of one particular war, the one in which there were fields and little woods full of neat rows of graves in Belgium and in which it was more than probable for two acquaintances to lose their sons at the same time and on the same battlefield (and consequently be buried in close proximity).[9]

Mansfield's use of ink as the killing weapon suggests that, as is the case with most human inventions, writing—that is using ink—can be both beneficial and deadly, and that what filled her life with pleasure and a sense of purpose, was the source of death and misery for many others. "The Fly" is, among other things, an expression of her belief that beyond the bullets, grenades, shrapnel, gas, tanks and disease, her brother and thousands of other young men and women were, in fact, killed by ink.

Bibliography

Assad, Thomas J. 1955. "Mansfield's 'The Fly'." *The Explicator* 14 (2): 23–25.

Bateson, Frederick W. and B. Shakevitch. 1962. "Katherine Mansfield's 'The Fly': A Critical Exercise." *Essays in Criticism* 12 (1): 39–53.

Bell, Pauline. 1960. "Mansfield's 'The Fly'." *The Explicator* 19 (3). Item 20.

---

[9] What might seem, especially to an outsider, as a rather implausible occurrence, was a hard fact of the British military system during the early years of the Great War. To motivate the young men to volunteer, they were placed with their friends and acquaintances in what is referred to as Pal Battalions. It was thus not uncommon that they would die on the same day and be buried close to one another. The practice was abandoned in the later years of the war. See Robinson (2011).

Bergson, Henri. 1910. *Time and Free Will: An Essay on the Immediate Data of Consciousness*. Translated by F.L. Pogson. London: George Allen and Unwin. https://ebooks.adelaide.edu.au/b/bergson/henri/time-and-free-will/chapter2.html.

Bledsoe, Thomas. 1947. "Mansfield's 'The Fly'." *The Explicator* 5 (7): 111–13.

Boyle, Ted E. 1965. "The Death of the Boss: Another Look at Katherine Mansfield's 'The Fly'." *Modern Fiction Studies* 11(2): 183–85.

Eliot, George. [1859] 2008. *Adam Bede*. London: Penguin Classics.

Fussell, Paul. [1975] 2000. *The Great War and Modern Memory*. Oxford: Oxford University Press.

Greenfield, Stanley B. 1958. "Mansfield's 'The Fly'." *The Explicator* 17 (1): 3–7.

Hagopian, John V. 1964. "Capturing Mansfield's Fly." *Modern Fiction Studies* 9 (4): 385–90.

Hanson, Clare. 2011. "Katherine Mansfield's Uncanniness." In *Celebrating Katherine Mansfield: A Centenary Volume of Essays*, edited by Gerri Kimber and Janet Wilson, 115–30. Basingstoke: Palgrave Macmillan.

Harris, Diana. 2014. "Milk, Blood, Ink: Mansfield's Liquids and the Abject." *Journal of New Zealand Literature* 32 (2): 52–67. Special issue, "Katherine Mansfield Masked and Unmasked," edited by Harry Ricketts and Anna Jackson.

Hart-Davis, Rupert, ed. 1983. *Siegfried Sassoon: Diaries, 1915–1918*. London: Faber & Faber.

Jacobs, Willis D. 1947. "Mansfield's 'The Fly'." *The Explicator* 5 (4): 63–65.

MacMillan, Margaret. 2013. *The War that Ended Peace: How Europe Abandoned Peace for the First World War*. London: Profile Books.

Meyers, Jeffrey. [1978] 2002. *Katherine Mansfield: A Darker View*. New York: Cooper Square Press.

Mitchell, J. Lawrence. 2014. "Katherine Mansfield's War." In *Katherine Mansfield and World War One*, edited by Gerri Kimber, Delia da Sousa Correa, W. Todd Martin, Alice Kelly, and Isobel Maddison, 27–41. Edinburgh: Edinburgh University Press.

---. 2011. "Katie and Chummie: Death in the Family." In *Celebrating Katherine Mansfield: A Centenary Volume of Essays*, edited by Gerri Kimber and Janet Wilson, 28–41. Basingstoke: Palgrave Macmillan.

---. 2004. "Katherine Mansfield and the Aesthetic Object." *Journal of New Zealand Literature* 22: 31–54.

New, W.H. 1996. "Mansfield in the Act of Writing." *Journal of Modern Literature* 20 (1): 51–63.

Oleson, Clinton W. 1961. "'The Fly', Rescued." *College English* 22 (8): 585–86.

Rea, J. 1965. "Mansfield's 'The Fly'." *The Explicator* 23 (9): 133–35.

O'Sullivan, Vincent. 2011. "Signing Off: Katherine Mansfield's Last Year." In *Celebrating Katherine Mansfield: A Centenary Volume of Essays*, edited by Gerri Kimber and Janet Wilson, 13–27. Basingstoke: Palgrave Macmillan.

Owen, Wilfred. 1920. "Dulce et Decorum Est." https://www.poets.org/poetsorg/poem/dulce-et-decorum-est.

Robinson, Bruce. 2011. "The Pals Battalions in World War One." http://www.bbc.co.uk/history/british/britain_wwone/pals_01.shtml.

Sassoon, Siegfried. 1918. "Base Details." http://www.bartleby.com/136/11.html.

Scutts, Joanna. 2009. "Battlefield Cemeteries, Pilgrimage, and Literature after the First World War: The Burial of the Dead." *English Literature in Transition, 1880–1920*, 52 (4): 387–416.

Shakespeare, William. 2005. *King Lear*. Edited by David Bevington and David Scott Kastan. New York: Bantam Books.

Soames, Mary, ed. 2001. *Winston and Clementine: The Personal Letters of the Churchills.* New York: Houghton Mifflin Company.

Stallman, Robert Wooster. 1945. "Mansfield's 'The Fly'." *The Explicator* 3 (6): 48.

Thomas, Joe D. 1961a. "Symbol and Parallelism in 'The Fly'." *College English* 22 (4): 256–62.

---. 1961b. "The Anatomy of a Fly." *College English* 22 (8): 586.

Todman, Dan. 2007. *The Great War: Myth and Memory.* London & New

York: Continuum.
Winter, Jay. [1995] 2010. *Sites of Memory, Sites of Mourning: The Great War in European Cultural History*. Cambridge: Cambridge University Press.
Woolf, Virginia. 1980. *Diary of Virginia Woolf,* Vol. 2, *1920–1924*. Edited by Anne Olivier Bell and Andrew McNeillie. New York: Harcourt Brace & Company.
Wright, Celeste Turner. 1955. "Genesis of a Short Story." *Philological Quarterly* 34 (1): 91–96.

Notes on Contributors

Erika Baldt is an Assistant Professor of English, literature programme coordinator, and Liberal Arts chair at Rowan College at Burlington County in New Jersey. Her research interests include modernism and cosmopolitanism, and she has published essays on Katherine Mansfield, Virginia Woolf, and Vita Sackville-West.

Maurizia Boscagli is Professor of English at the University of California, Santa Barbara. Her research interests include materialism, postfordist work, corporeality, and urbanism. She is the author of *Eye on the Flesh: Fashions of Masculinity in the Early Twentieth Century* (1996), *Joyce, Benjamin, and Magical Urbanism*, co-edited with Enda Duffy (2011), *Stuff Theory: Everyday Objects, Radical Materialism* (2014).

Ailsa Cox is Professor of Short Fiction at Edge Hill University, UK. Her books include *Alice Munro* (2004), *Writing Short Stories* (2005) and *The Real Louise and Other Stories* (2009). She is the editor of the journal *Short Fiction in Theory and Practice*.

Claire Davison is Professor of Modernist Studies at the Université Sorbonne Nouvelle, Paris, specializing in modernism's intermedial borders and boundaries—including translation/ reception of Russian literature in the 1910s; literary/musical modernism; and modernist soundscapes. Recent publications include *Translation as Collaboration: Woolf, Mansfield and Koteliansky* (2014).

Enda Duffy is Arnhold Presidential Dept. Chair of English at the University of California Santa Barbara. He is the author of *The Subaltern Ulysses* (1996) and *The Speed Handbook: Velocity, Pleasure, Modernism* (2009), which won the Modernist Studies Association Prize for the best book in Modernist Studies. He has edited *The Best Short Stories of Katherine Mansfield* (2011) and an edition of Joyce's *Ulysses* (2009).

Aimee Gasston completed her doctorate on modernist short fiction at Birkbeck, University of London, and is now a Birkbeck-Wellcome ISSF postdoctoral research fellow, working on a project about Elizabeth Bowen and literary stammering. She is Editorial Assistant for the Edinburgh University Press annual series, Katherine Mansfield Studies.

Elsa Högberg is a research fellow at Uppsala University. She is the author of *Virginia Woolf and the Ethics of Intimacy* (forthcoming, Bloomsbury Academic), and co-editor, with Amy Bromley, of *Sentencing Orlando: Virginia Woolf and the Morphology of the Modernist Sentence* (Edinburgh University Press, 2018). She is also editing a volume of essays entitled *Modernist Intimacies* (forthcoming, Edinburgh University Press).

Sydney Janet Kaplan is Professor of English and Adjunct Professor of Gender, Women, and Sexuality Studies at the University of Washington in Seattle. She is the author of *Circulating Genius: John Middleton Murry, Katherine Mansfield and D.H. Lawrence* (2010), *Katherine Mansfield and the Origins of Modernist Fiction* (1991), and *Feminine Consciousness in the Modern British Novel* (1975).

Janka Kascakova teaches English literature at the Catholic University in Ružomberok, Slovakia. Her research centres on modernism, the modernist short story, and fantasy literature. She is the author of numerous articles, book chapters, and a full monograph on Katherine Mansfield (2015), and the translator of her stories into Slovak (2013).

Gerri Kimber is Visiting Professor in English and Creative Writing, University of Northampton. She is Chair of the Katherine Mansfield Society and the author of *Katherine Mansfield: The Early Years* (2016), *Katherine Mansfield and the Art of the Short* Story (2015), and *Katherine Mansfield: The View from France* (2008). She is Series Editor of the 4 volume Edinburgh Edition of the Collected Works of Katherine Mansfield.

Todd Martin holds the Edwina Patton Chair of Arts and Sciences at Huntington University; he is co-editor of the yearbook series Katherine Mansfield Studies, and editor of *Katherine Mansfield and the Bloomsbury Group* (2016). He recently completed work at the Newberry Library as the Lester J. Cappon Fellow in Documentary Editing.

Ruchi Mundeja is Associate Professor in the Department of English at Lakshmibai College, University of Delhi. A doctoral candidate at Jawaharlal Nehru University, New Delhi, her research is primarily in the areas of modernist and postcolonial literatures. She has recently contributed a chapter to *Katherine Mansfield and the Bloomsbury Group* (2017).

Janet Wilson is Professor of English and Postcolonial Studies at the University of Northampton, UK. She has published widely on Katherine Mansfield and other New Zealand diaspora writers, and has recently co-edited *The Routledge Diaspora Studies Reader* (2017). She is Vice-Chair of the Katherine Mansfield Society, and co-editor of the *Journal of Postcolonial Writing* and the book series Studies in World Literature.

Index

A

"Abenddämmerung" *(Evening Twilight)* (Heine, H.), 169, 171-2
"Act of Wilful Defiance" (Sassoon, S.), 294
Adelphi, The, 140
adrenaline, 42-4, 47-8
Adventures of Elizabeth in Rügen, The (von Arnim, E.), 238
African, 13, 51-2, 60-1, 271
African American, 139, 155
Aiken, Conrad, 139
Ailwood, Sarah, 139
   Katherine Mansfield and Literary Influence, 139
"Aloe, The" (Mansfield, K.), 115
Alpers, Antony, 18, 113, 115-16, 210, 213, 234
"Am fernen Horizonte" (Heine, H.), 169, 171-2
America, 18-19, 55, 87, 139-40, 143-4, 146-8, 151, 221, 282
American Nervousness (Beard, J.), 41, 43
Andersen, Hans Christian, 20, 231, 241-50
   "Fir-Tree, The", 243-4, 246
   "Little Mermaid, The", 243
   "Old House, The", 246, 248
   "Snow Queen, The", 243, 248
   "Steadfast Tin Soldier, The", 243
Anthony and Cleopatra (Shakespeare, W.), 277

"As a Wife Has a Cow" (Stein, G.), 141
Ascari, Maurizio, 97
   Cinema and the Imagination in Katherine Mansfield's Writing, 97
Ashcroft, Bill, 22
Asheham House, 116, 118
Assad, Thomas, 287
"At the Bay" (Mansfield, K.), 21, 107, 117-18, 147, 150, 179, 219, 221-2, 271-7, 280, 282-3, 299
Athenaeum, 114, 121, 123, 127, 190
Australia, 13, 139, 145
Avinoff, Andrej, 154

B

Bailey, James, 93
   British Women Short Story Writers: The New Woman to Now, 93
Baker, Ida, 29, 189, 271
Bakhtin, M. M., 97
Baldt, Erica, 20
Banks, Joanne Trautmann, 133
Barnes, Djuna, 35
   Nightwood, 35
Barnett, L. Margaret, 257
Barthes, Roland, 273
Bartrick-Baker, Vere, 238
Bateson, Frederick W., 287
Battershill, Claire, 12
Beard, James, 41-4
   American Nervousness, 41, 43
Beauvoir, Simone de, 283
   Second Sex, The, 283
Beethoven, Ludwig van, 174
Begam, Richard, 52

Belgium, 265, 295, 301
Bell, Pauline, 287
Bellavite, P. A., 217
Benjamin, Walter, 85-8, 272
   "Some Remarks on Folk Art", 88
   "Storyteller, The", 272
   "Work of Art at the Time of Mechanical Reproduction, The", 86
Bennett, Arnold, 117
Bennett, Jane, 252
Benzel, Kathryn, 56
Beresford, J.D., 210
Bergson, Henri, 40, 42, 48, 211-12, 223, 251, 254-5, 260, 299
   Time and Free Will, 211
"Bergson's Theory of Art" (Hulme, T.E.), 254
Bernard, Claude, 40, 214
Besnault-Levita, Anne, 196
Bhagavad Gita, 20, 211-12, 224-5
Bibesco, Elizabeth, 188
Binkes, Faith, 209
Blake, William, 29
Bledsoe, Thomas, 287
"Bliss" (Mansfield, K.), 29, 31-2, 36-40, 43, 45-8, 65, 94, 128, 154, 278
Bliss and Other Stories (Mansfield, K.), 134
Blood (Galloway, J.), 103
"Blood" (Galloway, J.), 103
Boccaccio, Giovanni, 38
   Decameron, The, 38
Bodily Changes in Pain, Hunger, Fear and Rage (Cannon, W.), 42
Book of Songs (Heine, H.), 19, 161, 172, 237

Boscagli, Maurizia, 17
Bowen, Elizabeth, 196, 282-3
Bowring, Edgar A., 171
Boyle, Ted, 288
Brahms, Johannes, 172-4
Brennan, Teresa, 252
Brett, Dorothy, 118, 123, 146, 156, 188-9, 221
Bright, Laura, 299
British, 18, 21, 42, 93-4, 98-9, 110, 139-40, 257, 261, 266, 290, 297
British Short Story, The, 54
British Women Short Story Writers: The New Woman to Now (Young, E.; Bailey, J.), 93
Brooker, Peter, 59-60
Brown, Theodore M., 213
Browning, Robert, 19-20, 187, 189-91, 195-8, 200-1, 203, 205-6
   "My Last Duchess", 19, 187, 189, 197, 202-3, 205-6
Buch der Lieder (Heine, H.), 19, 161, 164-6, 169, 171, 173
Buck-Morss, Susan, 73
"Buckets of Blood" (Hadley, T.), 107
Burgan, Mary, 254
Byatt, A. S., 18, 93, 100-2, 104, 107, 109
   "On the Day that E.M. Forster Died", 100
   Oxford Book of English Short Stories, The, 93
   Sugar, 100
Byron, Glennis, 192-6

C

Canada, 145
"Canary, The" (Mansfield, K.), 104, 117, 262
Cane (Toomer, J.), 139, 155
Cannon, Walter, 42, 213-14, 218
   Bodily Changes in Pain, Hunger, Fear and Rage, 42
Canterbury Tales, The (Chaucer, G.), 30
Casanova, Pascale, 11, 23, 53, 67, 185-6, 190
   World Republic of Letters, The, 190
Castro, Joy, 141, 143-4, 146
Cather, Willa, 139
Century, The, 153
Chaplin, Charlie, 41
Chaucer, Geoffrey, 30
   Canterbury Tales, The, 30
Cheah, Pheng, 11-12, 20, 22
Chekhov, Anton, 45-6
Chelsea Rooming House (Gregory, H.), 145
Chevalier, Jean-Louis, 100-1
"Child of the Sea" (Mansfield, K.), 176
"Child Who Was Tired, The" (Mansfield, K.), 72, 79
Chopin, Frédéric, 174, 242-3
Christmas-Tree Land (Molesworth, M.), 20, 231-2, 235, 238-9, 244, 249
Churchill, Winston, 292
Cinema and Modernism (Trotter, D.), 96
Cinema and the Imagination in Katherine Mansfield's Writing (Ascari, M.), 97
"Coeur Simple, Un" (Flaubert, G.), 74, 76-7
Coleridge, Samuel Taylor, 196
Collected Letters of Katherine Mansfield, The (O'Sullivan, V.; Scott, M.), 30, 56-8, 67, 113, 115-16, 118-21, 123-4, 126-7, 132-4, 146, 178, 180, 188-9, 202, 221-2, 225-6, 242, 245, 251, 254, 256, 263-6, 271-2, 274-7, 279-81, 290, 294-5
Collected Poems of Katherine Mansfield, The (Kimber, G.; Davison, C.), 177
Conrad, Joseph, 34
Cornhill Magazine, 114
Coroneos, Con, 264
Cox, Ailsa, 13-14, 18
Crane, Walter, 13
Crane, William, 231
   Fifty Great Stories, 13
"Cup of Tea, A" (Mansfield, K.), 222

D

Damrosch, David, 11-12, 19, 185-7, 196, 206
   How to Read World Literature, 185
Darwin, Charles, 41, 44
   Expression of Emotion in Man and Animals, The, 41
"Daughters of the Late Colonel, The" (Mansfield, K.), 44, 98-100, 117, 221

Davidson, John, 189
  Rosary, The, 189
Davison, Claire, 14-15, 19, 64
  Collected Poems of Katherine Mansfield, The, 177
  Edinburgh Edition of the Collected Works of Katherine Mansfield. Vol. 4—The Diaries of Katherine Mansfield, including Miscellaneous Works, The, 166, 168, 171, 188-91, 237, 241
  Mansfield and Translation, 14
De Biasi, Pierre-Mark, 196-7, 206
"Dead, The" (Joyce, J.), 47
Death in Venice (Mann, T.), 31
Debussy, Claude, 174, 178
Decameron, The (Boccaccio, G.), 38
"Der Tod, das ist die kühle Nacht" (Heine, H.), 173, 237
Derrida, Jacques, 284
  "Signature Event Context", 284
Desire and Delight (Penny, F.E.), 297
Dickens, Charles, 84
  Old Curiosity Shop, The, 84
Dictionary of Physiology (Richet, C.), 215
"Die Einsame" (Mansfield, K.), 166, 168, 238
"Die Heimkehr" (Heine, H.), 165, 173
"Die Lorelei" (Heine, H.), 174
"Dill Pickle, A" (Mansfield, K.), 18, 94, 114, 117, 122-3, 130
"Discreet Journey, A" (Mansfield, K.), 116

Doane, Mary Ann, 85
"Doll's House, The" (Mansfield, K.), 72, 98, 107, 165, 282
"Doves' Nest, The" (Mansfield, K.), 102-3
Dowson, Ernest, 235-6
  "Visit, The", 236
Dreisch, Hans, 48
"Du bist wie eine Blume" (Heine, H.), 174-5
Duffy, Enda, 16, 36
Duhamel, George, 87
During, Simon, 66

E

Edinburgh Edition of the Collected Works of Katherine Mansfield. Vol. 3—The Poetry and Critical Writings, The (CW3) (Kimber, G.; Smith, A.), 15, 57, 117, 254, 297-8
Edinburgh Edition of the Collected Works of Katherine Mansfield. Vol. 4—The Diaries of Katherine Mansfield, including Miscellaneous Works, The (CW4) (Kimber, G.; Davison, C.), 166, 168, 171, 188-91, 237, 241
Edinburgh Edition of the Collected Works of Katherine Mansfield. Vols 1 and 2—The Collected Fiction, The (CW1 & CW2) (Kimber, G.; O'Sullivan, V.), 122, 124-8, 130-1, 148, 150, 155, 166, 168, 179, 187-8, 194, 198-200, 216-24, 233, 236,

238-9, 244, 246-9, 256-62, 272-9, 289, 291, 295
Edwards, Dorothy, 94
Einstein, Albert, 44
Eliot, T.S., 31, 45, 47, 71, 80, 88, 96, 146, 192, 194, 210, 287
   "Love Song of J. Alfred Prufrock, The", 31, 45, 192, 194
   "Waste Land, The", 47, 71, 96, 144
Elster, Ernst, 161
Emenyonu, Ernest, 13
Empathy and the Psychology of Literary Modernism (Hammond, M.), 193
energy, 16, 29, 36 41, 43-8
England, 13-14, 71, 98, 191
English Catalogue of Books, 12
"Escape, The" (Mansfield, K.), 18, 52, 56, 62-4, 114, 130-1, 154
Europe, 13-14, 17, 19-22, 52, 59, 162-3, 174, 267, 292, 296
"Evening Twilight" (Heine, H.), 167-8, 171
"Ex-Wife, The" (Smith, A.), 105-6
Expression of Emotion in Man and Animals, The (Darwin, C.), 41

F

Fairburn, A.D., 80
"Fairy Story, A" (Mansfield, K.), 248
fairy tale, 16, 20, 166, 231, 233, 241-2, 245, 248-50, 257-8, 260

"Family, The" (Latimer, M.), 19, 147
Fearing, Kenneth, 144, 153
Fee, Elizabeth, 213
feminism, 46, 85, 128, 133, 140-2, 146
Ferrall, Charles, 79
"Feuille D'Album" (Mansfield, K.), 117
Fifty Great Stories (Crane, W.), 13
Finnegans Wake (Joyce, J.), 141
"Fir-Tree, The" (Andersen, H.), 243-4, 246
Fitzgerald, F. Scott, 30
Flaubert, Gustave, 17, 74-7, 81, 189
   "Coeur Simple, Un", 74, 76-7
   Madame Bovary, 76
   Three Tales, 74
"Fly, The" (Mansfield, K.), 21, 287-90, 292-3, 298-301
Fontainebleau, 144, 152, 155
Ford, Henry, 41
France, 13, 15, 30, 41, 116, 123, 156, 162-3, 166, 266, 279, 293-5
Frankau, Gilbert, 298
   Peter Jackson, 298
Freud, Sigmund, 31, 58, 251-5, 257-61, 267, 274
   "Uncanny, The", 253, 257
Friedland, Louis S., 198
Fussell, Paul, 289

G

Galloway, Janice, 18, 100, 103-6
   Blood, 103
   "Blood", 103
   "Last Thing", 103-4
   "Scenes from a Life", 103

Galsworthy, John, 117
"Garden Party, The" (Mansfield, K.), 13, 73, 118, 131, 144, 244
Garden Party and Other Stories, The (Mansfield, K.), 221
Garsington Manor, 115, 127
Gasston, Aimee, 21, 255, 260
Gaudier-Brzeska, Henri, 209-10
Geiger, Wilhelm, 209-10, 226
"Germans at Meat" (Mansfield, K.), 257
Germany, 21, 238, 252, 256-7, 261-2, 264, 295
Gikandi, Simon, 52, 62
Goethe, Johann Wolfgang, 11, 175
  Weltliteratur, 11
Great Chronicle of Ceylon, The, 209
Great War *see* World War One
Greenfield, Stanley, 288
Gregory, Horace, 141-5
  Chelsea Rooming House, 145
"Grotesque" (Latimer, M.), 140
Guardian Angel and Other Stories (Latimer, M.), 141-2, 152
Gunn, Kirsty, 98
  My Katherine Mansfield Project, 98
Gurdjieff, G. I., 141, 145, 152, 154-6, 210

H

Hadley, Tessa, 18, 100, 105, 107, 109
  "Buckets of Blood", 107
  Sunstroke and Married Love, 107
Hagopian, John, 287-8
Hamlet (Shakespeare, W.), 30, 212
Hammond, Meghan, 193, 195, 223-5
  Empathy and the Psychology of Literary Modernism, 193
Hankin, 188
Hanley, James, 71
Hanson, Clare, 98, 114, 117, 121, 124, 128, 131, 251, 288
"Happy Christmas Eve, A" (Mansfield, K.), 244
Hardy, Thomas, 34
Harris, Diana, 288
Harvey, Graham, 252
Harvey, Melinda, 139, 255
  Katherine Mansfield and Literary Influence, 139
Haughton, Hugh, 80
Hawthorne, Nathaniel, 189
Hearth and Home, 247
Heidegger, Martin, 85, 87, 280
Heine, Heinrich, 19, 161-80, 237
  "Abenddämmerung", 169, 171-2
  "Am fernen Horizonte", 169, 171-2
  Book of Songs, 19, 161, 172, 237
  Buch der Lieder, 19, 161, 164-6, 169, 171, 173
  "Der Tod, das ist die kühle Nacht", 173, 237
  "Die Heimkehr", 165, 173
  "Die Lorelei", 174
  "Du bist wie eine Blume", 174-5
  "Evening Twilight", 167-8, 171
  "Homecoming, The", 165, 172

"Loreley, The", 171
Romanzero, 171
"To a Singer", 176
Helgesson, Stephan, 15, 22
Hemingway, Ernest, 140, 146
Moveable Feast, A, 140
Henderson, James Dougald, 272
Hensher, Philip, 14, 93-4, 97-100, 103, 106-7
Penguin Book of the British Short Story, The, 14, 93
Hiddleston, Jane, 186-7, 196
Hoberman, Ruth, 56
Hobsbawm, Eric, 72
Hoffmann, Brian B., 42
Högberg, Elsa, 21, 256
Holden, Philip, 12
"Homecoming, The" (Heine, H.), 165, 172
"House, The" (Mansfield, K.), 247
How to Read World Literature (Damrosch, D.), 185
Howard, N.P., 256, 261
Hulme, T.E., 254-5, 261
"Bergson's Theory of Art", 254
Hunter, Adrian, 54
Huxley, Aldous, 84
Vulgarity and Literature, 84

I

impressionism, 80, 84, 117-21, 123, 133-4
"In a Café" (Mansfield, K.), 126
In a German Pension (Mansfield, K.), 116, 195, 290
"In the Botanical Gardens" (Mansfield, K.), 113, 122-4, 126

Institute for the Harmonious Development of Man, 152

J

Jacob's Room (Woolf, V.), 116, 118, 134, 144
Jacobs, Willis D., 287
"Jakarta" (Munro, A.), 100
James, Henry, 33-4, 37
James, William, 33-5, 37, 42, 48
"What is an Emotion?", 33
Jameson, Fredric, 45
"Je ne parle pas français" (Mansfield, K.), 17, 29, 31, 45, 51-2, 56, 66, 155
Johnson, 211, 213
Joos, Martin, 213, 216
Journal of Katherine Mansfield (Murry, J.), 143
Journal of Postcolonial Writing, 11
Joyce, James, 16, 31-7, 42, 45-7, 83, 141, 190
"Dead, The", 47
Finnegans Wake, 141
Ulysses, 31-3, 35, 37-8, 43, 46-7, 144
Joyless Street: Women and Melodramatic Representations in Weimar Germany (Petro, P.), 85

K

Kampf, Louis, 146
Kane, Julie, 210-11
Kaplan, Sydney Janet, 18-19, 94, 96, 128, 267

Katherine Mansfield and the Origins of Modernist Fiction, 94, 142
Kascakova, Janka, 21
Katherine Mansfield and Literary Influence (Ailwood, S.; Harvey, M.), 139
Katherine Mansfield and the Art of the Short Story (Kimber, G.), 195
Katherine Mansfield and the Origins of Modernist Fiction (Kaplan, S.), 94, 142
Katherine Mansfield and the Postcolonial. (Ridge, E.), 139
Katherine Mansfield Notebooks, The (Scott, M.), 214, 225, 264, 282
Keats, John, 29, 180, 271
"Ode to a Nightingale", 29
"Kew Gardens" (Woolf, V.), 18, 113-16, 118-19, 121-34
Kimber, Gerri, 14, 20-1, 187, 191, 195-6, 279-80
  Collected Poems of Katherine Mansfield, The, 177
  Edinburgh Edition of the Collected Works of Katherine Mansfield. Vol. 3—The Poetry and Critical Writings, The, 15, 57, 117, 254, 297-8
  Edinburgh Edition of the Collected Works of Katherine Mansfield. Vol. 4—The Diaries of Katherine Mansfield, including Miscellaneous Works, The, 166, 168, 171, 188-91, 237, 241
  Edinburgh Edition of the Collected Works of Katherine Mansfield. Vols 1 and 2—The Collected Fiction, The, 122, 124-8, 130-1, 148, 150, 155, 166, 168, 179, 187-8, 194, 198-200, 216-24, 233, 236, 238-9, 244, 246-9, 256-62, 272-9, 289, 291, 295
  Katherine Mansfield and the Art of the Short Story, 195
  Mansfield and Translation, 14
King Lear (Shakespeare, W.), 292-3
Koteliansky, S.S., 15
Kuhn, Annette, 85
Kuhn, Walter, 145

L

Lady Margaret Hall, 234
"Lady's Maid, The" (Mansfield, K.), 72, 79, 104, 191, 194
"Last Thing" (Galloway, J.), 103-4
Latimer, Margery, 18-19, 140-56
  "Family, The", 19, 147
  "Grotesque", 140
  Guardian Angel and Other Stories, 141-2, 152
  Nelly Bloom and Other Stories, 141
  This Is My Body, 141-2
  We Are Incredible, 141

Lawrence, D.H., 31, 42, 44-5, 71, 94, 140, 142-3, 156
Pansies, 45
Sons and Lovers, 71
White Peacock, The, 45
Ledent, Bénédicte, 11, 13
Lee, Hermione, 98
Secret Self, The, 98
LeSuer, Meridel, 141-2
Letters *see* The Collected Letters of Katherine Mansfield
Letters of Katherine Mansfield, The (Murry, J.), 143
Lewis, Wyndham, 40, 44, 71
"Life of Ma Parker" (Mansfield, K.), 17, 72, 74, 80-2, 84, 86-8, 94, 117, 256, 262
Liggins, Emma, 54
Liszt, Franz, 172
"Little Governess, The" (Mansfield, K.), 96, 116
"Little Mermaid, The" (Andersen, H.), 243
London, 20, 46-7, 60, 94, 96-100, 143-4, 163, 188-9, 195, 209, 211, 233-4, 239, 241-2, 249, 257, 281, 294, 297-8
Loos, Anita, 145
"Loreley, The" (Heine, H.), 171
Lost Love, The (Owen, A.), 190
Loughridge, Nancy, 144, 152, 155-6
"Love Song of J. Alfred Prufrock, The" (Eliot, T.S.), 31, 45, 192, 194
Luhan, Mable Dodge, 156

M

McDiarmid, Hugh, 71
McDonnell, Jenny, 57
Macdowell, 173, 178
McGee, Diane, 258
McHale, Brian, 58
McKenzie, D.F., 133
McLaughlin, Ann L., 115, 118
MacLeod, Alison, 98
Morphologies: Short Story Writers on Short Story Writers, 98
MacMillan, Margaret, 292
McWilliam, Candia, 18
Madame Bovary (Flaubert, G.), 76
Mahāvaṃsa, The, 210, 222, 226
Maley, Willy, 53
Mallarmé, Stéphane, 272
"Man and His Dog, A" (Mansfield, K.), 262
Man and his Lesson, A (Maxwell, W. B.), 297
"Man Without a Temperament, The" (Mansfield, K.), 98
Mann, Thomas, 31
Death in Venice, 31
Mansfield and Translation (Davison, C.; Kimber, G.; Martin, T.), 14
Mansfield, Katherine, 11, 13-23, 29-33, 36-7, 40, 42-8, 51-67, 72-4, 79-82, 84-8, 93-110, 113-35, 139-48, 150, 152-6, 161-80, 187-206, 210-15, 217, 219-22, 224-6, 231-9, 241-67, 271-5, 277-84, 287-90, 292-301
"Aloe, The", 115

"At the Bay", 21, 107, 117-18, 147, 150, 179, 219, 221-2, 271-7, 280, 282-3, 299
"Bliss", 29, 31-2, 36-40, 43, 45-8, 65, 94, 128, 154, 278
Bliss and Other Stories, 134
"Canary, The", 104, 117, 262
"Child of the Sea", 176
"Child Who Was Tired, The", 72, 79
"Cup of Tea, A", 222
"Daughters of the Late Colonel, The", 44, 98-100, 117, 221
"Die Einsame", 166, 168, 238
"Dill Pickle, A", 18, 94, 114, 117, 122-3, 130
"Discreet Journey, A", 116
"Doll's House, The", 72, 98, 107, 165, 282
"Doves' Nest, The", 102-3
"Escape, The", 18, 52, 56, 62-4, 114, 130-1, 154
"Fairy Story, A", 248
"Feuille D'Album", 117
"Fly, The", 21, 287-90, 292-3, 298-301
"Garden Party, The", 13, 73, 118, 131, 144, 244
Garden Party and Other Stories, The, 221
"Germans at Meat", 257
"Happy Christmas Eve, A", 244
"House, The", 247
"In a Café", 126
In a German Pension, 116, 195, 290
"In the Botanical Gardens", 113, 122-4, 126
"Je ne parle pas français", 17, 29, 31, 45, 51-2, 56, 66, 155
"Lady's Maid, The", 72, 79, 104, 191, 194
"Life of Ma Parker", 17, 72, 74, 80-2, 84, 86-8, 94, 117, 256, 262
"Little Governess, The", 96, 116
"Man and His Dog, A", 262
"Man Without a Temperament, The", 98
"Marriage à la Mode", 62
"Married Man's Story, A", 102, 118, 215, 217-18, 220, 222, 255-6, 262
"Miss Brill", 18, 31, 45, 94, 113-14, 117, 119, 123-31, 133, 251, 255
"Modern Novel, The", 117
"Modern Soul, The", 177
"Mr Bennett and Mr Brown", 117
"Mr Reginald Peacock's Day", 115, 177
"My Lady Sits and Sings", 176
"Pictures", 94-8, 117
"Pine Tree, The", 234
"Pine-Tree, the Sparrow and You and I, The", 233
"Poison", 19, 187-91, 194-7, 205, 217-18, 220
"Prelude", 19, 29, 107, 115-17, 123, 128, 145, 147-50, 221, 251, 282
"Psychology", 94, 118, 126
"She", 234-5, 237

"Singing Lesson, The", 246
"Something Childish But Very Natural", 97
"Suburban Fairy Tale, A", 21, 252, 256-8, 260-2, 264-7
"Taking the Veil", 128
"Tiredness of Rosabel, The", 79, 94-5, 97
"Two Tuppenny Ones, Please", 94, 103
"Woman at the Store, The", 116, 134
Mantz, Ruth, 143, 279, 281
Mao, Douglas, 55
March-Russell, Paul, 54
Marey, Étienne-Jules, 41
"Mark on the Wall, The" (Woolf, V.), 57, 115-16, 118-19, 276
Marks, Sally, 261
"Marriage à la Mode" (Mansfield, K.), 62
"Married Man's Story, A" (Mansfield, K.), 102, 118, 215, 217-18, 220, 222, 255-6, 262
Martin, Todd, 14-15, 19, 55, 280
Mansfield and Translation, 14
Marx, John, 62
Maxwell, W. B., 297
Man and his Lesson, A, 297
Mendelssohn, Felix, 172
Menton, 188-9
"Metropolis and Mental Life, The" (Simmel, G.), 45
Meyers, Jeffrey, 188, 287, 299
Millin, Sara, 271
"Miracle Survivors" (Smith, A.), 106

"Miss Brill" (Mansfield, K.), 18, 31, 45, 94, 113-14, 117, 119, 123-31, 133, 251, 255
Mitchell, J. Lawrence, 298
"Modern Novel, The" (Mansfield, K.), 117
"Modern Soul, The" (Mansfield, K.), 177
Modern Times, 41
modernism, 11, 13-19, 21-3, 31-3, 35-8, 40-6, 48, 51-62, 64-7, 71, 73-4, 79-86, 88, 94, 97, 101, 103, 105, 113-14, 118, 120-1, 131, 133-4, 139-41, 144-7, 151, 163, 170, 174, 178, 181, 192-3, 206, 248, 250-4, 263-4, 267
Molesworth, Mrs., 231-3, 238-9, 241, 244, 249
Christmas-Tree Land, 20, 231-2, 235, 238-9, 244, 249
Monday or Tuesday (Woolf, V.), 116, 121
Monroe, Harriet, 144
Moore-Gilbert, Bart, 53
Moran, Patricia, 254
Moretti, Franco, 11, 44
Morphologies: Short Story Writers on Short Story Writers (MacLeod, A.), 98
Morrell, Ottoline, 113, 115, 118, 256, 266, 294
Moses, Michael Valdez, 52
Moss, Anita, 232
Moveable Feast, A (Hemingway, E.), 140
"Mr Bennett and Mr Brown" (Mansfield, K.), 117

"Mr Reginald Peacock's Day"
(Mansfield, K.), 115, 177
Mrs. Dalloway (Woolf, V.), 32, 35,
37, 43, 46-7, 118
Munch, Edvard, 31
"Scream, The", 31
Mundeja, Ruchi, 15-17, 23
Munos, Delphine, 11, 13
Munro, Alice, 100
"Jakarta", 100
Murry, John Middleton, 18, 30,
40, 46, 51, 67, 94, 123-4,
128, 140, 143-4, 152, 187-
9, 195, 202, 210-11, 222,
224-5, 262-3, 265, 274,
277-81, 290, 298
*Journal of Katherine
Mansfield*, 143
*Letters of Katherine Mansfield,
The*, 143
Murry, Richard, 126
Muybridge, Eadweard, 41
My Katherine Mansfield Project
(Gunn, K.), 98
"My Lady Sits and Sings"
(Mansfield, K.), 176
"My Last Duchess" (Browning,
R.), 19, 187, 189, 197,
202-3, 205-6
Mysticism, 20, 210-11, 213
mythology, 20, 171

N

Nelly Bloom and Other Stories
(Latimer, M.), 141
New Age, 115-17, 152, 254
New, W.H., 63, 80, 131, 293
New York, 141, 144-6, 152

New Zealand, 11, 13-14, 20-2, 39,
59, 80, 93, 98, 116, 139,
145, 163, 173, 191, 232,
239, 241, 282
Nietzsche, Friedrich, 235
Night and Day (Woolf, V.), 57,
114, 119, 121-2, 265
Nightwood (Barnes, D.), 35
North, Michael, 147

O

occultism, 210
O'Connor, Frank, 13
"Ode to a Nightingale" (Keats, J.),
29
O'Keeffe, Georgia, 145
Old Curiosity Shop, The (Dickens,
C.), 84
"Old House, The" (Andersen, H.),
246, 248
Oleson, Clinton W., 288
On Longing (Stewart, S.), 272
"On the Day that E.M. Forster
Died" (Byatt, A. S.), 100
Open Window, 248
Orage, A. R., 19, 152-4
"Talks with Katherine
Mansfield at
Fontainebleau", 153
Orlando (Woolf, V.), 118, 134
O'Sullivan, Vincent, 22, 93, 187,
196, 288
*Collected Letters of Katherine
Mansfield, The*, 30, 56-
8, 67, 113, 115-16,
118-21, 123-4, 126-7,
132-4, 146, 178, 180,
188-9, 202, 221-2,
225-6, 242, 245, 251,
254, 256, 263-6, 271-

2, 274-7, 279-81, 290,
294-5
*Edinburgh Edition of the
Collected Works of
Katherine Mansfield.
Vols 1 and 2—The
Collected Fiction, The*,
122, 124-8, 130-1,
148, 150, 155, 166,
168, 179, 187-8, 194,
198-200, 216-24, 233,
236, 238-9, 244, 246-
9, 256-62, 272-9, 289,
291, 295
*Oxford Book of New Zealand
Short Stories, The*, 93
Owen, Ashford, 190
Lost Love, The, 190
Owen, Wilfred, 260, 290, 296
"Strange Meeting", 260
*Oxford Book of English Short
Stories, The* (Byatt, A. S.),
93
*Oxford Book of New Zealand Short
Stories, The* (O'Sullivan,
V.), 93

P

Pansies (Lawrence, D.H.), 45
Paris, 40, 87, 143, 151, 163, 249,
277
Parker, Dorothy, 139
Parker, Robert, 173
Parsons, James, 174, 176, 178
Pater, Walter, 189, 234-5, 272
Payne, Evelyn, 234
*Penguin Book of the British Short
Story, The* (Hensher, P.),
14, 93

Penny, F.E., 297
Desire and Delight, 297
Peter Jackson (Frankau, G.), 298
Petro, Patrice, 85-6
*Joyless Street: Women and
Melodramatic
Representations in
Weimar Germany*, 85
Phèdre (Racine, J.), 102-3
Picaba, Francis, 36
Picture of Dorian Gray, The
(Wilde, O.), 238
"Pictures" (Mansfield, K.), 94-8,
117
"Pine Tree, The" (Mansfield, K.),
234
"Pine-Tree, the Sparrow and You
and I, The" (Mansfield, K.),
233
Poetry, 144
"Poison" (Mansfield, K.), 19, 187-
91, 194-7, 205, 217-18,
220
Polish, 15
Pope, Alexander, 196
Porter, Katherine Anne, 139
postcolonialism, 11-12, 16, 22,
52-3, 62, 67, 186-7, 206
Pound, Ezra, 44, 60, 80, 144, 146,
210
"Prelude" (Mansfield, K.), 19, 29,
107, 115-17, 123, 128,
145, 147-50, 221, 251,
282
Pride and Prejudice, 41
Proust, Marcel, 13
"Psychology" (Mansfield, K.), 94,
118, 126

Q

Queen's College, 144-5, 189, 233-4, 239
Queen's College Magazine, 238

R

Rabinbach, Anson, 41
"Racine and the Tablecloth", 100-2
Racine, Jean, 103
    Phèdre, 102-3
Rakosi, Carl, 144
Rankin, 139
Rea, J., 287
realism, 17, 73-4, 77, 80-1, 84, 86, 88, 97, 117
Rhythm, 116-17, 209-10, 212
Richet, Charles, 215-16
    Dictionary of Physiology, 215
Ridge, Emily, 139
    Katherine Mansfield and the Postcolonial., 139
Riekemann, Jane, 98
Rippmann, Walter, 234-6, 238, 248-9
Robbins, Bruce, 72
Robinson, Roger, 255
romance, 31, 38, 42, 47, 87, 114, 122, 128-9, 153, 161-2, 164-5, 169-70, 172, 174-8, 180, 192, 237, 253-4, 263
Romanzero (Heine, H.), 171
Rosary, The (Davidson, J.), 189
Ruddick, Marion, 231-3
Russell, Bertrand, 134, 211, 294
Russia, 13, 15, 71, 210
Rutherford, Ernest, 39

S

Sage, Lorna, 271
Said, Edward, 53, 186
Sammons, Jeffrey L., 178
Sandley, Sarah, 134
Sankar, S., 185-6
Sargeson, Frank, 93
Sartre, Jean-Paul, 281-2
Sassoon, Siegfried, 290, 294-5
    "Act of Wilful Defiance", 294
    "Scenes from a Life" (Galloway, J.), 103
Schoenberg, Arnold, 174
Schubert, Franz, 172, 174
    "Schwanengesang", 172
Schumann, Robert, 172
"Schwanengesang" (Schubert, F.), 172
Scott, Bonnie Kime, 14
Scott, Margaret
    Collected Letters of Katherine Mansfield, The, 30, 56-8, 67, 113, 115-16, 118-21, 123-4, 126-7, 132-4, 146, 178, 180, 188-9, 202, 221-2, 225-6, 242, 245, 251, 254, 256, 263-6, 271-2, 274-7, 279-81, 290, 294-5
    Katherine Mansfield Notebooks, The, 214, 225, 264, 282
"Scream, The" (Munch, E.), 31
Second Sex, The (Beauvoir, S.), 283
Secret Self, The (Lee, H.), 98
Selye, Hans, 43-4

sentimentality, 17, 60, 73-5, 77, 80-1, 83-6, 88, 130, 164-5, 174-5, 177
Seshagiri, Urmila, 52, 60
Shakespeare, William, 30, 278, 292-3
   Anthony and Cleopatra, 277
   Hamlet, 30, 212
   King Lear, 292-3
Shakevitch, 287
Shaw, Valerie, 275
"She" (Mansfield, K.), 234-5, 237
Shega, Joseph W., 214
Shieff, Sarah, 257, 266
"Signature Event Context" (Derrida, J.), 284
Simmel, Georg, 45, 83
   "Metropolis and Mental Life, The", 45
"Singing Lesson, The" (Mansfield, K.), 246
Skrbic, Nena, 56, 133
Smith, Ali, 18, 54, 64, 98, 100, 105-7, 271-2, 283
   "Ex-Wife, The", 105-6
   "Miracle Survivors", 106
   "True Short Story", 106
Smith, Angela, 114-15, 119, 125, 212, 214, 225, 254, 260
   Edinburgh Edition of the Collected Works of Katherine Mansfield. Vol. 3—The Poetry and Critical Writings, The, 15, 57, 117, 254, 297-8
Smyth, Ethel, 57
"Snow Queen, The" (Andersen, H.), 243, 248
Soames, Mary, 292
Sobieniowski, Floryan, 15

"Some Remarks on Folk Art" (Benjamin, W.), 88
"Something Childish But Very Natural" (Mansfield, K.), 97
Sons and Lovers (Lawrence, D.H.), 71
South Africa, 145, 271
Sri Lanka, 209
Stallman, Robert, 288
Stanton, Gareth, 53
Staveley, Alice, 114, 129, 133-4
Stead, C. K., 218, 220
"Steadfast Tin Soldier, The" (Andersen, H.), 243
Stein, Gertrude, 42, 141, 146, 175-6
   "As a Wife Has a Cow", 141
Stevenson, Randall, 58
Stewart, Susan, 272
   On Longing, 272
Stieglitz, Alfred, 145
"Storyteller, The" (Benjamin, W.), 272
Strachey, Lytton, 134
"Strange Meeting" (Owen, W.), 260
Stravinsky, Igor, 174
Studies in Prose and Verse (Symons, A.), 189
Studies in Prose in Verse (Symons, A.), 236
"Suburban Fairy Tale, A" (Mansfield, K.), 21, 252, 256-8, 260-2, 264-7
Sugar (Byatt, A. S.), 100
Sunflowers (Van Gogh, V.), 118
Sunstroke and Married Love (Hadley, T.), 107
Symons, Arthur, 189, 235-6, 249

Studies in Prose and Verse, 189
Studies in Prose in Verse, 236

T

Takamine, Jochiki, 42
"Taking the Veil" (Mansfield, K.), 128
"Talks with Katherine Mansfield at Fontainebleau" (Orage, A. R.), 153
tenderness, 16, 29-33, 37, 42, 48, 237
Tennyson, Alfred, 190, 196
This Is My Body (Latimer, M.), 141-2
Thomas, Joe D., 287-8
Three Tales (Flaubert, G.), 74
Time and Free Will (Bergson, H.), 211
"Tiredness of Rosabel, The" (Mansfield, K.), 79, 94-5, 97
"To a Singer" (Heine, H.), 176
To the Lighthouse (Woolf, V.), 17, 74, 77, 79, 83, 115, 134
Todman, Dan, 289
Tono Bungay (Wells, H.G.), 42
Toomer, Jean, 139, 141, 155-6
 Cane, 139, 155
transition, 140
Trotter, David, 96
 Cinema and Modernism, 96
Trowell, Garnet, 178
Trowell, Thomas, 161, 171-3, 178, 180
"True Short Story" (Smith, A.), 106
"Two Tuppenny Ones, Please" (Mansfield, K.), 94, 103

U

Ulysses (Joyce, J.), 31-3, 35, 37-8, 43, 46-7, 144
"Uncanny, The" (Freud, S.), 253, 257
"Unwritten Novel, An" (Woolf, V.), 115-16

V

Van Gogh, Vincent, 118
 Sunflowers, 118
Van Gunsteren, Julia, 80
Veblen, Thorstein, 72
Vechten, Carl Van, 145
Verlaine, Paul, 235
Versailles, Treaty of, 256, 266, 291, 295
Vice, Sue, 107
Vincent, Paul, 261-2
"Visit, The" (Dowson, E.), 236
vitalism, 40, 45-6, 48, 255
Vivekananda, 211-12
von Arnim, Elizabeth, 238
 Adventures of Elizabeth in Rügen, The, 238
Voyage Out, The (Woolf, V.), 114-15
Vulgarity and Literature (Huxley, A.), 84

W

Wagner, Richard, 174
Walkowitz, Rebecca L, 55
"Waste Land, The" (Eliot, T.S.), 47, 71, 96, 144
Waugh, Evelyn, 71, 79, 82
Waves, The (Woolf, V.), 115-16, 118, 134
We Are Incredible (Latimer, M.), 141

Wellington, 113, 123, 145, 171, 173, 232, 239, 241-2, 244, 299
Wells, H.G., 42, 117
  Tono Bungay, 42
Weltliteratur (Goethe, J.), 11
Welty, Eudora, 140
Wharton, Edith, 139
"What is an Emotion?" (James, W.), 33
"When the Wind Blows" (Woolf, V.), 134
White Peacock, The (Lawrence, D.H.), 45
Wilde, Oscar, 84, 192, 234-6, 238
  Picture of Dorian Gray, The, 238
Williams, Raymond, 70
Williams, William Carlos, 144
Wilson, Janet, 18, 52, 145, 255
Winter, J. M., 257, 265-6, 289
"Woman at the Store, The" (Mansfield, K.), 116, 134
Woman's Home Companion, 144
Woolf, Virginia, 16-18, 32-3, 35-7, 42, 47, 55-8, 66, 74, 77-9, 81, 84, 113-23, 125-34, 140, 163, 177, 191, 196, 210, 265, 276, 282-3
  Jacob's Room, 116, 118, 134, 144
  "Kew Gardens", 18, 113-16, 118-19, 121-34
  "Mark on the Wall, The", 57, 115-16, 118-19, 276
  Monday or Tuesday, 116, 121
  Mrs. Dalloway, 32, 35, 37, 43, 46-7, 118
  Night and Day, 57, 114, 119, 121-2, 265
  Orlando, 118, 134
  To the Lighthouse, 17, 74, 77, 79, 83, 115, 134
  "Unwritten Novel, An", 115-16
  Voyage Out, The, 114-15
  Waves, The, 115-16, 118, 134
  "When the Wind Blows", 134
  Years, The, 57
"Work of Art at the Time of Mechanical Reproduction, The" (Benjamin, W.), 86
working-class, 17, 63, 71-4, 76, 79, 81, 84, 107, 126, 296
world literature, 11-17, 19-20, 22, 53, 185-7, 190, 206
World Republic of Letters, The (Casanova, P.), 190
World War One, 22, 234, 260, 289-91, 295, 297
World War Two, 281
Wright, Celeste Turner, 287
Wullschlager, 243-5

Y

Years, The (Woolf, V.), 57
Youens, Susan, 174-5
Young, Emma, 93
  British Women Short Story Writers: The New Woman to Now, 93
Young, Robert, 185-7

Z

Zaturenska, Marya, 144

ibidem.eu